Understanding Conflict and Change in a Multicultural World

Other Titles by H. Roy Kaplan

The Myth of Post-Racial America: Searching for Equality in the Age of Materialism

Failing Grades: The Quest for Equity in America's Schools - Second Edition

Failing Grades: How Schools Breed Frustration, Anger, and Violence, and How to Prevent It

Understanding Conflict and Change in a Multicultural World

H. Roy Kaplan

ROWMAN & LITTLEFIELD
Lanham • Boulder • New York • London

Published by Rowman & Littlefield
A wholly owned subsidiary of The Rowman & Littlefield Publishing Group, Inc.
4501 Forbes Boulevard, Suite 200, Lanham, Maryland 20706
www.rowman.com

16 Carlisle Street, London W1D 3BT, United Kingdom

British Library Cataloguing in Publication Information Available

Library of Congress Cataloging-in-Publication Data

Kaplan, H. Roy.
Understanding conflict and change in a multicultural world / H. Roy Kaplan.
pages cm.
ISBN 978-1-4758-0766-0 (cloth : alk. paper) — ISBN 978-1-4758-0767-7 (pbk. : alk. paper) — ISBN 978-1-4758-0768-4 (ebook)
1. Culture conflict. 2. Multiculturalism. 3. Globalization—Social aspects. 4. Multicultural education.
I. Title.
HM1121.K36 2014
303.6—dc23
2013050448

Printed in the United States of America

Contents

Preface

This book is about the causes of human conflict and how we can attenuate, and, more importantly, avoid it. It is written to provide teachers and students with knowledge about the historical and contemporary sources of conflict in our world. It includes background information as well as maps to help readers understand issues that threaten our stability. The book is essential reading for the social sciences, an invaluable tool that lays the foundation for understanding our common heritage and future.

There is no magic elixir that can be added to the world's water supply to infuse reason and rationality. The knowledge contained in this manuscript *will* give readers the information necessary for reducing interethnic and interpersonal conflict that afflicts society and the classroom. As the world's population expands toward the projected nine billion mark by the end of this century, competition for space and natural resources magnifies tensions among rival ethnic and religious groups. Technological innovations, especially mass transportation and telecommunications, are bringing us into physical and ideological proximity.

Today, there are few places where people can live without the intrusion of ideas that threaten the status quo. We are witnessing the end of permanence and privacy. People from diverse societies are being thrust together at an unprecedented rate, leading to worldwide social upheavals. Traditional values and lifestyles are challenged by modernity and globalization. These tensions also surface in our classrooms as majorities and minorities exchange places in society.

Technology has improved the human condition, extending the lives of many people and relieving pain and suffering. But the speed through which technology diffuses through a social system has become a source of tension and stress. *Understanding Conflict and Change* identifies the processes: the dehumanization of work, population growth and immigration, ethnocentrism, racism, and religious fundamentalism, which are affected by technological innovation. These processes increase the level of conflict in society as readers will discover from analyses of the Middle East, Northern Ireland, and the former Yugoslavia.

Each chapter contains information about how increasing cultural diversity, interaction, and communication are heightening human conflict. Much of the analysis focuses on the United States, but international parallels are presented to demonstrate the universality of the concepts and challenges. These are life-and-death issues that affect every person on this planet. If we do not learn these lessons our future will be even more rent by unrest and violence, and our schools will reflect these tensions.

Chapter 1 combines historical, anthropological, and biological information about the common origin of our species to establish the premise that we are more alike than different. The human journey out of Africa that began over 60,000 years ago is likened to a global diaspora that is now being traversed through mass transportation and telecommunications. But mankind's journey to reunification is being impeded by myths and stereotypes that perpetuate racist and anti-Semitic behavior.

Chapter 2 explores the fallacy of myths about the natural intellectual superiority of Jews and the athletic prowess of dark-skinned people. These suppositions form the basis of prevalent prejudice and discrimination toward them and other groups. Although Jews account for only 0.2 percent of the world's population, they received 22 percent of the Nobel prizes between 1901 and 2011. Popular assumptions about Jewish intellectual accomplishments notwithstanding, Jewish achievements are not the result of superior genetic endowment, but the product of cultural and environmental (familial) influences.

While dark-skinned athletes seem to dominate the American sports scene in football and basketball, they play a relatively minor role in baseball (only 8 percent of major league players are black). They have a negligible presence in water and winter sports (but there currently are twenty-nine players of African and mixed African descent in the National Hockey League).

This discussion is presented to disabuse readers of stereotypical conceptions about these and other groups. It sets the stage for the larger conversation about the importance of recognizing basic biological and sociological facts that humans, regardless of color and ethnicity, are nearly genetically identical (99.8 percent common DNA). Observed physical differences are inconsequential in their effect on intellectual and athletic achievement. Culture, along with the opportunity structure and motivation, are the primary determinants of one's success.

These two chapters comprise Act 1, "Origins and Diaspora," of the human journey to reunification. They provide the foundation for the book by establishing our common genetic and geographic origins. They demonstrate that human cultural variations are the result of environmental differences. Act 2, "Bumps along the Road," presents a series of obstacles or challenges that are impeding the peaceful reunification of humanity. The changing nature and function of work creates competition for scarce resources and deprives people of meaningful experiences as work becomes a means to an end.

A discussion of national and international trends in population growth and immigration sets the tone for the next three chapters. They focus on the increasing influence of hate groups as population pressure and immigration thrust people from diverse cultures across borders and heightens tension when they compete for jobs and resources.

Along with the themes of the evolution of work and demographic pressure is the perplexing issue of religious fundamentalism. Intolerance of outsiders that emanates from ethnocentrism, the belief that one's group is superior to others, knows no boundaries as the text demonstrates through discussions of ongoing religious disputes in the Middle East, Northern Ireland, and the former Yugoslavia, despite the common genetic heritage of the disputants.

When Anders Brevik slaughtered seventy-seven people in Norway in July, 2011, he was protesting growing multiculturalism and what he perceived as the Islamization of the Western world. The murder of six Sikhs by Wade Page in Oak Creek, Wisconsin, in 2012 was another violent expression of rightist ethnocentric extremism. Readers will find similarities among left and right religious and political extremists. Both groups oppose the introduction of ideas and behavior deemed inimical to their own spiritual worldview.

Discussing such national and international movements is a precursor to Act 3, "Reunification," which presents information about the inevitability of human cultural diversity and contact. People and ideas are transmitted around the world at an unprecedented rate. Each year tens of millions of people travel across their country's borders, and 2.5 billion people interact regularly on the World Wide Web, sharing information, ideas, and their culture. These trends may be perceived as grave threats to traditional societies and fundamentalist religions who believe they have a monopoly over truth and morality. But the trends are inexorable and cannot be reversed.

The peoples of the world are indeed coming together as never before. Unless we attempt to understand and respect one another, the journey to reunification will be fraught with sorrow and grief. The final chapter, "How You Can Make Reunification a Reality," is a practical, proven guide, derived from the author's two decades of experiences in community organizing and conflict resolution. A postscript discusses ways teachers can introduce multicultural activities in their classrooms to promote tolerance, understanding, and respect.

Acknowledgments

This book is for my students and granddaughters. I dedicate it to them in the hope that they will learn the message that difference does not mean deficient. The beauty of human diversity gives us infinite choices and opportunities to engage and learn from one another. The journey to reunification can only succeed if we embrace and value our differences.

I would like to thank Lionel Lewis for comments about this work. He is a valued friend and colleague. Larry Jacobs of ESPN provided valuable comments about chapter two. My daughter-in-law, Tammy Jaycox Kaplan, and son, Ian, once again, gave me important editorial advice. My wife, Mary, has served as a constant companion and reinforced the value of inclusiveness to me for half a century.

My experience working with wonderful staff and colleagues in the National Conference of Christians and Jews helped me formulate my perspective on diversity, a desire that was instilled in me from birth by my parents.

Introduction

Our world is in turmoil—a cacophony of social and cultural clashes that grows louder each day. Intruding into our consciousness with the force of a runaway locomotive, cultural conflicts push us headlong into a future that appears bereft of reason and rationality. Traditional values and relationships appear to have yielded to the ephemeral. Groundedness has succumbed to the transient.

People are being exposed to myriad stimuli. They threaten to subsume their consciousness in a sea of data and minutiae, overwhelming their senses, drowning their sensibilities in a flood of emotions, stretching the brain's capacity to compartmentalize them.

Technology has become the arbiter of our time. Rather than enriching and serving people, it is transforming them by turning their lives into a succession of games. Gadgets occupy our time, minds, and hands. Using, consuming, and disposing of things *and people* have become the modus vivendi.

Fear is our zeitgeist—fear of others, fear of the present, fear of the future, but most of all, fear of change. How ironic that Western society, which prides itself on being a secular, technologically sophisticated civilization, is enmeshed in a conundrum of social, cultural, and political changes that threaten to rend it apart.

What is happening is the loss of permanency. Despite our affinity for the acquisition of things and ostentatious displays of consumption, even in the face of impending environmental disaster (global warming and depletion of natural resources such as potable water, oil, and precious metals), we yearn for a semblance of stability. The very newness proffered by technological innovation and gadgetry cannot fully eclipse our desire to order the world and interact with others in predictable ways.

It is this paradox, the conflict between our desire to consume on a selfish voyage into the future, and our craving for human stimulation with like-minded others, that is at the heart of this book. It is our thesis that the human journey, which began out of Africa over 60,000 years ago, led to a diaspora, a bifurcation of humans into many competing ethnic groups around the world.

Now through mass transportation and telecommunications humans are encountering and reengaging one another on an unprecedented scale. We have begun a journey toward the reunification of mankind. But this journey is complicated by ethnic, religious, and other cultural differences that, if not reconciled, will plunge our world into chaos. This book will help readers understand the sources of conflict among people on this planet. It will enable them to survive the journey toward the reunification of mankind.

Our optimistic assessment of the future will reveal how readers can create a civilization and schools where people respect and value one another despite cultural differences. The journey toward the reunification of mankind, though inexorable, will not be smooth. Along the way people will continue to encounter obstacles that impede the arrival at the final destination. How we cope with them will determine when we complete our rendezvous with our destiny—reuniting mankind after 60,000 years of diaspora.

PLAN OF THE BOOK

This book discusses historical and contemporary trends affecting people around the globe and focuses on the sources of conflict (e.g., population growth, immigration, racism, and religious fundamentalism) that threaten the peaceful reunification of mankind. Historical discussions of critical events are presented to illustrate the nature of past conflicts and how they were, or can be, peacefully resolved.

The book is organized into three sections representing parts of the human journey through time.

Act 1: Origins and the Diaspora

This section discusses scientific findings about the origin of mankind in Africa and the dispersal of humans around the globe and presents a review of biological and anthropological findings about our species, and Darwin's contribution to our understanding of heredity and environment through natural selection. The section also establishes the premise that humans are all members of the same species, nearly identical genetically. Race is a manmade construct that, to this day, is used to perpetuate the myth that one group is biologically superior to another.

Scientific findings tracing the origin and dispersal of our ancestors around the Earth are presented. A subsequent chapter explores popular mythology about the intellectual and athletic abilities of Jews and blacks. They are two groups that have been perennially stereotyped and discriminated against around the world.

Act 2: Bumps along the Road

This section reviews trends that impede the successful reunification of humans in a global multicultural society. In it, I discuss the sociological and psychological evolution of our species from ancient hominids who foraged for food to fiercely competitive people preoccupied with consumption and materialism. Outlining the changing nature, meaning, and function of work helps readers understand the relationship between social and economic security, competition, and the resurgence of racism.

This section includes a chapter on the demographic revolution and immigration to show how Western, predominantly white, societies are being affected by low birth rates and the influx of people of color from developing nations.

Religious conflict is a central focus of this section, and it discusses similarities and differences among the world's oldest and largest monotheistic religions, which have become a flashpoint for conflict in the twenty-first century. Religion is a powerful normative belief system that must be understood if mankind is going to survive the journey to reunification. Fear, prejudice, and orthodoxy do not have to be impediments to reconciliation if reasoned dialogue in search of common ground is sought.

Change is anathema to religious orthodoxy and people ensconced in their technological comfort zones. Materialism is the enemy of change because it feeds on conformity, stasis, and fear—fear of the unknown, fear of the stranger, fear of the loss of control over one's routine. Pluralism carries the promise of cultural salvation. Without it, life becomes an obsession with maintaining a modicum of mediocrity, living for existence without essence. A discussion of racism and hate groups demonstrates the extremes to which xenophobia and misplaced animosity toward people from different cultures can go.

Mass transportation and telecommunications are phenomena that provide a double-edged sword to society. While they enrich our lives by infusing ideas and technology, they challenge established moral and cultural values. The concept of cultural lag helps to explain resistance to scientific discoveries such as the birth control pill and the inability of people and societies to adjust to technological innovations.

Act 3: Reunification

This concluding section begins with a chapter on the role that population changes, technology, and telecommunications will play in the reunification of mankind. Religious fundamentalism will influence this event. A comparison between Islamic and Christian fundamentalist groups demonstrates similarities of methods and purpose.

This discussion is followed by an exploration of the concepts of freedom and control as they interact to influence the social psychological nature of our world. There is a fundamental paradox between freedom and control. It is found in all social systems. It represents a continuing struggle between the desire of humans to exercise freedom of speech and movement, and the necessity for society to impose order and stability to maintain equilibrium.

In an age of depletion of natural resources, competition among groups intensifies and precipitates restrictions on individual freedoms to maintain a semblance of order. If religious and ethnic groups cannot reach an accommodation with one another, will strong centralized governments impose order as in the former Yugoslavia or modern China? What kind of world will our posterity inherit if we are unable to learn to live together?

As human diversity and technological innovation seemingly spiral out of control, will governments, corporations, and special interest groups like the Tea Party and the Minutemen succeed in sacrificing individual freedom for the sake of returning to their conception of a desirable culture? This discussion will provide readers with insight into the positive and negative implications of this seemingly insoluble dilemma. I conclude that technological innovations in transportation and telecommunications will transcend attempts to stifle creativity, freedom of ideas, and movement, and, ultimately, lead to the reunification of mankind.

Some essential strategies must be implemented for the reunification to proceed peacefully. The final chapter explores the dilemma of engaging groups who are reluctant to participate in dialogue and interfaith activities because of ethnocentric and religious beliefs that deter them. I posit solutions so readers can create a more rational world by including people from different cultural backgrounds in their activities. Taking a proactive inclusive approach, "welcoming the stranger," is the antidote to hate and the salvation of the human species.

Act 1

Origins and the Diaspora

ONE

Africa

The Motherland and Human Diversity

If man's journey out of Africa could be expressed in terms of a year, imagine, then, that apes appear on New Year's Day. . . . Our first hominid ancestors to walk upright . . . would appear around the end of October. Homo erectus, who left Africa around 2 million years ago, would appear at the beginning of December. Modern humans wouldn't show up until around 28 December, and they wouldn't leave Africa until New Year's Eve! In an evolutionary eye-blink, a mere blip in the history of life on our planet, humans have left Africa and colonized the world.

—Spencer Wells, *The Journey of Man*

It's said that if you don't know where you're from, you won't know where you're going. This chapter establishes our common genetic and geographic heritage in Africa and demonstrates how we are more alike than different. Teachers should acknowledge ethnic differences of students while affirming important similarities.

AFRICA: WHERE THE HUMAN STORY BEGINS

Human life in the twenty-first century can quintessentially be characterized as variegated. The many hues and skin tones of mankind are only exceeded by the cultures and languages that abound around the globe. At the time of this writing there are 192 countries in the United Nations. The Human Relations Area Files, housed at Yale University, contain anthropological information on approximately two hundred cultures from different regions of the Earth, from the Akan of Ghana to the Yanoama of Venezuela and Brazil. But this is an incomplete picture of the disparate cultures that abound on this diverse planet. The United States alone is composed of nearly three hundred ethnic groups.

According to the Linguistic Society of America, there are approximately 6,809 known languages, a figure that is declining rapidly as the number of unspoken languages vanishes daily.[1]

Some experts contend that over half of the world's languages could be extinct by the end of this century.[2] It seems logical that each of these languages represents a different *ethnic group.* Language evolved as a method of communication among a group of people who lived together in a geographically delimited area where the inhabitants shared a common culture and value system.

One fascinating characteristic of these many languages, aside from their seeming diversity, is their similarity. Linguists have noted common rules of grammar that predominate around the world. Humans have the unique ability among animal species to form sentences and express themselves in logical, systematic ways. This finding should come as no surprise given the body of biological and paleoanthropological evidence that points to common human origins in Africa.

Recently, linguistic researcher Quentin Atkinson, using DNA and phoneme analysis of 504 languages, posited a credible theory linking common human origins and language to Southern Africa.[3] Research by geneticists and paleoanthropologists indicates that modern humans originated in Africa about 200,000 years ago. All humans on the planet are descended from a man and woman who lived in East Africa. The woman, known as Mitochondrial Eve, lived between 140,000 to 200,000 years ago. The man, Eurasian Adam, lived between 60,000 to 70,000 years ago.

Analyses of bones and genetic markers found in DNA (deoxyribonucleic acid) reveals that we all share genetic material from these two ancient ancestors. From the inspection of mitochondrial DNA (mtDNA), passed on from women to their offspring, and Y chromosomes passed on from fathers to their sons, scientists have concluded all humans are genetically linked to one another, sharing nearly 100 percent (99.98) of their DNA.[4]

Geneticist, Spencer Wells, who directs the Genographic Project for the National Geographic Society, is compiling a fascinating genetic roadmap of modern human movement around the world. Prior to what he calls "The Great Leap Forward," which represents the first major movement of modern humans out of Africa approximately 60,000 years ago, our ancestors were preoccupied with day-to-day survival. They were aided in their struggle for existence by several notable features. These distinguished them from other animals and simian cousins like monkeys and chimpanzees. Their large brains gave them the ability to think abstractly and creatively—to solve problems without relying on threat, fear and instincts.

As the Earth passed through alternative stages of warming and cooling, climatological changes forced our ancestors to adapt to topographical variations produced by wind, rain, heat, and cold. Animals that could not reach an accommodation with the vicissitudes of their environment disappeared and, as Darwin perceptively noted, fell by the wayside of history through the process of natural selection.[5]

Modern humans, like other hominid species, spent most of their time searching for food on the savannahs of East Africa. The weather at the time of their emergence was mild, and plants and animals were abundant. Living was, nevertheless, harsh, and the life span of these early humans was between twenty and thirty years.[6] Foraging for food was an integral part of the ancients' lives, as was the importance of passing on knowledge about the location of the most desirable scavenging sites—where and when the food could be found and the safety of consuming it.

Accomplishing these tasks required complex thought and speech patterns. The ability to communicate through speech is, in fact, a unique human characteristic facilitated through a combination of physiological and psychological developments. Researchers believe that modern humans' erect stature changed the anatomy of the skull and facilitated speech. The Foramen Magnum, the hole in the skull where the spinal cord passes through to connect with the brain, was at the back of the skull in hominids, who walked bent over prior to modern humans. Moderns' penchant for walking upright led to a realignment of the connection between the spinal cord and the brain at the bottom of the skull. This fortuitous connection in turn allowed the brain to expand and altered the shape of the skull. When man walked upright, the larynx moved deeper into the throat and further away from the soft palate, opening the oral cavity, which allowed resonant vocal tones.

Along with the larger brain that facilitated speech, words could be stored and recalled. Early hominid sounds were probably vowels with consonants added later.[7] Of course, being able to remember and relate facts about a region and its flora and fauna was of inestimable value to early man. This led to the development of languages, writing, and culture, further distinguishing characteristics between humans and other hominids and animals.

Although it is widely believed that early man was a savage hunter, anthropological evidence points to the conclusion that, initially, our ancestors spent a disproportionate amount of their time foraging for food. They wandered over the land gathering edible plants, insects, and, for those living near water, crustaceans and mollusks. The variety of plants and animals found in the lush savannahs of eastern Africa was the result of fortuitous circumstances. A combination of mild climate and an available water supply nurtured the efflorescence of indigenous plants and animals that became the staple fare of these ancient Paleolithic Homo sapiens.

In fact, the African continent was, and is, the most biologically diverse region of the world. So, too, are the humans who live there, even today. We know this from the genetic markers that allow us to trace the evolutionary path of our ancestors—mitochondrial DNA and the male Y chromosome. By analyzing these and estimating the time it takes for changes or mutations to occur in DNA, scientists have concluded that the biodiversity in Africa is the result of its age. The older the species, the more diverse is its DNA because it has had more time to mutate and evolve.

Human genetic variations occur along DNA strands called polymerases about once in every thousand. These mistakes or mutations provide a key to estimating how old a genetic line is. New mutations that persist in the genetic code of individuals (chromosomes) occur at the rate of twenty to thirty per generation. Geneticist Jonathan Pritchard of the University of Chicago estimates that beneficial mutations are diffused in a population in about 200 generations or roughly 5,000 years.[8] Counting the number of mutations provides a reasonable estimate of the age of a given genetic lineage.

Africans, particularly the San (previously known as bushmen)—who live in the area of the great African Rift Valley and the Kalahari Desert in the region of Botswana, Namibia, and South Africa—have DNA dating back to our earliest ancestors. Geneticist Wells contends that there is more genetic diversity within an African village than exists in the rest of the world.[9]

Not only do East Africans possess the most biologically diverse genetic markers, the language of some is among the most complex of any in the world. It contains 141 distinguishable sounds, compared to 31 in English.[10]

In addition to mapping the genetic origins of population groups, researchers use radiocarbon dating of bones and artifacts of our ancestors to trace the historical origin and convergence of languages in an attempt to demonstrate their commonalities.[11]

Linguist Joseph Greenberg and noted geneticist L. Luca Cavalli-Sforza, among others, attempted to elucidate the intricacies of human evolution by examining linguistic, genetic, and archeological evidence.[12] What emerges from the research of scholars who study human evolution is the incontrovertible conclusion that Africa was the ancestral home of mankind.

That is where our story begins. It is a story of change that has characterized our species from its inception. From evolutionary adaptations to environmental fluctuations that transformed deserts into wetlands, savannahs into deserts, plains into mountains, and created land bridges across oceans that permitted the migration of our ancestors and other animals from the Old World to the New. Along the way our ancestors spread genetic markers and cultural artifacts that left an indelible, if not always decipherable, record of their journey.

WHY HUMANS LOOK DIFFERENT

Looking at people from different parts of the world might lead one to conclude, as some scientists and philosophers did from the fifteenth through the twentieth centuries, that the wide variation in skin color and other external features such as height, hair texture, and the shape of the nose, eyes, and lips is indicative of distinct significant races among the peoples of the Earth. Prior to Darwin it was commonly believed that modern man had multiple origination sites around the world. This was known as the polygenist or multiregionalist theory. Darwin correctly posited the monogenist or common origin theory that depicted man as evolving from simian ancestors in one location. As we shall see, racists, eugenicists, and white supremacists staunchly defend the polygenist approach, which they use to explain not only physiological but social and psychological differences among groups of people.

Conclusions based on morphological variations are spurious. Apparent genetic differences among people are patently insignificant. There is only 0.2 percent genetic difference between any two people chosen randomly on the planet. As science writer Paul Hoffman points out, 85 percent of that diversity can be found in any local group of people. Supposed racial differences account for a fraction of the variation among individuals throughout the world.[13]

In our fascination and preoccupation with human variation we overlook the fact that humans have many more similarities than differences. We all breathe air, eat, and metabolize food. We have the same internal organs that can be exchanged along with blood, tissue, and bones. We think, have emotions, and feel pain.

The reason we look different from one another is related to our origin in Africa and the great genetic diversity of people there. When some of our ancestors left the African continent 60,000 years ago, they wandered around the planet and settled in places that provided them with food and shelter from the elements. At times their journey was hindered by natural boundaries such as mountains or bodies of water. Dwelling together for long periods of time had the effect of reducing the genetic diversity of their group, unlike their relatives who remained in Africa and exchanged genes with groups throughout the continent.

This process of isolation led to differences among the peoples of the Earth in two important ways. First, periodic mutations known as polymorphisms occurred in generations of isolated groups, often as adaptations to their environment. Second, the very act of isolation prevented them from exchanging and diversifying their gene pool with other humans. On the surface, these physiological variations may appear to presage significant differences among us. For hundreds of years, scientists, philosophers, eugenicists, and white supremacists have focused on these observable differences as prima facie evidence of racial differences *and* postulated theories rationalizing and justifying social inequality based upon them.

However seductive and convenient such theories have been, they are patently unscientific and fallacious. They misinterpret and misconstrue scientific facts. They focus on the marginal differences among us instead of the mass of ubiquitous characteristics that unite us as the species *Homo sapiens* (wise man). Later we will explore the underlying motivation of racism. Much of the foundation of modern eugenics and racism has been, and continues to be, a rationalization and justification for the perpetuation of social inequality, blaming victims of domination and exploitation for their predicament.

MAN: THE SOCIAL ANIMAL

Undeniably, humans prefer interacting with people who look and act similar to themselves. Such affinities arose from early man's migratory behavior. This led him to settle in discrete geographic areas cloistered from neighbors who might variously threaten the integrity of the group or encroach on their food resources. Through time, genetic drift (passing on genetic mutations in socially isolated groups) and natural selection (facilitated by adaptations to the environment along with generations of inbreeding), physical and cultural markers emerged that distinguished one group or clan from another.

Some of the most unique distinctions among these groups were not physiological but sociocultural. They represented their customs, traditions, ideological and religious beliefs, architecture, work and play. It is thought by some linguists that a mother language evolved into thousands of variations. This reflects the many cultural or ethnic groups, binding them together like blood into small- and large-scale social systems.

That man is a social animal is incontrovertible. Estimates place the number of modern humans at the beginning of the age of agriculture at ten million.[14] Considerable paleoanthropological evidence exists confirming that people gravitated toward one another and lived in groups. Whether for protection, collaboration, or camaraderie, people huddled together in small collectives that afforded them better opportunities to survive and thrive.

THE JOURNEY BEGINS

Once our ancestors learned to use tools, these collectives served to facilitate hunting the large animals that populated the savannahs where they lived. Hunting techniques and tools evolved with changes in terrain, season, and the depletion of game. As man improved his ability to kill wildlife, he was perforce, destined to expand his domain in search of food. This search and climatological changes led to a diaspora out of the motherland.

While some romantics might like to attribute man's journey out of Africa to his wanderlust, necessity led him to the Middle East. As luck would have it, there he found indigenous edible plants and animals as well as a congenial climate. These fortuitous circumstances played a vital role in the development of agriculture as anthropologist/geographer Jared Diamond demonstrated in his Pulitzer Prize–winning book *Guns, Germs, and Steel*.[15]

The narrow swath of crescent-shaped habitable land that ran some 1,200 miles across Southeast Asia through Syria, Iran, and southern Iraq where the Tigris and Euphrates empty into the Persian Gulf, was home to many native plant and animal species. They lent themselves to farming and domestication. Cereals such as varieties of wheat and barley, lentils, peas and chickpeas, flax, and muskmelons were indigenous to the area. They could be propagated, allowing nomadic hunter-gatherers to establish residences and grow food for a stable diet and adequate caloric intake.

Diamond notes that cereal crops grow fast, are high in carbohydrates, and yield up to a ton of edible food per cultivated hectare (roughly 2.5 acres). To this day they provide over half of all calories consumed around the world.[16]

Achieving a stable food supply meant that man had begun to master his environment. He was no longer subjected to the vicissitudes of climate and topography—at least in that part of the world. Judicious planting and harvesting of crops led to the accumulation of a surplus. This had the effect of creating a social and cultural revolution—the rise of cities. It is no accident, then, that the first known cities of Mesopotamia developed there over 6,000 years ago. The ancient city of Babylon was thought to have a population of 200,000 nearly 4,000 years ago.

Our early ancestors did not stop when they reached the proverbial Garden of Eden. They branched out into Asia and began populating other parts of the world. As science writer Steve Olson[17] documents, humans first moved into the Nile Valley and across the Sinai Peninsula into the Middle East perhaps as long as 100,000 years ago. This movement was followed by another migration 40,000 years later into India, southeastern Asia and Australia. Around this time our ancient ancestors also made their way into Europe and then, just 10,000 to 15,000 years ago, they walked across the Siberian land bridge and sailed down the coasts of North and South America.

One of the most intriguing attempts to document the journey of man out of Africa was conducted by geneticist Spencer Wells.[18] He provides a summary of the routes taken by our early ancestors by tracing their genetic markers in populations around the world. Looking at the prevalence and distribution of mtDNA and Y chromosome anomalies, Wells proposed that modern humans left East Africa by following a coastal route and ventured into the southern coast of Asia and then to Australia.

Once agriculture was developed, people could remain in the same location for greater periods of time, thus slowing the expansion of humans around the planet. Geneticist L. Luca Cavalli Sforza and archaeologist Albert Ammerman estimated that agricultural populations expand at the rate of one kilometer per year. Using this figure, it would take several thousand years for humans to move from northeastern Africa to the Bering Strait.[19]

The fact that all humans are closely genetically linked helps us understand why our basic biology is virtually identical. Physical differences such as skin color, the shape of our noses and eyes, and texture of our hair are the result of evolutionary processes that occurred over thousands of years. These changes happened because of human groups' genetic modifications that helped them live in geographically different environments.

Our ancestors originated in the same place (not spontaneously in different locations, as Old World philosophers, theologians, and scientists prior to Darwin speculated). This helps explain why humans look different—because they in-bred, lived separately from other groups, and adapted to their environment as they wandered around the planet. Yet, scientists have concluded that 90 percent of genetic variation among humans actually occurs on a given continent,[20] and Africa is the most genetically diverse region of the world.

Despite scientific evidence confirming the common origin of mankind, many people cling to myths about the supposed superiority and inferiority of "the other" (i.e., people from groups outside their own). Though based on false assumptions, these beliefs exert a great deal of social, psychological, and political power, affecting relationships between and among groups and societies, even nations.

At times such beliefs are expressed in the form of stereotypes about out-group members and individuals. At others they become part of the social fabric of society and form the normative structure of values affecting behavior and relationships. History is replete with examples of the mistreatment of outsiders despite scriptural admonitions in virtually every known religion to be gracious to strangers.

This book's thesis is that, while the world's population is expanding and becoming increasingly diverse, the many conflicts between ethnic groups that threaten peace and stability can be overcome if we as a species come to the realization that we are all related, descended from common ancestors in Africa. We have more similarities than differences.

Differences manifested through culture and value systems are not something we should fear. It is easier to live in peace and harmony than engage in continuous internecine warfare. We must realize that there are physical limitations imposed on us by the availability of raw materials. Cultural differences should be celebrated, not feared. Technological innovations have improved the quality of life of some people, but a significant proportion of the world's population lives in squalor. Ultimately, humanistic considerations must be invoked to reverse the detrimental effects of poverty and the fetish for materialism that is expanding from West to East.

Technology in itself does not solve problems—it often precipitates new ones (e.g., nuclear energy has led to horrific weapons and waste that threatens the planet). The world's problems, our problems, are, in the final analysis, human problems. The decisions about whether to develop and how to apply science and technology in society ultimately rest on social, psychological, and political considerations. They are human decisions informed by history, myths, and stereotypes that, if left unscrutinized, encumber human reason.

The history of mankind is replete with examples of man's inhumanity to his brothers and sisters. The motivation behind countless conflicts can be traced to competition for resources and self-aggrandizement, often at the expense of out-groups—people defined as different and deficient socially or technologically. Difference does not have to be juxtaposed with deficient. Wonderful, uplifting accounts of self-sacrifice, charity, and service are also interspersed in the story of mankind. By identifying the causes of conflict that threaten the harmonious journey of man toward reunification, we will, hopefully, be able to avoid past mistakes and spare our planet, its people, and our students a measure of misery. We now turn to an analysis of the way two groups of people, Jews and blacks, have been discriminated for eons and their adaptations to it.

SUMMING UP

- All humans originated in Africa.
- DNA research proves that all humans are related and more alike than different.
- Humans left Africa in waves beginning 60,000 years ago.
- Differences in physical appearance (e.g., skin color; hair texture; and the shape of the ears, nose, and lips) are the result of adaptations to the environment. They have no effect on human intellectual or athletic ability.

• The Fertile Crescent in Southeast Asia was the home of humans' first cities.

NOTES

1. Stephen R. Anderson, "How Many Languages Are There in the World?" Linguistic Society of America, 2004, accessed May 30, 2011, http://www.lsadc.org/info/pdf_files/howmany.pdf.

2. David Nettles and Suzanne Romaine, *Vanishing Voices* (New York: Oxford University Press, 2000).

3. Quentin Atkinson, "Phonemic Diversity Supports a Serial Founder Effect Model of Linguistic Expansion from Africa," *Science* 332 (April 15, 2011): 46–349.

4. See Wells, loc. cit., 2002, and John H. Relethford, *Reflections of Our Past: How History Is Revealed in Our Genes* (Cambridge, MA.: Westview Press, 2003), for a discussion of Y chromosome tracking and an overview of the genetic history of mankind. The National Geographic Society is conducting a worldwide analysis of DNA to delineate lines of origins and ancestry for all humans. See their website for information about this at www.genographic.org.

5. See the interesting summary of Charles Darwin's contributions in *Darwin's Sacred Cause*, by Adrian Desmond and James Moore (Boston: Houghton Mifflin Harcourt, 2009).

6. W. J. MacLennan and W. I. Sellers, "Ageing Through the Ages," *Proceedings of the Royal College of Physicians Edinburgh* 29 (1999): 71–75.

7. See "Evolution of Speech" at http://science.jrank.org/pages/6370/speech-evolution-speech.html, accessed November 7, 2010.

8. Pritchard, "How We Are Evolving," *Scientific American* 303, no. 4 (2010): 41–47.

9. Wells, *The Journey of Man* , 39.

10. Ibid., 56.

11. Joseph H. Greenberg, Charles A. Ferguson, and Edith A. Moravcsik, *Universals of Human Language*, 4 vols., (Palo Alto, CA: Stanford University Press, 1978); Meritt Ruhlen, *The Origin of Language* (New York: John Wiley, 1994).

12. Joseph H. Greenberg, Christy G. Turner II, and Stephen Zegura, "The Settlement of the Americas: A Comparison of the Linguistic, Dental and Genetic Evidence," *Current Anthropology* 25 (1986): 477–497; L. Luca Cavalli-Sforza, Alberto Piazza, Paolo Menozzi, and Joanna Mountain, "Reconstruction of Human Evolution: Bringing Together Genetic, Archeological and Linguistic Data," *Proceedings of the National Academy of Sciences* 85 (1988): 6002–6006; and L. Luca Cavalli-Sforza, *Genes, Peoples, and Languages* (New York: North Point Press, 2000).

13. Paul Hoffman, "The Science of Race," *Discover*, 1994, 4.

14. Wells, *The Journey of Man* , 151.

15. Jared Diamond, *Guns, Germs, and Steel* (New York: W.W. Norton, 1997).

16. Ibid., 125.

17. Op. cit., 3.

18. Wells, *The Journey of Man*.

19. Albert Ammerman and L. L. Cavalli-Sforza, *The Neolithic Transition and the Genetics of Populations in Europe* (Princeton, NJ: Princeton University Press, 1984).

20. Michael J. Bamshad and Steve E. Olson, "Does Race Exist?" *Scientific American*, December 2003, 78–85.

TWO

Different and the Same

*The Role of Heredity and Environment in Human
Intellectual and Athletic Achievement*

By virtue of being born to humanity, every human being has a right to
the development and fulfillment of his potentialities as a human being.
— Ashley Montagu

*Prevalent stereotypes about blacks and Jews lead to prejudice, discrimination,
and bullying. This chapter will help teachers set the record straight and empower
students to treat one another fairly when they learn the truth.*

A popular American cliché is that "white men can't jump," which is to
say that most people believe blacks are naturally superior athletes. Look
at all the black players in the National Football League (NFL) and the
National Baseball Association (NBA). They are bigger, stronger, and faster than whites, and they've got the numbers and bank accounts to prove
it. While blacks are lauded for their athletic prowess, Jews are stereotyped as shrewd investors, intellectually gifted lords over Wall Street and
the banking industry.

These conceptions may be flattering to some members of the respec-
tive groups. But people who believe them frequently subscribe to the
obverse position: blacks can't make it in the classroom, and Jews are
greedy and athletically challenged. Both sets of stereotypes are false, malicious distortions of reality. The following presentation may seem
counterintuitive to contemporary "wisdom," but the facts are incontrovertible in light of biological, social, and cultural forces that shape intellectual and athletic performance.

We focus on Jews and blacks to debunk prevalent misconceptions about two groups that have been discriminated throughout recorded history. Their plight serves to illustrate the kind of prejudice and propaganda used to isolate and dehumanize minorities around the world—techniques and arguments that, unfortunately, abound today.

Demythologizing fallacious assumptions about religious and ethnic groups is essential to overcome hostility toward "the other" on our journey toward reunification. Hopefully, through the intellect, reason, and nonviolence will ultimately prevail.

THE FALLACY OF RACE

Despite differences in appearance among individuals, scientists have established that there are no significant genetic differences in athletic or intellectual ability among the multitude of ethnic groups that populate our planet. Indeed, the very concept of race as a descriptor of physical differences among people has been abandoned by scientists. In light of genetic research, they have concluded that race is a social construct serving little substantive or heuristic value.

Yet, the term persists despite biological evidence that links humans to common origins with shared physiological characteristics. For example, the sickle cell gene, which originated as an evolutionary way of protecting humans from malaria, is found among Africans and about 8 percent of African-Americans, but also appears in Swedes. Noted geographer/anthropologist Jared Diamond presents evidence of many other anomalies that belie simplistic biological racial classificatory schemes.[1]

To be sure, humans are not all identical genetically. There is an increasing body of research that indicates some ethnic groups may have genetic predispositions to certain diseases such as hypertension, diabetes, and alcoholism. These diseases disproportionately afflict people of color (African-Americans, Native Americans, and Latinos), but epidemiological research reveals that it is difficult to attribute causality to ethnicity or the color of one's skin. Social factors such as poverty, nutrition, preventative behavior (e.g., exercise, health checkups, access to health care, and prejudice) also influence the prevalence and severity of these and other diseases.[2]

Scientists have even demonstrated that hypertension and heart disease as well as emotional/psychiatric disorders are affected by the stress people encounter living in densely populated, fast-paced societies. Anxiety; hostility; and fear of being rejected at school, on the job, or at home have also been linked to physical illnesses.

The adverse economic climate ushered in by the Great Recession of 2007–2010 exacerbated tension and conflict as economic insecurity increased among the world's population. Adding to these stressors was the ever-present specter of racism directed against people of color through-out the globe. Racism has been linked to increases in the level of anxiety referred to as the allostatic load. It is the burden of tension and stress people of color bear as they are scapegoated and become targets of op-pression (or assume they are being targeted because of past experiences). This phenomenon can heighten their susceptibility to hypertension, de-pression, other emotional disorders, and heart disease.[3]

The fact remains that humans, all humans, constitute a single species. They may have different skin color and hair texture, and other outward physiological differences (the shape of their nose, lips, and eyes), but there are no significant differences in the way their brains, internal and external organs, and systems function. We are all more alike than differ-ent—truly mtDNA Eve and Eurasian Adam's children.

The capacity for learning and achieving intellectual greatness is con-tained within humans who live in cosmopolitan cities as well as people inhabiting remote villages in rural areas in isolated parts of the world. Although science has confirmed this conclusion, myths abound about the purported genetic superiority of light-skinned people and the inferiority of dark-skinned groups. These false assumptions about human potential, motivation, and accomplishments create barriers to equality around the world. They perpetuate poverty and inequality, limit the lives of people, and deprive all of us of the fruits of their potential accomplishments.

IS THERE GENETIC VARIATION IN HUMANS?

Differences in achievement, defined in Western terms as scientific or ma-terialistic accomplishments, are related to the social and cultural environ-ment where people reside. As George Bernard Shaw's Eliza Doolittle in *Pygmalion* metaphorically demonstrated, and B. F. Skinner proved, it is possible to manipulate one's environment to influence behavior toward desired outcomes.[4] This belief lies at the heart of the wave of educational aids to enhance learning and achievement from prebirth through old age. It also goes for classroom learning environments.

Of course, there are biological limits that are genetically imposed on the extent of peoples' accomplishments. We're not identical in all ways, but the essence of potential human intellectual growth is essentially the same if one lives in Manhattan or on an archipelago in the South Pacific. The nature and extent of human endeavor is not so much the amount of cerebral genetic resources an individual or group has at its disposal, *but the influence of one's rearing and cultural priorities.*

Westerners ethnocentrically consider themselves the most civilized, sophisticated, and erudite inhabitants of the Earth. Yet, they could not survive in regions characterized by extreme heat or cold populated by indigenous people they deign to consider part of the same species. Historians, social scientists, and Holocaust survivors still ponder the enormity of barbarism, depravity, and crimes against humanity by the ostensibly most culturally advanced, civilized nation of the world, Germany. No ethnic group or nation has hegemony on creativity or evil.

The very fact that people look and behave differently has been the source of enormous human pain and suffering through the ages. Variations in language, clothes, and material culture that manifests itself in music, art, science, literature, and architecture, as well as nonmaterial ways of thinking and behaving (customs and traditions) distinguish one ethnic group from another. When, as we have seen, groups develop in isolation from one another, they not only develop different cultures but may have physiological differences. These occurred over thousands of years from living in different environments. These adaptations do not alter the basic genetic universality of humans. We are all basically physiologically the same.

DIFFERENCES AND HUMAN MISERY

Human groups have different appearances. Through the ages people attempted to explain intellectual and athletic accomplishments based on skin color, often using it as an indicator of intelligence. The flaw in such logic is the confusion between attributing outward structural/physiological differences among people as the cause of differences, instead of acknowledging that differences are derived from the effects of culture.

Human history is replete with instances of barbarism and genocide perpetrated against minorities whose behavior did not conform to the norms of the dominant group. Minorities have at times been tolerated by the dominant group. The Ottoman Turk Muslims allowed Christians and Jews and other religious minorities to practice their faith and traditions for six hundred years in the vast territory they controlled. Nevertheless, incidents of intolerance emanating from perceived genetic and cultural differences stand as hallmarks of human cruelty and inhumanity through the annals of history.

In the twentieth and twenty-first centuries we have seen massacres and genocidal rampages conducted against out-group minorities by the Turks (over 1.5 million Armenians killed between 1915 and 1923) and the Nazis (six million Jews and five million political dissidents, Gypsies, Jehovah's Witnesses, physically and mentally disabled between 1933 and 1945); in Nigeria (as many as three million Igbos killed in 1967), Cambodia (two million ethnic Chinese, Thai, Christians, Muslims, Buddhists, Vietnamese, and assumed dissidents between 1975 and 1978), Rwanda (800,000 mostly Tutsis by the Hutus from April to June 1994), Darfur (2003 to present 300,000 mostly black Africans); of Uighurs (Muslims) persecuted by the Han Chinese (present), Indians, and Pakistanis (1947 to present); and between Sunnis and Shiites in Iraq, Syria, and other Arab countries. We've also seen continued persecution of Christians, Muslims, Buddhists, Hindus, Jews, and other religious minorities in various countries today along with the traditional persecution of dark-skinned people by light-skinned ones.

If there is a common denominator among these sordid cases of crimes against humanity, it can be found in the attempt of the dominant cultural or color group to ridicule, belittle, and dehumanize the status of the minority. Emanating from religious, class, ethnic, or color differences, dominants attempt to denigrate minority contributions by disparaging them.

Derogatory labels and terms are used to further demarcate boundaries between the dominants and minorities. Minorities are imbued with ascribed statuses that carry negative attributes which label them as physically, morally, and intellectually deficient (e.g., the Dalit in India). We must try to understand the processes involved in the dehumanization of out-groups and the methods used to elevate dominants in order to avoid continuous civil strife around the world as culturally distinct groups increasingly interact.

INTELLECTUAL SUPERIORITY? THE CASE OF THE JEWS

Anti-Semitism originated from the crime of deicide purportedly committed by Jews. Dark-skinned people, on the other hand, have suffered from racist characterizations of them as intellectually inferior to light-skinned Europeans. This is because of misguided assumptions about their origin and appearance. Let's take a closer look at these assumptions.

Jews have been vilified for 2,000 years because of anti-Semitic demons that swirled in the heads of some gentiles. They nevertheless provided necessary services in predominantly Christian and Muslim societies as merchants, financiers, and, most importantly, scientists, artists, musicians, and scholars. As contributions to their adopted homelands around the world increased, and assimilation turned into amalgamation, stereotypes about them being different in some structural physical and psychological way persisted. Even in countries where they had resided for hundreds of years (e.g., Germany, Poland, Hungary, and Russia).

Jews had the unique status of being at once despised and envied, damned and praised, ostracized yet necessary. They were thought of, like the opine of the misogynist, as "you can't live with them, and you can't live without them." Perhaps no ethnic group has experienced as much travail or been more reviled and stigmatized than the Jews. Yet, like Christians and Muslims, they trace their lineage back to Abraham, who supposedly lived about 4,000 years ago. Since the Babylonian conquest of their nation in what is now Israel and Palestine nearly 2,600 years ago, they have been dispersed around the world.

Despite anti-Semitic propaganda, there is no stereotypical Jewish phenotype, no common Jewish morphology. There are light-skinned and dark-skinned Jews, Jews with blonde hair and blue eyes, and Jews with black hair and coal black eyes. There are Nordic, Aryan-looking Jews and Asian Jews with the epicanthic fold that narrows their eyes like their neighbors.

Jews have for centuries tended to live endogenously. This has resulted in certain polymorphisms that have created genetic markers (e.g., a Y chromosomal anomaly that distinguishes male Jewish priests (cohanim) from nonpriests and non-Jews). This trait proved that a black South African group called the Lemba were indeed of Jewish ancestry.[5] Common blood types and fingerprint whorls notwithstanding, these genetic eccentricities reveal little more than shared ethnicity. The overwhelming evidence demonstrates nearly identical DNA among all people, regardless of ethnic heritage. Our "out of Africa" lineage is older and more significant, and trumps more recent evolutionary sojourns.

Jews have, as people in other ethnic groups, learned to live, adapt, and cope with their neighbors and the various environments where they dwelled. Their trials and tribulations over 2,000 years of diaspora have been well documented. From the Roman conquest that led to the death of over 800,000 Jews during two revolts, the last one ending around 76 B.C.E. (before the common era), to the systematic genocide that liquidated six million European Jews during the Nazi Holocaust between 1933 and 1945 (two-thirds of the European Jewish population, including 1.5 million Jewish children), they have persevered.

Yet, this religious/ethnic group, numbering less than fifteen million people, just 0.2 percent of the world's population and 2 percent of the U.S. population, accounted for 22 percent (185) of the recipients of Nobel prizes between 1901 and 2011. Over a third (36 percent) of the Nobel recipients in the United States have been Jewish (as well as 38 percent of United States National Medal of Science winners). The figures are revealing in table 2.1.

The simplistic explanation for this anomaly would be to conclude that Jews are endowed with genetic abilities that are reflected in their accomplishments. While that reasoning may appeal to some people, it was inverted by anti-Semites who targeted them in state-sponsored pogroms in Europe for behaving differently from the majority. The reality is that after 2,000 years of persecution, Jews managed to survive and make important contributions to their adopted countries and the world—even if they were not always allowed or wanted to assimilate. And that is the key to understanding their achievements.

They were unable to fully participate in many of the countries they resided in. At times they were denied the right to vote, own property,

Table 2.1. Number of Jewish Nobel Laureates 1901–2010

Field	Percent of Jewish World Recipients	Percent of Jewish U.S. Recipients
Chemistry	20	29
Economics	41	53
Literature	12	27
Peace	9	10
Physics	26	37
Physiology/Medicine	27	40

*Figures are for people of full, three-quarters and half Jewish lineage. Source: Jewish Nobel Prize Winners, http://www.jinfo.org/Nobel_Prizes.html. (Reprinted with permission.) See also Richard Nisbett, Intelligence and How to Get It (New York: W.W. Norton, 2009), chapter 9 for more statistics on this point.

and participate in guilds and other occupations that could provide them with security and social mobility. Jews turned inward, embracing asceticism and scholarship. Studying Jewish law and the Bible, Talmud, and Torah became the focus of their lives. It was this emphasis that led to creative thinking that challenged and questioned their existence. Rewarding children for scholarship and intellect became the cornerstone of Jewish educational attainment.

Christians eschewed materialism and financial pursuits, obeying the admonition of Matthew 19:24, "It is easier for a camel to pass through the eye of a needle than for a rich man to enter the kingdom of God," and Matthew 6:24, "No man can serve two masters . . . God or Mammon (Greed)." Jews filled the vacuum and became merchants, bankers, and moneylenders. Despite the need for such people, Christians loathed these pursuits, recalling Christ's tirade against Jewish merchants and moneylenders in the Temple: "Jesus entered the Temple and began to drive out all the people buying and selling animals for sacrifice. He knocked over the tables of the money changers and the chairs of those selling doves," Matthew 21:12.[6]

What emerged from this sentiment was a classic case of blaming the victim. Jews were denied opportunities to participate in culturally sanctioned activities. At times they were treated as outcasts, ostracized, and forced to live in ghettos, shtetls, and "beyond the pale of settlement." They focused on intellectual, scholarly endeavors and trade. They pursued their Abrahamic religious tradition, including at times, speaking a central and eastern European language derived from Hebrew, German, and Slavic called Yiddish.

While being rejected and denied full participation in many European countries, they were stigmatized and castigated for being different. Their very reaction to ostracism, which was often forced upon them, was used as an indication of their difference and marked them as unwilling to assimilate. It was not Jewish genes but Jewish culture that produced some of the world's greatest minds.[7]

How Did Jews Manage to Succeed?

After all, what is a Jew but a human being who is the sum of his or her environmental opportunities and motivation to succeed? Insight into the reason for the high level of Jewish achievement appeared in research conducted by Andrew Cherlin and Carin Celebusky. Writing in the *Journal of Marriage and Family*, they concluded, after reviewing National Opinion Research center surveys between 1972 and 1980, covering representative samples of 12,280 people, that "overall, the differences between Jewish and non-Jewish families are more modest than many previous writers have suggested. However, in the domain of childbearing and childrearing Jews do seem to be different; they tend to follow a strategy well suited to enhancing their children's social, economic, and intellectual achievements."[8]

The researchers found that Jews instilled a higher level of motivation and desire to achieve in their children than Protestants and Catholics. They took satisfaction from their children's achievements. Jews were more likely to value self-determination and self-direction for their children, emphasizing autonomy that could lead to accomplishments in society. Coupled with the smaller size of Jewish families, such motivation helps to explain high levels of Jewish achievement.

After a thorough review of psychological research on intelligence, psychologist Richard Nisbett concluded that, although Jews have the highest average IQ of any ethnic group, their intellectual success is due to their culture and environment, which emphasize scholarship and achievement.[9]

No genetic markers have been identified linking achievement to ethnicity. The explanation of Jewish achievement confirms the importance of sociocultural, learned experiences for children and the role of family and early educational opportunities on later outcomes in life. The obverse of this thesis, that deprivations experienced in early childhood can impair academic achievement, has been amply demonstrated by contemporary research. The National Assessment of Educational Progress, known as "The Nation's Report Card," reveals that more than 40 percent of the variation in average reading scores and 46 percent of the variation in average math scores in the United States is related to poverty.[10]

It is not genes or nature that is the key factor in the Jewish equation for success, but society, that is, nurture. The wonder about Jewish accomplishments through the ages is that they were able to achieve success despite restrictions placed upon them by contemptuous anti-Semites.

Even after expulsion from England in 1290, France in 1306, Spain in 1492, Norway in 1687, and many other countries,[11] they managed to survive, endure, thrive, and be readmitted, often becoming integrated and assimilated into their new homeland. The fact that Jews had lived in Germany for more than a thousand years, a nation reputed to have achieved the highest level of culture and civilization, still confounds scholars of the Holocaust and torments survivors.[12]

Anti-Semitism was a product of supposed Jewish involvement in deicide. Religious dogma, reaction to Jewish customs and traditions, and antipathy to Jewish claims of a Covenant with God denoting them as the "chosen people," were also components in it.

Jews have been persecuted for more than 2,000 years based on criteria used to single them out as genetically different from the non-Jewish population. This sentiment reached its climax with the eugenics movement in the first half of the twentieth century, culminating in the Nazi's attempt to characterize Jews as *Untermensch* (a subhuman species). Ideological and pseudoscientific propaganda then fueled nascent anti-Semitism in occupied European countries, leading to their mass extermination.[13]

Philosopher George Santanya wrote, "Those who ignore history are condemned to repeat it." In the case of Jews, repeated stereotyping and demonizing has led to discrimination, acts of brutality, and genocide. It also calls to mind Jewish resilience, an ethnic group's ethos to survive and thrive against formidable obstacles. There is no Jewish gene for brilliance—no genetic explanation for their contributions to the world. Jewish triumphs have come at great sacrifice measured in blood, sweat, and tears.[14]

ORIGIN OF MYTHS ABOUT BLACKS

Just as Jews have been stereotyped as brilliant intellectual overachievers, the obverse is said about dark-skinned people, especially African-Americans. Early attempts to classify groups of people as superior and inferior escalated in the 1700s and became a fascination of Europeans who had an obsession for ranking people in beauty and intelligence.[15] Not surprisingly, they always put themselves at the pinnacle of their classificatory schemes.

Noted Swedish biologist Carolus Linnaeus (1707–1778) was the first person to develop a taxonomic scheme for classifying living organisms in his *Systema Naturae*, published in 1735. Linnaeus was principally concerned with plants. His biological taxonomy is still used today. It fell to the German researcher, Johann Friedrich Blumenbach (1752–1840), the "father of scientific anthropology," to create the first comprehensive human classificatory scheme. In his *On the Natural Varieties of Mankind*, published in 1776, Blumenbach declined to rank order the types he created for mankind based on superiority or inferiority: Caucasian (white), Mongolian (yellow), Malayan (brown), Ethiopian (black), and American (red). He did, however, infer differences in temperament and motivation. These concepts influence to this day stereotypes about people of color.

The field of scientific anthropology was an attempt to understand the diverse behavior of people in situ, that is, where they lived. It was an important contribution to the fledgling social science. Despite attempts of scientists to render their work value-free, pressures of the prevailing political climate at times distort concepts and intentions. Such was the fate of early anthropology.

Figure 2.1. Man ape, from Angola[16]

As European travelers returned from voyages to distant places around the world, they brought back sketches and commentaries of the "strange" inhabitants they observed.

Figure 2.2. A Hottentot family [17]

The practice of labeling indigenous dark-skinned people as primitive and even subhuman became commonplace in the context of the ethnocentric European perspective that stereotyped other cultures as inferior. The rationale for this was threefold: from the European perspective, they were more technologically advanced by virtue of being able to travel to "undeveloped" parts of the world—proof that their culture and belief system was naturally superior to what many considered depraved, soulless, primitive, and less civilized species of mankind.

Secondly, the European penchant for decimating, subjugating, and enslaving indigenous people required a corresponding rationalization to justify the degradation of foreigners and the expropriation of their property. This rationalization took shape in the reasoning of clergy like the Spaniard Juan Gines de Sepulveda. In the sixteenth century he argued before a junta created by King Charles V of Spain that indigenous people were inferior and they and their property belonged to their conquerors.[18]

A third motive in the plundering of distant lands and peoples was the evangelical thrust of Christianity. This was led by sycophantic monarchs and clergy intent on expanding state and religious properties. Such rationalizations served to inspire and motivate some of the explorers and conquistadors during the sixteenth and seventeenth century. It undoubtedly led to destruction and misery among indigenous peoples in the Americas and Africa. Along with the rise of mercantilism and capitalism, these concepts not only provided the motivation for the subjugation of indigenous people, they justified it.

It may seem like a stretch to link such concepts to contemporary stereotypes about people of color. But a persistent common thread depicting dark-skinned people as ignorant, simianlike, and incapable of being civilized persists in European and North American societies to this day. Perhaps it is a remnant of Blumenbach's classification that cited those people dwelling by the Caucasus Mountains in Asia Minor as the "most beautiful race of men." Although he remarked positively on the accomplishments of Africans, it was this designation of whites that became the standard by which beauty and grace were defined. As Europeans invaded the far corners of the globe, they not only infused their technology but their culture with its religion, ethics, orientation to work, and physical appearance. This permeated, and often perversely affected, indigenous populations.

The fact that European standards of aesthetics were unapproachable by indigenous people denigrated their culture. In effect, this established a castelike system that, to this day, relegates people of color to a subservient position in a social hierarchy they cannot hope to transcend. No matter how hard they work, no matter how much time and money they spend attempting to transform themselves into European clones, they still are considered outcasts in white-dominated societies.[19]

There is an ancient Chinese proverb that says, "He who wins the war and invents the printing press may write history and establish cultural norms in the most flattering way." The spoils of war encompass more than material possessions. They intrude into the unconsciousness of people, influence thought, and set standards and normative ways of thinking and behaving. They dominate the vanquished in ways far beyond those attained by the sword and the gun.[20]

We will explore this phenomenon later in our discussion of the unification of mankind. It should be noted that the bias favoring white culture and standards of beauty over the aesthetics and culture of indigenous people, who were subjected to colonization and exploitation by Europeans, has had a lasting impact on their perceptions of, and relationships with, white people.

To this day, some people of color in the United States and indigenous people around the world are hostile toward whites because of the rapacious, avaricious, and exploitative behavior of Europeans bent on conquering the planet for the sake of God, King, and Mammon. Such beliefs form the basis of a deep distrust of whites and a repugnance of their culture. These feelings have been, and will continue to be, expressed in various forms of protest ranging from peaceful to violent terroristic attacks on Westerners and their surrogates.[21]

EXPLORING THE MYTH OF THE BLACK ATHLETE

Maybe it is white narcissistic infatuation with the belief they are naturally superior that gnaws at their egos when they observe dark-skinned people performing extraordinarily on playing fields around the world. This was an ironic turn of events in view of eighteenth- and nineteenth-century chauvinistic British and European perceptions of indigenous "colored" peoples as physically and intellectually inferior to whites.

When colonial powers conquered Africa, Asia, Australia, and the Americas, they viewed the inhabitants as lower species on a phylogenetic scale that had white Europeans at the top. This reasoning emanated from the polygenetic hypothesis, which held that God created white Europeans in his own image, but other, lesser species of men and women were also created around the world.[22]

It was not until Charles Darwin's treatises *On the Origin of the Species*[23] and *The Descent of Man*[24] that an alternative, monogenetic theory was proposed. It gave credence to the modern view that all living humans are descended from a man and woman who lived in Africa thousands of years ago. Even after Darwin's ideas gained credibility, popular racist stereotypes about the genetic physiological and intellectual inferiority of people of color persisted and permeated the policies and treatment of indigenous people in colonized lands. Even today, only a minority of people in the United States and Great Britain subscribe to Darwin's findings, despite its acceptance among scientists as the seminal basis of understanding biology.[25]

Some writers regaled the virtues of noble savages as rugged individuals who mastered their environment. But racist ideologies depicting indigenous people as physically unfit and morally degenerate dominated the thinking of Europeans and influenced policies of colonial powers. For example, Comte Joseph Arthur de Gobineau, recognized as the founder of modern racist theory, wrote about the physical and intellectual inferiority of dark-skinned people in his 1856 treatise, *The Moral and Intellectual Diversity of Races*.[26]

When indigenous people of color were not barred from participating in sports, they were ridiculed for their lackluster performance or scorned for their purportedly inferior strength and stamina. Compared to white Europeans, who ostensibly represented the highest level of intellectual and physical perfection, indigenous people were disadvantaged because of their supposedly inferior genes. These beliefs became the underpinning that perpetuated white conceptions of racial superiority. They justified restrictions impeding full access to and participation in European sports (e.g., soccer, cricket, rugby, and track) and helped establish a psychological framework that bolstered white self-perceptions about their superior athletic prowess and invincibility on the playing field.

Denying people of color equal opportunities to participate in white-dominated sports (recruitment, training, nutrition, coaching, equipment) helped perpetuate the European perception of their own physical superiority by creating a sports-centered self-fulfilling prophesy. How could the outcome be otherwise in the face of blocked opportunities and restrictions placed on aspiring indigenous participants? When black and brown athletes began to gain prominence in athletic competition, their success was explained as evidence of their closeness to nature, primitiveness, and ability to endure the pain of demanding training that European and other white competitors could not.[27]

Even more malevolent in its impact on the opportunities of people of color in the United States and around the world has been the persistence of the white ideology that holds there is an inverse relationship between their athletic performance and intellectual ability, what Professor John Hoberman calls the "Law of Compensation." This belief has not only impeded the full participation of athletes of color in white-dominated sports around the world, it has restricted them to certain sports and positions within them (e.g., it was not until the late 1960s that blacks were allowed to play quarterback in the NFL). It nourished white racist sentiments about the criminal proclivities of uncivil athletes of color who surfaced in professional sports such as American football and basketball.[28]

Even today, athletes of color are ridiculed by fans in Europe who make monkey noises and throw bananas on the field in soccer matches. The situation became so serious that FIFA, the world governing body of football (soccer), conducted a campaign to curtail racism during the 2010 World Cup in South Africa,[29] and antiracist banners are still displayed at soccer matches in Europe.

Equally unfortunate and disastrous is the belief by many children of color that their best opportunity for success runs through the athletic field rather than the classroom. Euphoria exists among some African-Americans over their contemporary dominance of some sports. But the white grip on economic and political power remains virtually impervious to change.[30]

The relevance of this discussion to our thesis cannot be overstated. The social and psychological implications of racist stereotypical conceptions of people of color influence our perceptions of one another throughout the world. White conceptions of beauty, religion, and morality have come to symbolize the desirable standard. They have been inculcated into indigenous cultures conferring representations of what is acceptable and preferable, even though they may not be attainable.

Faced with the imposition of values and standards that may be alien, antithetical, and even inimical to indigenous cultures, people of color may seek advancement by pursuing dominance and recognition in athletic endeavors. These hold out the tantalizing promise of success denied them through participation in the social, economic, and political spheres of activity. The fact that their chance of making it as a professional athlete is comparable to winning a lottery matters little. When compared to the materialistic hype that pervades the airwaves and suffuses the minds of wannabe pros with prospective multimillion-dollar incomes, luxurious limousines, high-priced clothes, and glamorous women — the twenty-first century American Dream through athletic prowess exerts a strong pull.

African-Americans and Professional Sports

In the United States, African-Americans were restricted from participating in professional sports like baseball, basketball, and football, and relegated to Negro leagues until the mid-twentieth century. Today, they have seemingly come to dominate these sports. But the reality is something quite different when you take a closer look and consider the population base from which the players are drawn; cultural influences on athletic participation; the attitudes of coaches, management, and owners of teams; fallacious beliefs about genetics and athletic ability; the difficulty in trying to ascertain someone's racial/ethnic identity; and the ubiquity of performance-enhancing substances. These issues are highlighted in the following discussion.

American football is often viewed as the epitome of toughness and athletic prowess.[31] There are 1,696 players on the thirty-two professional football teams in the National Football League (NFL). The league barred black players for decades. Currently, 67 percent of the players are black, (and a surprising 2 percent are Polynesian). Looking at these numbers, one might conclude that nature has made dark-skinned people physically suited for the sport. But one must not overlook the role of culture, history, and social and psychological forces in the development of athletes and their choice of sports.

Clearly, professional sports in the United States, especially football, basketball, and some events in track are dominated by people of color. Journalist Jon Entine contends that men of west and east African descent have a biological/genetic edge that contributes to their supremacy in jumping and running.[32] Contrary to this view, historian John Hoberman contends, "Such ideas about the 'natural' physical talents of dark-skinned peoples, and the media-generated images that sustain them, probably do more than anything else in our public life to encourage the idea that blacks and whites are biologically different in a meaningful way." This mindset is destructive to African-Americans and society in general.[33]

Looking at past depictions of people of color as intellectually inferior to whites, Hoberman fears racial stereotypes about black athletic superiority perpetuate racist thinking. After analyzing historical and physiological evidence about purported racial genetic differences in athletic ability, he concluded,

> Having examined nerve fibers, muscle fibers, bone density, human growth hormone, the male sex hormone, and more, we have found that the data are only as dangerous as the evolutionary scenarios they evoke, and that such scenarios originate less in our knowledge of human biology than in an imaginary realm that has been shaped by *National Geographic*, Tarzan films, and what we believe about the worst horrors of American slavery.[34]

The recent analysis of sport physiology research by journalist David Epstein presents evidence of small genetic differences among ethnic groups, especially runners, but he is careful to temporize his remarks with the caveat that culture has an important role in athletic success.[35]

Though journalist Entine devotes his tome to enumerating the records held and outstanding performances of people of African descent, he fails to comprehend the scientific fact that there are more variations in performance within a group than between groups. Furthermore, varying sources estimate as much as 35 percent of African-American genes are derived from whites, depending on the region, from vestiges of slavery and miscegenation. These genes are predominantly from white males. Obversely, population geneticist Mark Shriver estimates that as many as fifty million whites in the United States have at least one black ancestor.[36]

Some writers unknowingly perpetuate the myth of separate racial groups when, in reality, there is only one race, *Homo sapiens*. Voluminous statistics revealing differing levels of athletic achievement do not reflect underlying racial differences. They may indicate differences between ethnic groups who, for social and psychological reasons, as much as physiological ones, choose to participate, train, and compete in certain sports.

As with any large distribution of people, there are exceptions on both ends of the bell curve of normal distribution. Most individuals fall in the middle range. Coaches and owners, as well as the public, have become fixated on the outliers of the distribution. They seek exceptionalities and cultivate specific types, characteristics, and specializations for a given sport (e.g., football).

These specializations are often not transferable to other sports. The ability to perform specializations (e.g., batting or throwing a baseball or catching a football) can be linked to body types. In some instances these can be improved through training, coaching, and diet, leading to superior functioning (e.g., quickness, speed, stamina, flexibility, accuracy, agility, strength). What proponents of the superiority of the black athletic perspective overlook is the *range of specializations* and abilities within every ethnic group on the planet, *as well as the ability to think clearly and creatively and make decisions under pressure in a competitive situation.*

Comprehension, including creativity of thought and the ability to make critical decisions instantaneously on the athletic field is not contingent on the color of one's skin, religion or ethnicity. It is distributed randomly throughout the species, manifested like courage, fortitude, humility, and honor as the noble acts of men and women in the struggle for greatness and survival.

Many young African-American men participate in football and basketball because they view it as their ticket to success. Inner-city boys are heavily recruited into these sports, just as young Polynesians see football as their way to fame and fortune. The Mormon Church proselytizes heavily in Polynesia, offering educational opportunities at an extension of Brigham Young University in Oahu, Hawaii. Their sojourn to the mainland receives a boost if they are inclined to play football.

The Keys to Success: Motivation and Opportunity

Any attempt to ascertain the formula for the athletic and intellectual achievement of people must include the impact of motivation and opportunity in their lives: how hard a person is willing to work to accomplish his/her goals and what kind of obstacles must be overcome to achieve them. Blacks were excluded from most professional sports in the United States (football's NFL until 1946, baseball's major leagues until 1947, and basketball's NBA until 1950). They played in their own leagues, at times against white teams.

The success of black athletes when they entered white professional leagues helped to increase the opportunities for other minorities in the previously white-dominated world of professional sports. Blacks were denied opportunities to gain admission to financially remunerative positions in the corporate sector. They were also prevented from obtaining the requisite academic skills that would enable them to compete with whites for positions in leading colleges and universities.[37] They faced government policies that discouraged them from obtaining federal college grants under the World War II GI Bill of Rights.[38] Quotas also prevented them from entering all-white colleges and universities. It isn't surprising that many pursued careers in sports.[39]

This option has been one of the most misunderstood and unfortunate choices blacks have pursued. Misunderstood because blacks' seeming success on the playing field has fed into sports management stereotypes about their genetic superiority in athletics over whites. This is reflected in Entine's work.[40] Such faulty logic not only underestimates the powerful pull that the prospect of fame and fortune has on blacks, it disregards the crucial role that culture plays in the choice and mastery of a given sport.

In the final analysis, choosing to engage in a sport is a cultural choice. It is a function of its intrusion into the consciousness of the population (i.e., its desirability and its accessibility [expenses and the ease with which potential participants can engage in it]). Even more unfortunate has been the African-American and white fascination with black athletes to the exclusion, and even denigration, of black intellectual accomplishments.[41]

Major league baseball (MLB) is a good example. Management's values, a country's culture, the opportunity structure, and motivation intersect to create a market for the dreams of an ethnic group. The Dominican Republic, a country with less than ten million people that shares the island of Hispaniola with Haiti, has produced over four hundred major league baseball players. It accounts for approximately 20 percent of contemporary players. With an average per capita income of less than $3,000, there is a tremendous incentive for young men to find a way out of poverty on the island.

The success of Dominican athletes in the U.S. major leagues created a self-fulfilling prophesy. Teams recruit players heavily in the Dominican Republic in the belief that Dominicans possess superior talent for baseball. Twenty-nine of the thirty major league teams have training facilities there. The Dominican winter baseball league is renowned for its high level of play. The entire country is immersed in the culture of the sport, and this sentiment, along with the prospect of a better life, has catapulted many young men—such as Ozzie Virgil (the first Dominican to enter the major leagues in 1953); Felipe, Matty, and Jesus Alou; Julian Javier; Manny Mota; Pedro Borbon; Cesar Cedino; Juan Marichal; and Sammy Sosa—into celebrity status. What a pity Haitians prefer soccer![42] The social and psychological implications of this phenomenon make it obvious that genetics take second place to cultural influences.

Why Whites Dominate Some Sports

If we look at the predominantly white sport of tennis, we find some wealthy families sending their children to "academies" to study with coaches like Nick Bollettieri in Bradenton, Florida. They hope they will become successful like his former students Boris Becker, Jim Courier, Andre Agassi, Monica Seles, and Maria Sharapova.

It's difficult for the public to see the parallels in these examples because they are confused by the rhetoric of racism with its genetic explanation for athletic performance. Yet, white dominance of swimming, golf, tennis, skiing, and baseball (with only 8 percent African-American players) are, like black domination of football and basketball, products of the same set of processes: motivation, opportunity, access to resources, and culture.

The fact that hardly any dark-skinned athletes participate in the Winter Olympics doesn't mean that whites have genetic endowments leading to superiority on the slopes or in the rink. In fact, in 2013, there were twenty-nine players of African ancestry in the National Hockey League (NHL), most raised in cold climates where ice, snow, and hockey are found, demonstrating that dark-skinned people can achieve high levels at such sports.

What, then, accounts for white dominance in water sports? First, in white-dominated countries like the United States, blacks were forbidden or discouraged from swimming at public beaches. They were also unable to live in close proximity to the water because of the high cost of property and restrictions preventing even affluent blacks from living in such areas. Even after restrictions against blacks (and Latinos and Jews) were lifted, fees were assessed, reducing accessibility to swimming areas. Unlike Jews, they did not possess the capital to build or purchase clubs. The combination of these conditions served to diminish black participation in water sports, not myths about them having heavier bones or denser fast-twitch muscles.

Racism among Management and Coaches

If athletes gravitate to specific sports, so, too, do the attitudes of management and coaches about them and the positions they are supposedly suited for. Believing certain ethnic groups are naturally superior in some sports and positions, they focus their attention on recruiting and placing athletes with supposedly genetic affinities for them as we have seen in the case of Dominican baseball players.[43]

Successful black athletes were molded through investments of time, money, and resources into the types of athletes management was seeking without acknowledging or comprehending the influence of environmental contingencies. Owners and coaches were responsible for creating the very types of athletes they desired. The more successful they became at discovering young athletes like Dominican baseball and inner-city football players, the more they intensified their efforts to identify future stars for their team among such groups—a perfect illustration of the self-fulfilling prophesy.

This phenomenon has a psychological counterpart among white youth who, as a *Sports Illustrated* study demonstrated, choose sports in which they believe they will succeed. Such decisions were made in part based upon their perception of coaches' biases and the amount of black participation—again creating a self-fulfilling prophesy, excluding themselves from sports like football and basketball.[44]

Demythologizing Superiority in Sports

It is difficult to avoid arguments about who is the best athlete, what ethnic group produces the best players, or what team is the best in the world. It is easy to fall into the trap of believing that one ethnic group is naturally superior to another when looking at participation and win rates. One has to remain detached—to overcome ethnocentric bias and public pressure about the natural superiority of this or that athlete or ethnic group in a specific sport.

The key to debunking sport mythology lies in where you live. The supremacy of a particular ethnic group in a given sport does not mean that they are genetically superior. Their achievement is comprehensible when we consider the popularity, availability, and affinity for the sport in a specific area. Given these variables, people of varying ethnicities, colors, and cultures share the limelight of athletic and intellectual prowess. Athletes are motivated to train and succeed in a sport after considering these choices. They make rational (economic) decisions to participate.

Cricket and soccer, staples of the English, who dominated the sports for many decades, were introduced around the world through colonization. Today, despite the establishment of the sports in England, countries such as India and Australia rival her in cricket, and the English haven't won a World Cup in soccer since 1966. Brazil is the only country to have won five World Cups. What race are Brazilians?

If you were one of the 2.2 billion viewers of the 2010 men's World Cup, you would have seen a wide variety of players in shapes, sizes, and colors among the thirty-two teams in the tournament. The average number of goals scored in the sixty-four game tournament was 2.27 per game. The most goals were scored by Germany (sixteen), followed by the Netherlands (twelve), the runners-up in the tournament. Spain, the winning team, scored only eight goals, behind Argentina's ten and Uruguay's eleven. Ghana, the lone African team to make it into the round of sixteen, scored only five, as did the United States. The highest scorer of the tournament was Diego Forlan, a light-skinned player from Uruguay, with five goals.

Watching the teams running up and down the fields throughout the host country, South Africa, you did not see one side totally dominating another with superior speed, agility, stamina or strength. While some teams may have been a bit taller than others, some of the stars in the competition were among the smallest athletes on the pitch. Often the difference between winning and losing was just one goal, with a number of games being decided by overtime shootouts. So too was the 2011 Women's World Cup won by a highly skilled Japanese team over the bigger and highly touted U.S. squad.

Some small ethnic groups have hegemony over certain sports. Why are Basques the best jai alai players in the world? The three million people who live in the region that borders Spain and France from the Mediterranean Sea in the west to the Pyrenees in the east are infatuated with and dominate the sport. Does that mean that they have a gene that makes them superior jai alai players? If we give little credence to such a statement, why should we assume that Dominicans are genetically superior baseball players or Austrians and Norwegians genetically superior at Alpine events or Australians naturally better in tennis or swimming? What of the supposed genetic superiority of Kenyan and Ethiopian distance runners or African-Americans and Polynesians in football? Does the Italian fondness for bocce ball mean they have a genetic predisposition for bowling and baseball—sports in which they have excelled?

Be careful before you jump to conclusions about this. There may indeed be overrepresentation of certain ethnic groups in specific sports, but that *does not* prove genetic intervention. The penchant of football and basketball coaches to recruit blacks is recognition of blacks' interest in and dedication to those sports *and* their popularity among African-Americans, as well as the rewards they offer to young men from impoverished backgrounds.

To what extent coaches and management understand (or care about) the complex dynamics of this situation is not known. We had a glimpse of their stereotypical views in an ABC television *Nightline* interview in 1987 between host Ted Koppel and Al Campanis, then general manager of the Los Angeles Dodgers.

Koppel asked Campanis about the dearth of blacks in managerial positions on and off the field in baseball, to which he replied, "I know that they have wanted to manage, and many of them haven't managed. But they are outstanding athletes, very God-gifted and wonderful people. . . . They are gifted with great musculature and various other things. They are fleet of foot and this is why there are a number of black ballplayers in the major leagues." Koppel seemed dismayed by Campanis's response and pressed him again about the lack of African-Americans in the front office. Campanis responded, "It's just they may not have some of the necessities to be, let's say a field manager, or perhaps, a general manager." At the time, forty years after Jackie Robinson integrated major league baseball, there were no black managers, general managers, or owners. Although Campanis apologized, he was forced to resign two days later.[45]

Major league baseball has made some changes since then. In 1999, Bud Selig, commissioner of baseball, mandated that teams seeking managers must interview a person of color in the process. At the start of the 2012 season, five of the thirty major league teams were managed by people of color (two African-Americans and three Latinos). Three general managers were of color (one Latino and two African-Americans) and 21.9 percent of senior administrative staff jobs were held by people of color. However, there are no black team owners (Ervin "Magic" Johnson is a minor partner with the Guggenheim Group that owns the Los Angeles Dodgers) and only one team is owned by a Latino (Arturo Moreno owns the Los Angeles Angels).

African-Americans have fared better in managerial positions in the National Football League, perhaps as a result of a similar policy, the Rooney Rule, implemented in 2003. Named for its progenitor, Dan Rooney, whose family owns the Pittsburgh Steelers, the rule stipulates that teams interview at least one minority person in the process of filling a head coach position.

At the start of the 2012 season, there were five African-American head coaches in the NFL and one Latino. There were also five African-American and one Latino general managers. For the first time, a person of color, Pakistani-born Shahid Khan, is a majority owner of an NFL franchise, the Jacksonville Jaguars. People of color were employed in sixteen senior administrative positions in the league's teams.[46]

The National Basketball Association is by far the most egalitarian professional sports league in the United States. At the start of the 2011–2012 season, 47 percent of the head coaches were African-American. Twenty-six percent of the general managers and 22 percent of the senior administrative officers were people of color. African-Americans held 13 percent of CEO/president positions in the league. Only one NBA team is majority-owned by an African-American, the NBA Charlotte Bobcats, whose principal owner is former basketball superstar Michael Jordan.[47]

Interestingly, four baseball teams are owned by Jews as well as eight NFL teams, nine NBA teams, and three NHL teams. The commissioners of the NBA, NHL, and MLB are Jewish. After Jews immigrated to the United States in large numbers at the turn of the twentieth century, many, like blacks later, sought advancement through sports and entertainment. Jews were commonly found in prizefighting, baseball, basketball, and football, despite stereotypes to the contrary. Fourteen Jewish athletes played in major league baseball during the 2012 season, eight in the NHL, six in the NFL, and two in the NBA.[48]

What Really Makes a Great Athlete?

A wide array of athletes from different ethnic and sociocultural backgrounds participate *and excel* at a cornucopia of sports. This demonstrates athletic proficiency as well as commitment, motivation, and perseverance. Social, cultural, and organizational pressures also predispose athletes to engage in one sport over another.

Athletic proficiency in one sport may not transfer into others. Few high-caliber athletes are able to compete in multiple sports. Remember when Michael Jordan, arguably one of the greatest basketball players in history, tried to play professional baseball? He was assigned to the Birmingham Barons, a Class AA minor league team of the Chicago White Sox. After hitting .202, he gave up on his dream of playing in the major leagues after one year.

But did you know that Jordan failed to make his Laney High School varsity basketball team in Wilmington, North Carolina, in his sophomore year? He worked hard, grew four inches, from 5'11" to 6'3," and the rest is history. Motivation is one of the cornerstones of proficiency in intellectual and athletic achievement.

Jordan's inability to make it to the major leagues of baseball also points to the specialization required to become proficient at a given sport. Some sports require speed, others dexterity, still others endurance, quickness, agility, hand/eye coordination, heftiness, or diminutiveness. Who are the best athletes in the world? *It depends on the sport*, because each one emphasizes different specialized abilities, and rarely can an athlete excel at a high level in more than one.

One notable exception was Jim Thorpe, who was born in 1887 in a one-room home in Prague, Oklahoma. His father was a farmer, and his mother was a Native American, a Pottawatomie and a direct descendant of the Sauk and Fox Chief Black Hawk. In the Olympic Games of 1912 in Belgium, Thorpe won the pentathlon and decathlon. He later played baseball for the New York Giants, Cincinnati Reds, and Boston Braves. He also played professional football for six teams, including the Canton Bulldogs and Cleveland Indians.

Thorpe's Olympic medals were taken away because he played semi-professional baseball prior to competing in the Olympics. But he didn't let that deter him from achieving on and off the athletic field, teaching and coaching Native Americans, public speaking, and compiling one of the most incredible careers of any athlete. In 1950, the Associated Press named him the greatest American football player *and* the greatest overall male athlete. ABC television christened him the greatest athlete of the first half of the twentieth century. He died of a heart attack in 1953. In 1982, twenty-nine years after his death, his medals and Olympic records were restored.[49]

What makes a great athlete like Thorpe? Surely, he had a genetic gift, but how widely is it found among other Native Americans? Or, for that matter, did his abilities come from his father's side or his mother's? How can we determine whether one of the best shortstops in baseball, Derek Jeter, gets his athletic talent from his white mother or African-American father or the best golfer, Tiger Woods, derived his ability from his Thai mother or African-American father?

Can we assume that it is solely the genetic endowment of the single black parent that accounts for the success of these athletes? Did parental support, coaching, family and community resources, training, and opportunity for competition play a role in their success?

Even more confusing is our definition of athletic achievement. The records of hockey star Wayne Gretzky stand out as a monumental accomplishment—2,857 career points, including an amazing 215-point season. Speaking of points, Wilt Chamberlain's one-hundred-point game in March 1962 against the New York Knicks may never be broken, or, for that matter, Ty Cobb's .366 career batting average or Nolan Ryan's seven no-hitters or Cy Young's 511 wins or Jerry Rice's 22,895 receiving yards in football.

One would think that the real test to determine the world's greatest athlete would be the Olympic decathlon. U.S. athletes have fared well in this event. In 1948 and 1952, Bob Mathias, a white man, won in London and Helsinki. He was followed in 1956 by Milt Campbell in Melbourne and in 1960 by Rafer Johnson in Rome, both African-Americans. In 1968, Bill Toomey, a white male from the United States, won in Mexico City, and in 1976 a white American male, Bruce Jenner, won in Montreal. In 1996, American Dan O'Brien, an adopted child who is Finnish and African-American, won when the games were in Atlanta. In the Bejing games in 2008, Brian Clay, an American, whose mother is Japanese and father is African-American, won, and in the London games of 2012, twenty-four-year-old Ashton Eaton, whose mother is white and father is African-American, took first place over his teammate, Trey Hardee (white), two-time world champion, who took the silver medal.

One of the greatest decathlon athletes is Daley Thompson, a black man born in England. Along with Bob Mathias, they are the only two athletes to win the Olympic decathlon twice.[50] Thompson has the distinction of holding the world, Olympic, Commonwealth, and European decathlon titles simultaneously. He was undefeated in the event for nine years.

But perhaps you think endurance is the mark of the greatest athlete. Which sport would you pick to demonstrate that? How about the Tour de France, a bicycle event that lasts three weeks and covers about 2,000 miles. A white American, Lance Armstrong, won a record seven times, but the sport of cycling was dominated by Marshall "Major" Taylor, an African-American in the 1890s, and he didn't employ blood doping and performance-enhancing drugs.

Distance running is an interesting phenomenon. Long dominated by white males, perhaps the greatest of his time was Paavo Nurmi of Finland. In 1925 he set two world records in one hour, running the mile and 5,000 meters in Madison Square Garden in New York. He competed in three Olympic Games from 1920 to 1928, winning nine gold and three silver medals and setting twenty-five world records. Ethiopian Haile

Gebrselassi was one of the greatest contemporary runners in the world. He set twenty-seven world records and competed in four Olympics, winning the gold medal twice at 10,000 meters.

Time is an important factor in the development and success of athletes. Are the athletes of today superior to those of the past? Bigger, faster, stronger . . . of course, and the records prove that point. In fairness, each new generation of athlete can only be compared to his or her peers. Diet, coaching, training, resources (including pharmaceuticals and rehabilitation) change, and with them their influence on athletic performance.

Researchers at the Tuck School of Business at Dartmouth College have been able to predict the medal outcome of Olympics with 95 percent accuracy by factoring in a country's population and per capita Gross Domestic Product (GDP). GDP is the best predictor of a country's Olympic performance, even though some sports are nation specific and may have a larger pool of athletes to draw on.

Past medal success is also a good predictor of future success because past investments in producing successful medalists pays off in future wins over their careers. Host countries win an additional 1.8 percent of the medals beyond that predicted by GDP alone because of their mobilization of resources. This demonstrates once again the importance of societal values in the performance of athletic (and intellectual) achievement.[51]

The field of distance running is dominated today by Ethiopian and Kenyan runners. This fact can be partially explained once again by their motivation to succeed, rigorous training, and quality coaching. Journalist Jon Entine contended there is a genetic factor that contributes to their success and the success of African-American and Jamaican sprinters.[52]

He acknowledged that illegal drugs were being used to boost athletic performance, but concluded his tome by heaping adoration on the African-American track star Marion Jones. She won five medals at the Sydney Olympics in 2000. Jones was later convicted of lying to federal agents about her use of performance-enhancing drugs. In addition to forfeiting medals and prizes, she served six months in prison.

In view of subsequent revelations and allegations about widespread use of performance-enhancing drugs by athletes of all colors and ethnicities, one might reasonably assume that today, many athletic records are suspect, in effect rendering attempts to compare accomplishments within and among different ethnic groups pointless.

Why Do We Care about Athletic Ability?

A common assumption of sports fans around the world is that dark-skinned athletes are superior to light-skinned ones. This belief is, at its most elemental level, inherently racist and anti-intellectual. As we have demonstrated, there are no significant biological differences among the many ethnic groups around the world. All humans share 99.98 percent identical DNA. The obvious differences in skin color; height; weight; hair texture; and the shape of one's eyes, ears, or nose are polymorphisms that developed through generations of inbreeding and separation from other ethnic groups. They are not related to basic human genetic variation in intellectual or athletic ability. There is just as much intellectual and athletic variation within an ethnic group as there are among them.

Despite scientific evidence to the contrary, many coaches and sports fans still believe that some groups possess superior athletic ability over others. An astute critic of racism in sports perceptively observed, "The world of sport has become an image factory that disseminates and even intensifies our racial preoccupations."[53] Racial stereotypes of black athletes in the media not only impede the performance of white athletes, they are detrimental to blacks by portraying them as essentially physical and primitive.[54] Such depictions diminish black intellectual achievements in science, business, and the arts.

People of color have also made enormous contributions to the intellectual and business foundations of our civilization. The facts are indisputable but often ignored or denigrated by ethnocentric, chauvinistic, or ignorant people. They are fearful of and ill-prepared for the coming merger of mankind that transcends national, social, and psychological boundaries.[55]

That one ethnic group has attained intellectual or athletic notoriety is not the result of genetic endowment. It results from a complex set of variables. These include motivation for and opportunities to engage in an activity; the location where a person resides; cultural preferences, expectations, encouragement and rewards for engaging in one sport or intellectual endeavor over another; and timing, which determines when a particular activity is appropriate and available. These variables are bound up in a combination of familial and peer pressures, which are combined with social and structural situations that promote or prevent an individual or group from achieving success in the classroom or on the field.

The question remains, if people are all related and nearly identical genetically, and observed differences in facial features, hair, and stature are the result of biological adaptations to one's environment over time, then doesn't it make sense that some ethnic groups have evolved physically and psychologically, giving them superior athletic and/or intellectual abilities? The answer lies in the very nature of our society—our mixing and mobility. Through the ages we have moved and interbred so much that there is no pure strain, no one physical or intellectual type that stands alone as innately superior or inferior.

Yet, the search for elusive genes that supposedly confer physical and psychological superiority goes on. An article by Max Fisher in the April 2012 *Atlantic* sought to attribute Kenyan long distance runners' success to a mysterious genetic endowment and downplayed cultural and psychological influences on their performance.

The Nazis propounded the myth of Aryan supremacy. That was debunked by Jesse Owens, a young African-American, when he won four gold medals in the 1936 Olympics in Berlin. Certainly, there are hereditary differences among ethnic groups in size, shape, and ability. But trying to generalize from isolated outlying athletic or intellectual types is like trying to predict the winning ticket in the lottery based on past winning numbers. Each draw and sequence of numbers is independent of all prior draws. They have no influence on future numeric appearances. Human genetic variation is so mixed and complex as to nullify attempts to select traits in a systematic way for the purposes of selective breeding.

The eugenics movement, popularized at the turn of the twentieth century by Houston Stuart Chamberlain, Madison Grant, and Lothrop Stoddard,[56] bemoaned the "mongrelization" of Western society and culture. Immigration of eastern Europeans, most notably Jews, was thought to represent low culture and morals. The movement received a deathblow from the horrors perpetrated under Nazism in the 1930s and 1940s. It stands as a sordid chapter in human history that resulted in the murder of six million Jews and five million disabled Germans, political dissidents, Jehovah's Witnesses, and Gypsies—people persecuted not for what they did, but for who they were.

There undoubtedly is an element of heritability that accounts for the athletic and intellectual achievement of some individuals. But the range of abilities in every ethnic group approximates the bell curve of a normal distribution with variations ranging from low to high accomplishments. The majority of people cluster at the midpoint. When Jews were blocked from full participation in American society in the early to mid-twentieth century, they sought success and recognition through intellectual endeavors as they had throughout the last 2,000 years. So, too, did the Irish, Italians, Poles, and other eastern Europeans who were similarly stereotyped as morally and intellectually backward.

As we move into the twenty-first century, African-Americans and Latinos, confronting the same types of obstacles, are demonstrating that they can compete beyond the playing field when given the opportunity. Elsewhere around the world, the awakening underclasses strive to achieve a semblance of the good life that Western society has monopolized. We can expect to see more competition as the world's population increases and natural resources become scarce and precious.

When faced with life choices, individuals weigh the range of possible outcomes of action or inaction. The path they take is not the result of genetic endowment, but of the complex of ideas that we call our culture and heritage. That one ethnic group may appear to excel on the stage of life is far less attributable to genes than who wields power and privilege. It is also based on conscious decisions about the likelihood that action will result in success or failure and produce the desired rewards in relation to the sacrifices made to obtain them. [57]

Such reasoning is the product of social, psychological, and economic considerations. Throughout history they have been embedded in cultural and ethnic traditions that have been misinterpreted as reflections of racial genetic differences in intellectual and athletic ability.

After an erudite review of the literature on intelligence, psychologist Richard Nisbett concluded that culture and the environment accounts for black/white differentials in IQ. Raising children in an upper-middle-class environment can increase their IQ scores twelve to eighteen points! He observed, "geneticists say there is no such thing as a single point estimate for heritability. Heritabilty is dependent on the particular population and the particular circumstances in which it is examined." [58] Simply stated, "the environment almost completely swamps heredity." [59] And for the poor, "only 10 percent of the variation in intelligence is driven by heredity, which means that improving the environment of children born into poor families could have a big effect on intelligence." [60]

The purpose of this discussion has been twofold: to demonstrate the underlying racist connotations inherent in assumptions about reputed superiority and inferiority of ethnic groups, blacks, and Jews in intellectual and athletic endeavors and to help readers understand the common genetic bonds all humans share and the potentialities they possess for intellectual and athletic achievement. The list of accomplishments on and off the athletic field by Jews and blacks is commendable. It is all the more remarkable in light of the obstacles they have had to overcome in their quest for equality. A quest that is reflected in the changing nature and orientation to work that is transforming societies around the world. We now turn to a discussion of this agent of change.

SUMMING UP

- Race is a social construct invented to justify the domination and exploitation of others.
- No significant differences exist in intellectual or athletic ability between light and dark-skinned people.
- Jewish intellectual accomplishments are based on Jewish emphasis on scholarship and child-rearing practices.
- Black and Latino athleticism is not biological, but the product of social and cultural forces.
- Students of all colors can improve their academic performance given the opportunity to experience quality teaching environments.

NOTES

1. Jared Diamond, "Race without Color," *Discover*, November 1994, 34–40.
2. See the landmark survey of the causes and effects of racial health disparities, *Unequal Treatment: Confronting Racial and Ethnic Disparities in Healthcare* (Washington, DC: National Academies Press, 2003).
3. See the discussion of this phenomenon in Tim Wise, *Colorblind* (San Francisco: City Lights Publishers, 2010), and H. Roy Kaplan, *The Myth of Post-Racial America* (Lanham, MD: Rowman & Littlefield Education, 2011).
4. B. F. Skinner, *Beyond Freedom and Dignity* (New York: Alfred A. Knopf, 1971).
5. David Goldstein, *Jacob's Legacy: A Genetic View of Jewish History* (New Haven, CT: Yale University Press, 2008).
6. See http://bible.cc/matthew/21–12.htm.
7. For example, Moses, Christ, Maimonides, Spinoza, Marx, Freud; scientists Boas, Bohr, Born, Einstein, Franklin, Oppenheimer, Teller, Salk; artists Chagall, Modigliani, Segall, Max; musicians Bernstein, Gershwin, Mahler, Streisand. See Charles Silberman's *A Certain People* (New York: Summit Books, 1985) for accomplishments of American Jews through most of the twentieth century and Steven L. Pease's *The Golden Age of Jewish Achievement* (Sonoma, CA: Deucalion, 2009) for a synopsis of Jewish achievements over the last two hundred years.
8. Andrew Cherlin and Carin Celebusky, "Are Jewish Families Different? Some Evidence from the General Social Survey," *Journal of Marriage and Family* 45, no. 4 (1983): 903.
9. Richard E. Nisbett, *Intelligence and How to Get It: Why Schools and Culture Count* (New York: W.W. Norton, 2009).
10. For an analysis of the effect of social class on educational attainment, see Helen F. Ladd and Edward B. Fiske, "Class Matters, So Let's Just Admit It," *St. Petersburg Times*, December 25, 2011, 4P. For statistics on the effects of poverty on learning, see "Reading, Literacy, and Education Statistics," *The Literacy Company*, at http://www.readfaster.com/education_stats.asp, and the homepage of the National Assessment of Educational Progress at nces.ed.gov/nationsreportcard/.
11. See http://www.biblebelievers.org.au/expelled.htm for a list and dates of the expulsion of Jews from nations around the world.
12. See James Carroll's *Constantine's Sword: The Church and the Jews* (Boston: Houghton Mifflin, 2001) for an analysis of the Roman Catholic Church's historical relation to the Jews and a recent analysis of anti-Semitism by Phyllis Goldstein, *A Convenient Hatred: The History of Anti-Semitism* (Brookline, MA: Facing History and Ourselves National Foundation, 2011).
13. See "How Many Jews Were Murdered" for a list of Jews killed by country in the Holocaust at http://history1900s.about.com/library/holocaust/bldied.htm.
14. Despite Jewish contributions to the world, anti-Semitism persists, often covert, but at times surfacing in the alcohol-induced rants of celebrities like actor Mel Gibson and John Galliano of Christian Dior.
15. See an excellent review of this in Stephen Jay Gould, *The Mismeasure of Man*, revised and expanded edition (New York: W.W. Norton, 1996).
16. Man ape, from Angola, presented to Fredric Henry, Prince of Orange, from N. Tulpius M.D circa 1752.
17. A Hottentot family (from Thomas Herbert's 1638 *Some Yeares Travels into Divers Parts of Asia and Africa*). See https://netfiles.uiuc.edu/rwb/www/teaching/engl209/outlines/outline24.html.
18. See: Bonar Ludwig Hernandez, "The Las Casas-Sepulveda Controversy: 1550–1551," at http://userwww.sfsu.edu/~eph/2001/hernandez.html.
19. See, for example, Ellis Cose, *Rage of a Privileged Class: Why Do Prosperous Blacks Still Have the Blues?* (New York: Harper Perennial, 1994). African-Americans and other dark-skinned people around the world are targeted by cosmetic companies for hair products and skin bleaching creams, playing on the theme that successful people have

European features and light skin. See the video by Kiri Davis at http://video.google.com/videoplay?docid=1091431409617440489#; also "Fair and Handsome" skin whitening cream ads in India at http://www.youtube.com/watch?v=Okqd9zaI698; and the "My Black is Beautiful" campaign waged by Procter and Gamble at http://myblackisbeautiful.com/.

20. Consider the implication of psychologists Claude Steele and Joshua Aronson's research in this regard, which demonstrates the negative effects of labeling and stereotyping on the academic performance of women and minorities. Claude M. Steele and Joshua Aronson, "Stereotype Threat and the Intellectual Test Performance of African-Americans," *Journal of Personality and Social Psychology* 69, no. 5 (1995): 797–811; Claude M. Steele, "Thin Ice: 'Stereotype Threat' and Black College Students," *The Atlantic,* August 1999, 44–54.

21. Martinique-born black liberationist author Frantz Fanon was one of the most ardent critics of white colonialist behavior. See his classics *The Wretched of the Earth* (New York: Grove Press, 1965); *Black Skin, White Masks,* revised edition (New York: Grove Press, 2008).

22. See Gould, *The Mismeasure of Man*; John Hoberman, *Darwin's Athletes: How Sport Has Damaged America and Preserved the Myth of Race* (Boston: Houghton Mifflin, 1997); and Jon Entine, *Taboo: Why Black Athletes Dominate Sports and Why We're Afraid to Talk about It* (New York: Public Affairs, 2000), for discussions of the supposed inferiority of dark-skinned people.

23. Charles Darwin, *On the Origin of the Species* (London: Murray, 1859).

24. Charles Darwin, *The Descent of Man,* 2 vols (London: Murray, 1871).

25. A survey in Britain found only 25 percent of adults believed Darwin's ideas were "definitely true," with another 25 percent saying they were "probably true." Riazat Butt, "Half of Britons Do Not Believe in Evolution, Survey Finds," *Guardian,* February 1, 2009, http://www.guardian.co.uk/science/2009/feb/01/evolution-darwin-survey-creationism. In the United States, Gallup Polls have consistently revealed that nearly half the adults reject Darwin's ideas. In 2001 only 12 percent of people polled believed that humans evolved from other life forms without the involvement of God. See David Quammen, "Was Darwin Wrong?" *National Geographic Magazine,* November 2004, at http://ngm.national/geographic.com/ngm/0411/feature1/. A recent PEW survey reported 40 percent of people in the United States don't believe that humans evolved over time.

26. Joseph Arthur de Gobineau, *The Moral and Intellectual Diversity of Races* (Philadelphia: J. B. Lippincott, 1856).

27. See Hoberman, *Darwin's Athletes,* for an elaboration of these points, and Entine, *Taboo,* chapter 5. Gould, *The Mismeasure of Man,* 142–151, poses a similar concept called "recapitulation theory" first propounded by the nineteenth-century German zoologist, Ernst Haeckel, which blossomed into a racist belief that dark-skinned people represented beings on the lower, earlier rungs of human development. One of the finest analyses of racism and imperialism in sport is C.L.R. James's *Beyond a Boundary,* new edition (London: Serpent's Tail, 2000).

28. For a history of black athletic participation in the United States, see William C. Rhoden, *Forty Million Dollar Slaves* (New York: Crown Publishers, 2006).

29. To see the anti-racist ceremony prior to each match in the World Cup, go to http://www.youtube.com/watch?v=DjHFJYUb4MA. Despite this effort, racism persists on European pitches. For a review of recent incidents, go to http://www.cnn.com/2013/01/04/sport.

30. For example, in the United States, only five of the Fortune 500 corporations were headed by a person of color in 2011: Ursula Burns, Xerox Corporation; Kenneth Chenault, American Express; Clarence Otis Jr., Darden Restaurants; Donald Thompson, McDonalds; and Ronald Williams, Aetna. In 2011, there were no African-Americans in the U.S. Senate and only two Latinos. Only three African-Americans have been elected governors of states since the Civil War. The U.S. Supreme Court has had only two African-Americans and one Latino in its 221-year history.

31. Yet research indicates the most difficult athletic action is hitting a baseball. See "The Force of Gauge: The Most Difficult Act in All Sports," at http://www.projectview.org/mathandbaseball/mostdifficultactinallsports.htm.

32. John Entine, *Taboo*.

33. John Hoberman, *Darwin's Athletes*, xiv.

34. John Entine, *Taboo*, 240.

35. David Epstein, *The Sports Gene: Inside the Science of Extraordinary Athletic Performance* (New York: Current, 2013).

36. John Relethford, *Reflections of Our Past* (Boulder, CO: Westview, 2003); Steve Olson, *Mapping Human History: Genes, Race and Our Common Origin* (Boston: Mariner Books, 2002); Mark D. Shriver et al., "Ethnic-Affiliation Estimation by Use of Population-Specific DNA Markers," *American Journal of Human Genetics* 60 (1997): 957–964; Esteban J. Parra et al., "Estimating African-American Admixture Proportions by Use of Population-Specific Alleles," *American Journal of Human Genetics* 63 (1998): 1839–1851.

37. For an analysis of structural/institutional effects on black attainment, see William Julius Wilson, *More Than Just Race* (New York: W.W. Norton, 2009).

38. See Ira Katznelson, *When Affirmative Action Was White* (New York: W.W. Norton, 2005), and Carol Anderson, *Eyes Off the Prize* (New York: Cambridge University Press, 2003), for discussions of racist federal policies toward minorities.

39. Jews were also restricted from entering colleges and universities by quotas, although not as widely as blacks. See Jerome Karabel, *The Chosen: The Hidden History of Admission and Exclusion at Harvard, Yale and Princeton* (Boston: Mariner Books, 2006).

40. Entine, *Taboo*.

41. See Hoberman's analysis of this phenomenon in *Darwin's Athletes*.

42. For a discussion of baseball in the Dominican Republic, see Paul Clammer, Michael Grosberg, and Jens Porup, *Dominican Republic and Haiti* (Oakland, CA: Lonely Planet, 2008). For a glimpse of why major league teams recruit heavily in the Dominican Republic and elsewhere in Latin America, see Corey Brock, "Padres Reach Out to Dominican Republic: 'Taj Mahal of Training Facilities' to Open Wednesday in Najayo," *MLB Network*, at http://mlb.mlb.com/news/article.jsp?ymd=20080428&content_id=2604573&vkey=news_sd&text=jsp&c_jd=sd.

43. Similar attitudes can be found in the preference of many U.S. college soccer coaches for foreign players, again confirming the importance of culture, motivation, and training over natural athletic ability.

44. S. L. Price, "Whatever Happened to the White Athlete?" *Sports Illustrated*, December 8, 1997, 32–55.

45. Eric Johnson, "Nightline Classic: Al Campanis," at http://abcnews.go.com/Nightline/ESPNSports/story?id=3034914.

46. See Richard Lapchick, "The 2012 Racial and Gender Report Card: National Football League," at http://tidesport.org/RGRC/2011/RGRC_NFL_2012_Final.pdf. Also see Douglas C. Proxmire, "Coaching Diversity: The Rooney Rule, Its Application and Ideas for Expansion," at http://acslaw.org/Advance%20Spring%2009/Coaching%20Diversity.pdf.

47. For more information, see Richard Lapchick, "The 2012 Racial and Gender Report Card: National Basketball Association," at http://tidesport.org/RGRC/2012/2012_NBA_RGRC_FINAL%20FINAL.pdf.

48. These numbers are estimates since leagues protect the privacy of players and some players do not release information about their religious affiliation, some have no religious preference, and some are children of mixed marriages.

49. "Jim Thorpe: World's Greatest Athlete," at http://www.cmgww.com/sports/thorpe/bio2.htm.

50. Thompson won in 1980 and 1984.

51. Andrew B. Bernard and Meghan R. Busse, "Who Wins the Olympic Games: Economic Resources and Medal Totals," *Review of Economics and Statistics* 86, no. 1 (2004): 413–417.

52. Entine, *Taboo.*

53. Hoberman, *Darwin's Athletes,* xiv.

54. See Claude M. Steele and Joshua Aronson's work on stereotype threat, "Stereotype Threat and the Intellectual Test Performance of African-Americans."

55. For a review of black inventors and their contributions to society, go to the Black Inventor Online Museum at http://www.blackinventor.com/. For a list of Hispanic contributors to the United States go to "Contributions of Americans of Hispanic Heritage," at http://www.neta.com/~1stbooks/dod2.htm. See also, Mary Bellis, "Top 10 Mexican Inventors," investors.about.com, at http://inventors.about.com/od/famousinventors/tp/mexican.htm, and "Famous Hispanic Inventors," investors.about.com, at http://inventors.about.com/od/hispanicinventors/Famous_Hispanic_Inventors.htm. A scholarly search for African-American scientists and inventors can be undertaken at http://www.ipl.org/div/pf/entry/78530.

56. Houston Stewart Chamberlain, *Foundations of the Nineteenth Century,* trans. John Lees (New York: John Lane Company, 1911); Madison Grant, *The Passing of the Great Race* (New York: Charles Scribner's Sons, 1916); Lothrop Stoddard, *The Rising Tide of Color against White World-Supremacy* (New York: Charles Scribner's Sons, 1920).

57. The most incisive critique of attempts to classify humans by purported physiological characteristics was done by the late Harvard scientist Stephen Jay Gould in *The Mismeasure of Man.* Gould's treatise uncovers historical and contemporary pseudoscientific schemes that denigrate and stigmatize marginalized groups for the purpose of perpetuating white privilege and dominance of society's elites.

58. Nisbett, *Intelligence and How to Get It,* 22.

59. Ibid., p.31.

60. Ibid., p. 194.

Act 2

Bumps along the Road

THREE

How Work Transformed Society and Created Social Inequality

Without work all life goes rotten. But when work is soulless, life stifles and dies.

—Albert Camus

Work is indeed a four-letter word, but its evolution has had an enormous impact on who we are, what we do, and the way we relate to one another and our students.

THE ROLE OF WORK THROUGH THE AGES

The Biblical admonition "By the sweat of thy brow shalt thou eat bread" reverberates through the history of mankind as a standard of individual self-worth and the communal obligation to be a productive member of society. The modern obsession with productivity and acquisitiveness was not always the cultural imperative of our forbearers. For the ancients, work was a necessity for survival. As the nature and function of work evolved in the Occident, it nurtured a system of class and status associated with the increased division and specialization of labor. This was used to extend the power and privilege of a select group of property owners.[1]

The quest for land and resources led to the domination and exploitation of dark-skinned indigenous workers in their homelands. As mercantilism and capitalism spread, workers in faraway lands were depicted as physically, intellectually, morally, and culturally inferior. Work evolved from an intrinsically meaningful and necessary part of life to an instrumental means to an end. With this evolution in its meaning and function came a chauvinistic Occidental worldview that stereotyped other cultures as primitive.

47

There is a certain arrogance associated with the kind of work one does in Western society. It can be apprehended in even the most elementary forms of interaction between people as when they first meet and exchange greetings and basic information about themselves. "Who are you?" is invariably followed by "What do you do?" This is an attempt to ascertain one's status relative to others in social settings defined by the prevailing cultural importance of the work one does.

In Western societies there is a preference for intellectual over manual work. This is because these countries have largely evolved from manufacturing things to producing and processing ideas and providing services. Not all workers in these postindustrial jobs are equally rewarded for their efforts or held in the same regard.

There is a persistent bias against working with one's hands as opposed to working with one's head. This intellectual elitism is reinforced by so-called professional organizations that purportedly promote high standards of practice and ethics among their members ostensibly to maintain quality, professional service. Much like the ancient Greek ideal, thinking occupations became the most highly esteemed (and rewarded), with the bias against physical labor relegated to the helots and supposedly less intellectually capable members of society.

Despite occasional protestations about the dignity and virtue of work (one recalls the observation of President Richard Nixon that "scrubbing floors and emptying bedpans has as much dignity as the Presidency"), Western society has come to place a priority on intellectual endeavors and rewards them commensurately. Estimated lifetime earnings of high school graduates in the United States are $1.2 million, compared to bachelors' degrees with lifetime earnings of $2.1 million, masters' with $2.5 million, doctoral degrees with $3.4 million, and professionals with $4.4 million.[2]

The disdain for manual work, despite the necessity for it (e.g., growing food, building and cleaning homes and businesses, caring for children, sick and elderly, protecting communities from crime and fire, maintaining society's infrastructure—roads, bridges, buildings) created a cult-like obsession with certification and degrees to the monetary and social detriment of physical work. Paradoxically, many of the so-called professional organizations like teaching and medicine have become mired in the materialistic ethos of our time. Today they more closely approximate trade unions. For example, the American Medical Association (AMA), founded in 1847 "to promote the art and science of medicine for the betterment of the public health," devoted much of its first 125 years trying to keep the public health in private hands. At various times it campaigned against Red Cross blood banks, compulsory vaccinations for childhood diseases, and health maintenance organizations.

The two most prominent professional teacher organizations are the American Federation of Teachers and the National Educational Association. Like the AMA, their reluctance to admonish and remove incompetent, unethical, and even criminal associates raises serious questions about their commitment to professional standards and the provision of quality services.[3]

The Western emphasis on work became a means for obtaining materialistic pleasures using the working classes at home and abroad to get them. Meanwhile, they were stereotyped as intellectually and culturally inferior because their predominant mode of production was manufacturing and low-tech services. This ideological mindset occurred in conjunction with a value system that supported the belief in inevitable progress. Now, using, consuming, and disposing of things *and people* became the Zeitgeist. It promised the good life to whites who viewed the working class and people of color as biologically inferior, expendable resources, and, in time, competitors in the global marketplace.

HOW THE WEST WON

The story of how the West came to dominate the rest of the world and feed off its human capital and resources is a fascinating tale. By a combination of luck,[4] ideology,[5] and ingenuity borne of necessity (survival in the face of a hostile environment), the Occident developed a technological edge over the rest of the world. Scientists and writers[6] have described the human exodus from Africa that began about 60,000 years ago.

It is imperative to understand the pattern of early human migration because it established human genetic lineages and contributed to cultural efflorescence. This led to the accumulation of a surplus that affected living arrangements. These in turn were spurred by the development of religious and ideological values that provided the foundation for the development of the role of work and its subsequent use in the domestication of plants and animals and the rise of feudalism, mercantilism, and capitalism.

Human Migration out of Africa

As we noted earlier, modern humans originated in Africa about 200,000 years ago. About 60,000 years ago, spurred by a variety of forces ranging from wanderlust to climatological shifts, humans began to a search for new hunting and gathering prospects. Some of our ancient ancestors commenced a migration that eventually took them throughout the world. The dispersion of people and subsequent isolation of some groups over thousands of years led to polymorphisms, or genetic mutations. For the most part these affected exterior characteristics (e.g., skin color, the shape of eyes, ears, noses).

Research by Richard Lewontin[7] and Luca Cavalli-Sforza, Paolo Menozzi and Alberto Piazza[8] confirmed the existence of different blood types and other polymorphisms among different ethnic groups around the world. One of the most significant conclusions of their work was the fact that 85 percent of human variation exists *within* any specific group. This finding reduces propositions about supposed racial differences to absurdity. More current genetic analyses of DNA confirm the blood type conclusions and reveal the universality of humanity and its common ancestral heritage in Africa.[9]

For the purpose of our discussion, it is noteworthy that scientists have found distinct polymorphisms in different ethnic groups around the globe. These are traceable to human migrations: 41,000 years for divergence between Africans and East Asians, 33,000 for Africans and Europeans, and 21,000 years for Europeans and Asians.[10] Nevertheless, all humans (*Homo sapiens*) have over 99 percent identical DNA, making suppositions about differences in athletic and intellectual ability illogical and *false*, as we have demonstrated.

So the question remains, if humans are virtually genetically identical, why did some groups of people develop different and supposedly superior technology? Bluntly, why, from a Western ethnocentric perspective, did European, and later North American, civilizations develop sophisticated market-based economies and higher standards of living compared to indigenous people in Africa, Asia, and Central and South America?

To understand the complexity of this issue we must go back in time to explore the migratory movement of humans as they surged out of Africa. Estimates place the intrusion of humans into the Middle East between 50,000 and 70,000 years ago.[11] We are able to trace the movement of our early ancestors by the spread of mtDNA and Y chromosomes in paleo-anthropological and fossilized findings.[12]

Traveling close to the shoreline, they found an abundance of edible plants and animals that could be domesticated, combined with a temperate climate (the lush African savannahs were drying up, forcing them to shift their hunting and gathering activities). This 1,200 mile strip of land became referred to as the Fertile Crescent. It is part of a larger 75,000 square-mile region known as the Levant, which runs along the Mediterranean Sea from latter-day Iraq and the Persian Gulf through Syria, Jordan, Lebanon, and Israel. Geographer Jared Diamond contends that "the Fertile Crescent was perhaps the earliest center of food production in the world, and the site of origin of several of the modern world's major crops and almost all of its major domesticated animals."[13]

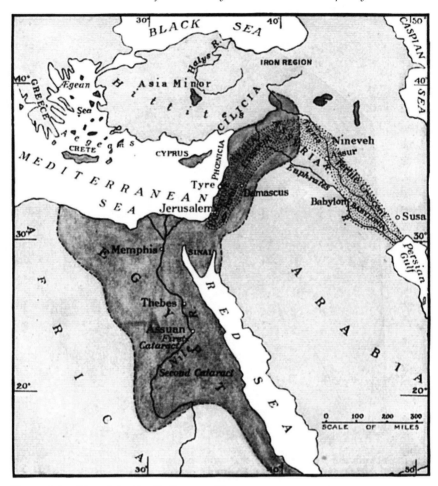

Figure 3.1.   Map of the Fertile Crescent [14]

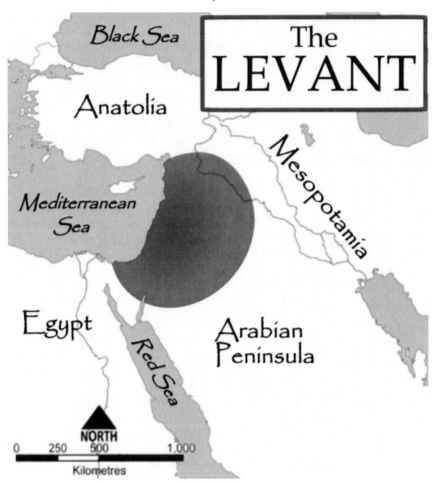

Figure 3.2.   Map of Levant[15]

THE RISE OF NATIONS AND TRANSFORMATION OF SOCIETY

The domestication of crops and animals created a dramatic change in the nature of human societies. The nomadic way of life yielded to more stable living and family arrangements. Fields were planted, cultivated, and harvested. For the first time, food surpluses were achieved. This reduced the number of people needed in agricultural endeavors. Villages grew into towns, and towns blossomed into cities. Historians generally agree that the first large-scale cities of 10,000 or more people developed in ancient Mesopotamia, or what is now known as Iraq.

Changes in the nature of work, and man's relationship to it, created a necessity for coordinating, distributing, and administering the activities of citizens of these larger aggregations of people. Life's chores, demands, and obligations that were previously attended to in family, clan, and tribal associations could no longer be left to the vicissitudes of chance and the whims of nature and goodwill of the inhabitants. People left the arduous demands of producing food on their land in search of new opportunities. They sought more comfortable lifestyles and the protection afforded by greater numbers of inhabitants in the cities. But they had to voluntarily surrender some of their freedom in exchange for the protection of the city and state.

This transition from independent, free-willing citizens to law-abiding subjects of states became the focus of philosophical discussions as states grew into countries and countries into empires. Feudalism, with its hereditary titles and perquisites, gave monarchs the power to impose their will on citizens exacting obedience and submission for the price of protection.

The desire for increased wealth and power fueled the expansion of markets. Feudalistic systems morphed into mercantilist nation-states and capitalistic modes of production and consumption. An early glimpse of this debate can be apprehended in the writing of Aristotle around 350 years B.C.E. when he addressed Nicomachean Ethics—a discussion that portends the contemporary hedonistic/materialistic preoccupation of citizens with being able to obtain "the good life," which he deemed "the end of the city-state."[16]

Later, other philosophers like Hobbes, Locke, and Rousseau debated the proper role of monarchs.[17] They considered the role of power, authority, and the rights and responsibilities of rulers and citizens. Tension between individual rights and government's prerogatives and responsibilities is still hotly debated around the world. In the United States it became integrated into the Constitution. This reasoning is reflected in the tripartite distribution of power between the legislative (Congress), judicial (courts), and the executive (president) branches, and in the Bill of Rights. Subsequent amendments were added to ensure protections of speech, press, and assembly for citizens as well as providing for the common defense and welfare of residents.

The framers of the U.S. constitution received inspiration from English forbearers (e.g., the Magna Carta [1215]). They also borrowed concepts from the Six Nations Confedercy's compact. This group of northeastern Native Americans drafted rules of confederation to ensure cooperation and rights for Indians living in the region of central and upstate New York in the sixteenth and seventeenth centuries.[18]

There has always been tension between citizens (the governed) and the State (the governors). For the sake of obtaining safety and security, citizens have, throughout history, voluntarily or through coercion, relinquished some of their freedom to the State for the maintenance of stability and the social order. While some people resisted diminutions of their freedom, others recognized, as the philosophers, the necessity for order and control as a political reality.

REGULATING WORK AND PEOPLES' LIVES

Complex social organizations today, often disparagingly referred to as bureaucracies, arose as a mechanism to control the division and specialization of work. They provided for the elevated needs and expectations of the inhabitants of cities. Legal rules and regulations, specialists, and formalized methods of administering and providing for the needs and wants of citizens were introduced. Rationality and efficiency were sought to manage burgeoning populations.

These manmade social creations were flawed from the outset. In their quest for the rationalization of production and distribution of goods and services, they assumed that participants within the organization were ideologically committed to the organization's goals. Since the Industrial Revolution, owners, managers, and supervisors of work organizations have been trying to assess and harness the energy of workers by cajoling, prodding, promising, threatening, and punishing employees. The fields of scientific management, human engineering, personnel (now human resources), human accounting, human relations, job enrichment, industrial democracy, etc., all evolved as attempts to understand and outflank workers' imperfect commitment to their jobs.[19]

The Bond between Religion and Work

A corollary religious and ideological trend emerged that bolstered and extolled the virtue of work while eschewing materialism and ostentatious displays of wealth. This was a prevalent theme in Calvinism and other forms of aesthetic Protestantism of the seventeenth and eighteenth centuries. Throughout Western Europe an ethic arose that elevated industriousness and deferred gratification (self-sacrifice for later rewards— personified by the belief in the Doctrine of the Elect and predestination).

The belief in an afterlife was a powerful method of social control, especially when some people embraced a supralapsarian versus an infralapsarian perspective.[20] The latter held that the ultimate destiny of people was already decided by God in his infinite wisdom. The former perspective maintained that one's actions would ultimately determine one's fate after death. This perspective became the normative undergirding for nascent capitalism, and, ultimately the foundation of modern European and North American economic activity. It formed the value system upon which Western societies perceive themselves as more industrious, worthy, and deserving than other regions of the world.[21]

Work in Antiquity

The very nature and function of work in the twenty-first century has, for most people, come to be synonymous with tension, stress, competition, and conflict. Work is often viewed as an instrument for the domination and exploitation of individuals, even whole continents such as Africa. We must collaborate in the transformation of work into a positive, meaningful activity. It should not exploit people and nature if we hope to bridge the cultural chasm preventing the unification of mankind.

We need to understand the historical role that work has played in the development of modern systems of production and consumption. Understanding the temperament of contemporary workers and how the nature of work and the production/consumption nexus affects relationships among people and countries is also important.

From the earliest stirrings of our cave-dwelling ancestors who bore clubs upon their shoulders and shuffled after assorted game to put on the rock for dinner (when they were not being pursued themselves), to modern office workers who trudge in and out of cars, planes, subways, trains, and buses in quest of bread for the table, life has been a never-ending struggle for survival and security. Work has been the most socially acceptable method for obtaining it.

Man's definition of work has evolved as he has mastered his environment and developed new forms of production and consumption. Particularly in the West, with its emphasis on achievement, progress, and materialism, work became the catalyst for the domination and exploitation of the individual. This trend occurred first in Europe and then spread like a plague that decimated indigenous populations around the world. It trapped them through religious and ideological bonds that led to the exploitation of their resources and the stultification of generations.

The work of our Paleolithic ancestors was almost exclusively for survival. Living in small, loosely organized bands of individuals, they spent a large part of their waking hours gathering food and later hunting. It wasn't until the Neolithic era between 8000 and 6000 B.C.E. that farming and domestication of animals occurred.

Ancient man developed tools that enabled him to survive and dominate his environment. It was this ability that distinguished him from other animals. But the tools were crude, and no significant surpluses existed in Paleolithic times, so people lived precarious hand-to-mouth existences. Neolithic people did, however, domesticate animals and grow crops. Women were usually tasked with agricultural chores to free men to develop more specialized tools for hunting and other activities. As agriculture became more sophisticated, crafts emerged.

Work in pre-industrial societies was unfettered by bureaucratic rules and regulations without the pressures and constraints of time. As early humans evolved, they learned to make and use tools. This afforded them the opportunity to gain a semblance of control over their environment and develop a food surplus.

From early food gatherers and hunters to modern telecommuters, work was, and remains, an essential means of survival. It not only provided sustenance, it set the natural rhythms of life. As English historian E. P. Thompson[22] noted, prior to the development of time pieces, people worked as long as there was light, from dawn to dusk.

Man's relationship to his work was primarily intimate. It was a means of sustenance and survival. Yet, it was also a source of satisfaction and identity because he had control over the productive process. Such societies were task-oriented, as Thompson noted: "The working day lengthens or contracts according to the task—and there is no great sense of conflict between labour and 'passing the time of day.'"[23]

The struggle for survival necessitated long hours of backbreaking toil. In the absence of clocks and electricity one worked from sunup to sunset, blurring the distinction between work and nonwork. As anthropologist Walter Neff pointed out, "Even when the hunt has been successful and the men are presumably merely 'sitting about the campfire,' they are usually occupied with something—making an arrow, chipping an arrowhead, shaping a scrapper, etc."[24]

Actually, work as we know it is a fairly recent development, evolving in the past 10,000 years. The rise of cities increased the necessity for greater agricultural productivity and the division of labor. Work became associated with remuneration, changing the relationship between people and their tasks.

Historian Arnold Toynbee observed, "The hunter or food gatherer who disciplined himself into becoming a cultivator became conscious, as a result of this economic revolution, of work in contrast to idleness, rest, play and leisure."[25] But the distinction between work as an activity that stimulates the mind and body that provides sustenance, as distinct from expending energy for remuneration in the employ of someone else— what we may refer to as labor—had not yet developed.

In ancient times, even warfare took a backseat to the essential activity of subsistence. Many of the wars of antiquity were brief or adjourned during the growing season to allow peasant soldiers time to plant their crops. Protracted conflicts such as the Peloponnesian War had devastating effects on peasants and the economy as historian Claude Mosse has shown.[26]

Work and the Industrial Revolution

With the coming of the Industrial Revolution, man's relationship to his work was altered. As Marx observed, natural relationships were disrupted by the specialization and division of labor that led to a loss of autonomy and control and, ultimately, dissatisfaction and alienation. The evolution of the nature and function of work has had a profound effect on the social and psychological state of mankind as well as the nature of society. This transformation, as we will see in chapter 4, plays an important role in population shifts and immigration trends that threaten the stability of societies around the world.

As Western societies developed technologically, work was transformed from an end to a means. Society and the relationships among people were altered. Humans began using and consuming things and objectifying and manipulating one another for the satisfaction of their personal needs and wants. This phenomenon personified Aristotle's contempt for capitalist forms of production, "that which consists in exchange is justly censured; for it is unnatural, and a mode by which men gain from one another."[27]

Marx also believed that modern work

> converts the labourer into a crippled monstrosity, by forcing his detail dexterity at the expense of a world of productive capabilities and instincts; just at in the States of La Plata they butcher a whole beast for the sake of his hide or his tallow. Not only is the detail work distributed to the different individuals, but the individual himself is made the automatic motor of a fractional operation, and the absurd fable of Menenius Agrippa, which presents man as a mere fragment of his own body, becomes realized.[28]

Marx and Engels noted this phenomenon when they observed that peoples' lives are shaped around the nature of the process of production. A man's work constitutes his mode of life. "As individuals express their life, so they are. What they are, therefore, coincides with their production, both with what they produce and with how they produce."[29]

Marx maintained that capitalist societies assign workers to particular activities by necessity to maximize production. As society grows the inhabitants split into classes based upon the nature of the work they do. This becomes the division of labor that influences their life opportunities and lifestyles.

As work becomes fragmented to increase productivity for expanding markets and meet the rising level of competition at home and abroad, workers (the proletariat) are exploited by the propertied class (bourgeoisie). Basic conflicts were thought to arise between these two classes around the process of production and consumption. Marx contended that in capitalist societies all "natural relationships" are perverted, as they become "money relationships."

One can better comprehend Marx's condemnation of modern work by considering the time he was writing. When he and his colleague, Friedrich Engels, called for workingmen around the world to unite in 1848, a series of riots and revolutions were sweeping through Europe. France, Germany, Italy, Austria, Hungary, and Czechoslovakia were all experiencing social unrest, as the working classes sought greater representation in government, property rights, improved living and working conditions, and freedom. By focusing on work as the fulcrum that balanced the life chances of individuals, Marx was able to link the increasingly depersonalized, fragmented nature of work to the domination and exploitation of workers through capitalist production.

Deprived of their autonomy, workers labored in dull, dangerous, and deleterious conditions. They were meagerly compensated for their risk of life and limb in the Industrial Revolution, which introduced machines into the world of work on a large scale for the first time in history. Living in unhealthy, crowded cities, workers experienced the profound condition of alienation.

Marx believed that man's creative desire to maximize his potentialities through meaningful activities (his term was *Selbstbestätigung*, or self-realization, which predated Abraham Maslow's concept of self-actualization by one hundred years) was blocked, making the life of the proletariat stultifying, degrading, and deplorable.

As revolutionaries, Marx and Engels believed that the only way for the proletariat to improve this situation was for them to revolt. They should seize the means of production and redistribute private property. This would restore harmony in the world of work and society. "The revolution is necessary, therefore, not only the ruling class cannot be overthrown in any other way, but also because the class *overthrowing* it can only in a revolution succeed in ridding itself of all the muck of ages and become fitted to found society anew."[30] Establishing a communist society would abate the alienation of the proletariat, for then there would be no need for forced specialization:

> Nobody has one exclusive sphere of activity but each can become accomplished in any branch he wishes, society regulates the general production and thus makes it possible for me to do one thing to-day and another tomorrow, to hunt in the morning, fish in the afternoon, rear cattle in the evening, criticize after dinner, just as I have a mind, without ever becoming hunter, fisherman, shepherd or critic.[31]

In hindsight, we know that the duo did not foresee the important role that labor unions and democratic governments would play in redressing workers' grievances. Technological changes also improved the quality of working life. And they did not foresee the substitution of ruling capitalist oppressors with Communist Party functionaries who were equally exploitative and ruthless.[32] Nevertheless, the cogency of their argument delineating the transformation of the nature and function of work and the exploitation of workers was prescient.

THE DISPARITY OF WEALTH

In more than a century and a half since they urged workingmen to unite in *The Communist Manifesto*,[33] there has been a continued accretion of wealth in the hands of a Western corporate elite dominated by white males. A corresponding centralization of political and military power that ensures the perpetuation of the status quo to the detriment of women and people of color,[34] has also occurred.

Recent analyses of wealth disparity in the United States reveal an increasing centralization of income in the hands of fewer people. Today, the top 1 percent of wage earners in the United States control 23 percent of the income in the nation. The top 10 percent of pretax income-earning Americans control half of the nation's wealth. An estimated $400 billion of pretax income flowed *from* the bottom 95 percent of wage earners to the top 5 percent during the first decade of the new millennium.[35]

Each year *Forbes Magazine* publishes a list of the wealthiest four hundred Americans. In order to make the list, your net worth must be a minimum of $1 billion. Only one person of color, Oprah Winfrey, is on it.[36]

THE PERSISTENCE OF BUREAUCRATIZATION

It is difficult to encapsulate the nature of modern work into a single form or model. Western capitalist nations have, however, seen a diminution of manual laborers and manufacturing workers. They have been relegated to an underclass of peripatetic unskilled and semiskilled laborers at home and abroad, often recruited from developing countries in Asia, Africa, Central and South America.

A large percentage of the modern labor force works in complex bureaucratic organizations. In the United States, half the private sector labor force (nearly fifty million people) work in firms employing five hundred or more workers. Another 17 percent of the labor force work for local, state, and federal governments.[37]

More workers in developed nations are working on flexible schedules. They telecommute from their homes and satellite offices. But the vast majority of workers are still employed in standardized, routinized, and regimented work organizations. They are characterized by the same types of authoritarian leadership structures described by Weber over a century ago. Many are being administered by scions of the founders of these organizations.[38]

The Telework Research Network reports that 70 percent of workers in the United States commute to work all the time. However, it is estimated that 40 percent of them hold jobs that could be done at home. Currently, 2 percent (2.8 million) people, not including the self-employed, consider their homes the primary place of work. Twenty to thirty million people work from home at least one day a week. A quarter of employees said they could, if allowed, do as much as 80 percent of their work at home.[39]

There is always room at the top for the ambitious and talented. But control of work organizations remains in the hands of a few people who attend the same prep schools and universities, intermarry, and form the core of the contemporary power elite.[40] Power still resides at the top despite the growth of flexible time, telecommuting, job enrichment, and quasidemocratic programs.

The decline of the union movement in the United States, as witnessed by the introduction of antiunion legislation in several states in 2011 (e.g., Wisconsin, Minnesota, Indiana, Florida, Ohio) does not augur well for the future of industrial democracy. Workers' autonomy, the restoration of meaning in the world of work, and social equality has been put on hold. Occupy Wall Street and similar protest movements across the United States[41] represent a reaction to this trend.

WORK, MATERIALISM, AND PREJUDICE

In effect, workers in advanced industrial societies have reached an accommodation with their jobs—a quid pro quo relationship that recognizes the instrumental arrangement they have committed to. They sell their time and energy for rewards that may satisfy their materialist needs and desires. These goods and services are often purchased at the expense of people of color at home and abroad who manufacture them in deleterious environments (e.g., Bangladesh), and they are still believed to be intellectually and culturally inferior compared to Eurocentric standards of beauty and technology.

The Western fetish for natural resources satisfied through the domination and exploitation of developing nations persists, and so, too does the stereotypical view of dark-skinned people who supply them. Only a balance of social and economic forces reversing the lopsided flow of material and human capital on Spaceship Earth can restore harmonious relations.[42] Pressure on workers to maintain increasingly unsustainable levels of production and consumption will continue as demographic changes increase the population of the developing world. The depletion of natural resources, increasing cost of our materialist ethos, and interaction of diverse cultures is creating unprecedented conflict among nations.

WHAT HATH WORK WROUGHT?

Through work and work organizations (bureaucratic structures) Westerners exported their technology and dominance of nature to lesser-developed civilizations. This led to the domination and exploitation of the people and their natural resources. In that sense, Western ideology is not only expansionist, it is parasitic. It preys on the land and people of other places for what Westerners casually, even naively assume to be their prerogative. It is a rationalization, an entitlement, complete with an ideology and religion that views other cultures as inferior, expendable, subordinate, and servile for the satisfaction and maintenance of Western materialism. For example, with about 5 percent of the world's population, the United States consumes a quarter of the world's energy and one-third of the world's nonreplenishable natural resources. [43]

White, European-based societies have, for generations, treated dark-skinned people from developing nations as economic resources and targets. They have predatorily exploited them as markets, used them as cheap labor, and objectified them as subjects of research.

In Africa, for example, colonial powers extracted natural resources and people to fuel the social and industrial appetites of Europeans and North Americans. Some twelve to fifteen million Africans were kidnapped from their homeland and sold in the trans-Atlantic slave trade from the mid-1400s to the late nineteenth century. The institution of slavery was a method of obtaining cheap labor for the extraction and production of raw materials in colonized lands (Africa; North, Central, and South America; and the Caribbean).

To undergird the practice of chattel slavery, Westerners fabricated a religious ideology that portrayed people in less-developed civilizations as soulless pagans and primitives. Spanish Catholic theologians Gines de Sepulveda and Bartolomé de las Casas debated this belief system in the sixteenth century regarding whether it was appropriate to subject indigenous people and expropriate their resources. [44]

There is a long and sordid history of medical experimentation, particularly in testing the efficacy of pharmaceuticals, by white-dominated North American and European companies using dark-skinned surrogates. For example, birth control pills thirty times stronger than those used today were tested on Puerto Rican women beginning in the mid-1950s. [45] The notorious IUD, the Dalkon Shield, was dumped on foreign markets by manufacturer A. H. Robbins after slumping sales in the United States and negative publicity about its safety arose in the early 1970s. Over $12 billion in lawsuits from 327,000 women alleging harm from the device were levied against Robbins, which filed for bankruptcy and established a $2.47 billion trust fund for claimants. [46]

Then there was the infamous U.S. Public Health Service's Tuskegee medical experiment. It withheld treatment for forty years of 399 black men suffering from syphilis to determine the effects of the disease on the body. [47]

One of the most callous illustrations of white American corporate disdain for dark-skinned people is manifested in the marketing of tobacco products to minority youth in the United States and abroad, in effect foisting harmful products on children for the sake of profit.[48]

THE JUSTIFICATION OF WHITE SUPREMACY

Western (white) ethnocentrism, traceable back to Blumenbach's unfortunate early characterization of Caucasians as the most beautiful and superior form of mankind,[49] led to a haughtiness among whites referred to as "white privilege."[50] This attitude is a form of white entitlement. It simultaneously conveys an arrogance and paternalism toward other cultures and dark-skinned people, who are viewed as culturally and biologically inferior. It is manifested in obliviousness toward their sensibilities borne from centuries of colonialism and imperialism. This attitude has led to instrumental relationships where Westerners view other societies, their inhabitants, and their resources, as legitimate targets of exploitation.

The late Harvard biologist Stephen Jay Gould portrayed the white male infatuation with denigrating people of color (and women) as a form of biological determinism that placed them on top of all other groups deemed biologically inferior. Gould illustrated the point by quoting Englishman David Hume (1711–1776):

> I am apt to suspect the negroes and in general all other species of men (for there are four or five different kinds) to be naturally inferior to the whites. There never was a civilized nation of any other complexion than white, nor even any individual eminent either in action or speculation. No ingenious manufacturers amongst them, no arts, no sciences.[51]

Using the concept of recapitulation, late-nineteenth-century scientists attributed the supposedly infantile intellectual development of women and people of color to their being stuck on lower levels of the evolutionary ladder. They blamed the victims for their social problems and adverse life chances.

Biological determinists likened women and dark-skinned people to infants and children, lacking in the qualities of maturity and reason held by white European males: "Dealing with peoples who represent the same stage in the history of the development of the race that the child does in the history of the development of the individual. The tropics will not, therefore, be developed by the natives themselves."[52]

The colonialist disdain for dark-skinned indigenous people can be summed up in the words of Rudyard Kipling:

> Take up the White Man's burden—
> Send forth the best ye breed—
> Go bind your sons to exile
> To serve your captive's need;
> To wait in heavy harness,

On fluttered folk and wild —
Your new-caught, sullen peoples,
Half-devil and half-child. [53]

The Occidental infatuation with science and technology, coupled with the ideology of progress, led to the perception of other cultures and people as expendable. Work was the mechanism that diffused and imposed Western technology and values. It led to the denigration of nonwhite cultures throughout the world.

Only recently, with the diminution of natural resources (oil, water, rare earth minerals) have Westerners begun to sense that "their" world is changing. As the depletion of these resources continues,[54] burgeoning populations in developing nations are becoming aroused about injustices that characterized their past and threaten their present and future. Indigenous movements have destabilized traditional Western-influenced autocratic tyrannical regimes (e.g., Egypt, Tunisia, Syria, Yemen, Libya, Bahrain, Ivory Coast, Venezuela, Bolivia, Nicaragua). They reflect scarcity borne of competition, which may further incite animosities between the Western "haves" and the developing world's "have nots."

Capitalistic attempts to expand markets through advertising aim to increase materialism. Diminishing raw materials heretofore exploited of, by, and for the West exacerbate animosities between the wealthy fraction of the world's population and the majority poor. The World Bank estimates that there are 1.345 billion people living on $1.25 or less a day. According to the United Nations Food and Agricultural Organization, 925 million people (13 percent of the world's population) are undernourished. [55]

The End Poverty Campaign calculates that poverty accounts for more than 50,000 deaths a day—eighteen million annually. The disparities between "have" and "have not" nations are striking. The gross domestic product (GDP) of the poorest forty-eight nations in the world is less than the combined wealth of the world's *three richest individuals*. Twenty percent of the world's population in developed nations consumes 86 percent of the world's goods. This statistic is more outrageous when we consider that the poorest 40 percent of the world's population accounts for only 5 percent of global income, compared to three-fourths of the world's income controlled by only 20 percent of the richest individuals on the planet. In fact, the average annual income of this richest 20 percent of the world's population is fifty times higher than the poorest 20 percent. [56]

The continuation of this situation will heighten suspicions between ethnic groups and nations as they vie for an expanded portion of the diminishing resource pie. Struggles for power and privilege may well become the norm. Western attempts to maintain hegemony over raw materials under the guise of globalization are recognized as latter-day imperialistic excursions. They will be rejected by indigenous people seeking to retain a greater portion of their resources, precipitating higher prices as demand outstrips supply.[57]

Bolstered by economic necessities and ideological currents, populist indigenous movements to preserve the homeland against the "evil, rapacious West," will heighten tensions. The white, Western minority and the growing nonwhite majority will clash in what is becoming a religious, ideological, and environmental zero-sum game. This threatens the stability and existence of civilization. We now look at trends that imperil the peaceful reunification of mankind. We begin with the movement of masses of people across national borders in a modern-day quest for better lives.

SUMMING UP

- The nature of work has changed from a source of sustenance to status.
- Today, working with one's hands is viewed as less important than intellectual activities.
- European domination of the world was the result of technology based on cultural forces, not superior intellect.
- Karl Marx and Friedrich Engels criticized the exploitation of workers in industrial societies.
- Most workers, like teachers, work in complex organizations where they are subject to many rules and regulations.
- The disparity in wealth in the United States and around the world is reflected in high rates of poverty, illiteracy, and adverse health.

NOTES

1. For a synopsis of this phenomenon, see Gerhard E. Lenski, *Power and Privilege: A Theory of Social Stratification* (Chapel Hill: University of North Carolina Press, 1984).

2. Jennifer Cheesman Day and Eric C. Newburger, "The Big Payoff: Educational Attainment and Synthetic Estimates of Work-Life Earnings," Current Population Reports, U.S. Census Bureau, U.S. Department of Commerce, July 2002.

3. Research reveals that a very small percentage of physicians account for the majority of malpractice claims in the United States. One report based on an analysis of 35,000 physicians found that, of those with two or more malpractice payouts since 1990, only 7.6 percent were disciplined and only 13 percent of physicians with five or more medical malpractice payouts were disciplined. See the National Practitioner Data Bank reported in HealthGrades at http://www.healthgrades.com/media/dms/pdf/hgfirstnationalphysicianmalpracticedatabase.pdf(accessed May 25, 2011). Incompetent teachers are also shielded from discipline. For example, just ten out of 12,000 teachers were fired in Hawaii in 2010. In Pinellas County, Florida, with 7,300 classroom teachers, only six tenured teachers were fired between 2005 and 2009. Nearby Hillsborough County, the eighth-largest school district in the United States with 13,000 classroom teachers, fired just ten tenured teachers during this time. In New York City, just 88 out of 80,000 teachers were fired for poor performance between 2007

and 2008, and in Chicago, just 0.1 percent were discharged between 2005 and 2008 ("Finding Out about Fired Teachers Almost as Hard as Firing Them," accessed May 25, 2011, http://www.eiaonline.com/intercepts/2011/04/22/finding-out-about-fired-teachers-almost-as-hard-as-firing-them/; Ron Matus, "It's Hard to Fire Teachers, Even if They Are Bad," *St. Petersburg Times*, March 29, 2009, accessed May 25, 2011, http://www.tampabay.com/news/education/k12/article987898.ece; "Protecting Bad Teachers," accessed May 25, 2011, http://teachersunionexposed.com/protecting.cfm).

4. Jared Diamond, *Guns, Germs, and Steel* (New York: W.W. Norton, 1999).

5. Max Weber, *The Protestant Ethic and the Spirit of Capitalism* (New York: Charles Scribner's Sons, 1958).

6. John Relethford, *Reflections of Our Past* (Cambridge, MA: Westview Press, 2003); Spencer Wells, *The Journey of Man* (Princeton, NJ: Princeton University Press, 2003); Steve Olson, *Mapping Human History* (Boston: Mariner Books, 2002).

7. Richard Lewontin, "The Apportionment of Human Diversity," *Evolutionary Biology* 6 (1972): 391–398.

8. Luca Cavalli-Sforza, Paolo Menozzi, and Alberto Piazza, *The History and Geography of Human Genes* (Princeton: Princeton University Press, 1994).

9. One of the clearest presentations of these phenomena can be found in geneticist Spencer Wells's *The Journey of Man*.

10. Wells, *The Journey of Man*, 24.

11. A recent discovery of teeth resembling those of *Homo sapiens* was found in a cave in Israel and dated at about 400,000 years ago. More research is needed to confirm this finding, which could switch the origin of the site of early humans from Africa to Asia, but the preponderance of evidence points to the theory of African origins. See Israel Hershkovitz et al., "Middle Pleistocene Dental Remains from Qesem Cave [Israel], *American Journal of Physical Anthropology* 144 (April 2011): 575–592.

12. Along with Wells (*The Journey of Man*), another incisive summary of the journey of ancient people is presented in James Shreeve, "The Greatest Journey Ever Told: The Trail of Our DNA," *National Geographic Magazine*, March 2006, 61–73.

13. Diamond, *Guns, Germs, and Steel*, 134.

14. See ancienthistory.about.com/od/neareast/ss/110708ANE_10.htm.

15. See http://en.wikipedia.org/wiki/File:The_Levant_3.png.

16. Aristotle, *Politics, III*, trans. Benjamin Jowett, http://classics.mit.edu.

17. Thomas Hobbes, *The Leviathan* (1660), http://oregonstate.edu; John Locke, *Second Treatise of Civil Government* (1690), http://www.constitution.org/jl/2ndtreat.htm; Jean Jacques Rousseau, *The Social Contract or Principles of Political Right*, trans. G. D. H. Cole (1762), http://www.constitution.org/jjr/socon.htm.

18. The six nations were Onondaga, Cayuga, Mohawk, Oneida, Seneca, and Tuscarora.

19. For an enunciation of the characteristics of bureaucracies, see Max Weber, *Economy and Society* (Berkeley: University of California Press, 1978).

20. Further discussion of these concepts can be found at "What Is Infralapsarian, Supralapsarian, and Sublapsarian?" Got Questions.org, http://www.gotquestions.org/lapsarianism.html; and Phillip R. Johnson, "Notes on Supralapsarianism and Infralapsarianism," http://www.spurgeon.org/~phil/articles/sup_infr.htm.

21. The definitive analysis of the effect of Protestantism on the development of capitalism was done by Max Weber, *The Protestant Ethic and the Spirit of Capitalism* (New York: Routledge, 2001), http://xroads.Virginia.edu/~hyper/weber/WeberCH1.html. An early example of these values in North America came during the Great Awakening, which began in the American colonies in the 1730s, creating a religious revival that emphasized traditional ascetic Protestantism. The classic sermon of pastor Johnathan Edwards, "Sinners in the Hands of an Angry God," delivered July 8, 1741, in Enfield, Connecticut, demonstrated the normative power of suprlapsarianism (available at http://www.ccel.org/ccel/edwards/sermons.sinners.html).

22. E. P. Thompson, "Time, Work-Discipline, and Industrial Capitalism," *Past and Present* 38, no. 1 (1967): 56–97.

23. Ibid, 60.

24. Walter Neff, *Work and Human Behavior* (New York: Atherton, 1968), 52–53.

25. Arnold Toynbee, *A Study of History*, vol. 1 (Oxford: Oxford University Press, 1954), 8–9.

26. Claude Mosse, *The Ancient World at Work*, trans. Janet Lloyd (London: Chatto and Windus, 1970).

27. Aristotle, *Politics*, in *The Basic Works of Aristotle*, ed. Richard McKeon, (New York: Random House, 1941), 1141.

28. Karl Marx, *Capital*, vol. 1 (New York: Penguin Classics Edition, 1992), 481–482.

29. Karl Marx and Friedrich Engels, *The German Ideology*, ed. C. J. Arthur (New York: International Publishers, 1947), 42.

30. Karl Marx and Friedrich Engels, *The German Ideology*, in *The Collected Works of Karl Marx and Frederick Engels*, vol. 5 (Progress Publishers, Moscow, 1976), 52–53.

31. Marx and Engels, *The German Ideology* (International Publishers, 1947), 53.

32. For an analysis of this phenomenon, see Milovan Djilas, *The New Class* (Boston: Mariner Books, 1982).

33. Karl Marx and Friedrich Engels, *Manifesto of the Communist Party*, trans. Samuel Moore (1888), http://www.marxists.org/archive/marx/works/1848/communist-manifesto/.

34. For analyses of this phenomenon, see C. W. Mills, *The Power Elite* (New York: Oxford University Press, 2000); Ferdinand Lundberg, *The Rich and the Super Rich* (New York: Lyle Stuart, 1968); G. William Domhoff, *Who Rules America?* (New York: McGraw-Hill, 2005); Gabriel Kolko, *Wealth and Power in America* (Westport, CN.: Greenwood Press, 1981).

35. See: H. Roy Kaplan, *The Myth of Post-Racial America* (Lanham, MD: Rowman & Littlefield Education, 2011), 141–148; Lawrence Mishel, Jared Bernstein, and Heidi Shierholz, *The State of Working America: 2008–2009* (Washington, DC: Economic Policy Institute, 2009); Thomas Piketty and Emmanuel Saez, "Income Inequality in the United States, 1913–2002," November 2004, http://elsa.berkeley.edu/~saez/piketty-saezOUP04US.pdf; Emmanuel Saez, "Striking It Richer: The Evolution of Top Incomes in the United States (Update Using 2006 Preliminary Estimates)," University of California Department of Economics, March 15, 2008, http://elsa.berkeley.edu/~saez/saez-UStopincomes-2006prel.pdf; Thomas M. Shapiro, Tatjana Meschede, and Laura Sullivan, "The Racial Wealth Gap Increases Fourfold," *Institute on Assets and Social Policy Research and Policy Brief*, The Heller School for Social Policy and Management, Brandeis University, May 2010, http://www.insightcced.org/uploads/CRWG/IASP-Racial-Wealth-Gap-Brief-May2010.pdf; Amaad Rivera et. al., *State of the Dream 2009: The Silent Depression* (Boston: United for a Fair Economy, 2009); Paul Taylor, Richard Fry, and Rakesh Kochar, "Wealth Gaps Rise to Record Highs Between Whites, Blacks, Hispanics," PEW Research Center, July 26, 2011, http://www.pewsocialtrends.org/2011/07/26/wealth-gaps-rise-to-record-highs-between-whites-blacks-hispanics/; A succinct overview of relevant research on this topic can be found in G. William Domhoff, "Wealth, Income, and Power," *Who Rules America?* http://www.2ucsc.edu/whorulesamerica/power/wealth.html. Retrieved 1/4/12. Timothy Noah's *The Great Divergence* (New York: Bloomsbury Press, 2012) outlines the growing problem of inequality in the United States and provides approaches for diminishing it. Nobel Prize economist Joseph E. Stiglitz's *The Price of Inequality: How Today's Society Endangers Our Future* (New York: W.W. Norton, 2012) provides a sobering analysis of the nature and effects of income disparity in U.S. society.

36. See, for example, "The Forbes 400, 2010: The Richest People in America," *Forbes*, http://www.forbes.com/wealth/forbes-400/list.

37. Lyman Morales, "Gov't. Employment Ranges from 38% in D.C. to 12% in Ohio: Federal, State, or Local Government Employs 17% of U.S. Workers Nationally," August 6, 2010,http://www.gallup.com/poll/141785/gov-employment-ranges-ohio.aspx.

38. For a look at the composition and interlocking of corporate boards in the United States, see http://thescreamonline.com/commentary/comment4-3/theyrule/theyrule.

html and Richard Zweigenhaft and G. William Domhoff, *Diversity in the Power Elite* (New Haven, CT: Yale University Press, 1999).

39. http://www.teleworkresearchnetwork.com/telecommuting-statistics. In early 2013 Marissa Mayer, the new CEO of Yahoo, created a controversy by requiring all of the company's telecommuters to report to work in the office, demonstrating the locus of power still resides there.

40. See Zweigenhaft and Domhoff, *Diversity in the Power Elite*.

41. For an elaboration of the goals and methods of the Occupy Movement, go to http://occupywallst.org/about/.

42. This term was used by the futurist R. Buckminster Fuller. For further information about his concerns for the ecology and survival of our planet, see his *Operating Manual for Spaceship Earth*, ed. Jamie Snyder (Zurich: Lars Müller Publishers, 2008).

43. An acerbic critic of this process was Martinique-born Frantz Fanon. See his *The Wretched of the Earth* (New York: Grove Press, 1965).

44. See Kaplan, *The Myth of Post-Racial America*, 23–26, for a synopsis of their discussion.

45. Some critics contend that some of the motivation for this project emanated from the eugenics movement and a desire to curtail the population growth of the island. For an example, see Angela Davis, "Racism, Birth Control, and Reproductive Rights," in *From Abortion to Reproductive Freedom: Transforming a Movement*, ed. Marlene Gerber Fried (Boston: South End Press, 1990), 15–26.

46. Gina Kolata, "The Sad Legacy of the Dalkon Shield," *New York Times*, December 6, 1987, and Milt Freudenheim, "Dalkon Shield Trust Fund," *New York Times*, August 8, 1988.

47. See James H. Jones, *Bad Blood: The Tuskegee Syphilis Experiment* (New York: Free Press, 1993), and Susan M. Reverby, ed., *Tuskegee's Truths: Rethinking the Tuskegee Syphilis Study* (Chapel Hill: University of North Carolina Press, 2000).

48. "Tobacco Industry's Targeting of Youth, Minorities and Women," American Heart Association, http://www.americanheart.org/presenter.jhtml?identifier=11226; Derek Yach and Douglas Bettcher, "Globalisation of Tobacco Industry Influence and New Global Responses," *Tobacco Control* 9 (2000): 206–216. A survey of tobacco use in sixteen countries recently revealed the disastrous effects of predatory marketing on the public health of three billion people. See Gary A. Glovino et al., "Tobacco Use in 3 Billion Individuals from 16 Countries: An Analysis of Nationally Representative Cross-Sectional Household Surveys," *Lancet* 380, no. 9842 (2012), 668–679.

49. Johann Friedrich Blumenbach, *The Anthropological Treatises of Johann Friedrich Blumenbach: De Generis Humani Varietate Nativa*, ed. and trans. Thomas Bendyshe (London: Longman, Green, Longman, Roberts and Green, 1865), http://campus.udayton.edu/~hume/Blumenbach/blumenbach.htm.

50. For a discussion of the nature of white privilege, see Peggy McIntosh, "White Privilege: Unpacking the Invisible Knapsack," *Independent School* 49, no. 2 (1990), 31–36; Allan G. Johnson, *Privilege, Power, and Difference*, 2nd ed. (New York: McGraw-Hill, 2006); Paula Rothenberg, ed., *White Privilege: Essential Reading on the Other Side of Racism*, 2nd ed. (New York: Worth Publishers, 2005). Also see the writing of Tim Wise, such as *White Like Me* (New York: Soft Skull Press, 2004).

51. Quoted in Stephen Jay Gould, *The Mismeasure of Man*, revised and expanded ed. (New York: W.W. Norton, 1996), 72.

52. B. Kidd, *The Control of the Tropics*, quoted in Gould, *The Mismeasure of Man*, 147.

53. Rudyard Kipling, athttp://www.wsu.edu/~wldciv/world_civ_reader/world_civ_reader_2/kipling.html.

54. In 2012, the GDP of China (population 1.3 billion) rose 2 percent; of India (population: 1.2 billion)—5.4 percent; of Brazil (population 195 million)—1 percent; of Indonesia (population 243 million)—6.3 percent; of the United States—2 percent.

55. "2011 World Hunger and Poverty Facts and Statistics," *Hunger Notes*, (http://www.worldhunger.org/articles/Learn/world%20hunger%20facts%202002.htm.)

56. End Poverty Campaign, "Facts on World Hunger and Poverty," *Hearts and Minds*, http://www.heartsandminds.org/poverty/hungerfacts.htm.

57. Two of the most incisive accounts of corporate rapaciousness of developing countries are Anthony Sampson's *The Sovereign State of ITT* (New York: Stein and Day, 1973) and *The Seven Sisters: The Great Oil Companies and the World They Shaped* (New York: Viking Press, 1975). Pulitzer Prize–winning author Daniel Yergin's book *The Prize: The Epic Quest for Oil, Money and Power* (New York: The Free Press, 2008) and Steve Coll's *Private Empire: ExxonMobil and American Power* (New York: Penguin Press, 2012) update and corroborate Sampson's earlier analysis of Big Oil. Jacob Hacker and Paul Pierson's book, *Winner-Take-All Politics: How Washington Made the Rich Richer and Turned Its Back on the Middle Class* (New York: Simon & Schuster, 2010), describes how power, wealth, and influence are wielded in the United States to the detriment of the working-class majority. Abroad, Venezuela's recently deceased Hugo Chevez, Brazil's Lula Da Silva, Bolivia's Evo Morales, Nicaragua's Daniel Ortega, Argentina's Cristina Fernandez De Kirchner, Uruguay's Tabare Vazquez, and recently deposed Fernando Lugo of Paraguay are all left-leaning leaders who demanded changes in the way their countries do business with developed nations. For a discussion of this trend, see Jorge G. Castaneda "Latin America's Left Turn," *Foreign Affairs*, May/June 2006, 28–44.

FOUR

Upsetting Equilibrium

Population Pressure and Immigration

The superior power of population cannot be checked without producing misery or vice.

—Thomas Malthus

*The composition of our society and classrooms is changing, and with change
comes the imperative to rethink and restructure our view of the world, ourselves,
and our students.*

OUR EXPLODING POPULATION

Conflict from encounters with hostile groups have regularly occurred
during mankind's relatively brief time on this planet. The competition for
natural resources and the struggle for survival are reaching the crisis
stage in the human journey. The increase in the large number of working-
age people, especially youth, has created restlessness. Job creation and
opportunities for better living languish in the acrid air of autocratic
governments mired in undemocratic traditions. Witness the demonstrations of the 2011 Arab Spring across the Middle East. The August 2011
riots in England linked racism and unemployment as youth rampaged
against a stolid English closed social system. The Brazilian riots in June
2013 also reflect these trends, as does continued unrest in Egypt.

The growing scarcity of raw materials only heightens the perceived
needs of large numbers of people to obtain them. The proliferation of
information about goods and services that fall beyond the ability of youth
to afford them (half of the world's population lives in poverty and one-
fifth are severely undernourished) heightens their desire for better lives,

increasing migration across the globe. As the unemployed and underemployed search for better lives, they come into conflict with indigenous populations who view them as threats to their cultural norms.

The world's population reached seven billion in October 2011, and it will hit nine billion by 2050. At its current annual growth rate of 1.15 percent, seventy-seven million people are added each year. At this rate, the world's population will double in about fifty years.

The pace of population growth is more easily comprehended when we consider that it took more than 60,000 years for modern men and women to reach 300 million just 1,000 years ago. In 1700 there were 600 million people. The earth's population reached one billion around 1800. By 1900 there were 1.5 billion inhabitants on the planet.

A second billion was added from 1900 to 1950, and in just forty years (1990) the population doubled from 2.5 billion to five billion. The annual rate of the world's population growth rate has leveled off since its high of over 2 percent in the early 1960s. Its current rate of growth has led to varying projections as high as twelve billion by the end of this century.

HOW CHINA AND INDIA CONFRONT POPULATION GROWTH

There used to be some sentiment for unfettered population growth in developing nations. Today, few responsible leaders promote such policies. Governments of developing nations learned that sheer numbers of impoverished, underfed, and uneducated people are more of a liability than an asset. In fact, China and India, whose population together accounts for nearly a third of the world's people, have active population control programs. In 1979, China began the controversial one child per family program, coercing and cajoling couples through financial incentives, tax policies, penalties, and subsidies to limit their families to one child.

Even before the implementation of this policy, the Chinese government realized that population control was essential. With only 7 percent of the world's arable land and about 18 percent of its population, it was obvious that something was needed to stem the tide of population growth. Interestingly, the most notable decline in China's population growth occurred *before* the implementation of its one child policy. Between 1970 and 1979 the government emphasized "late, long, and few" — late childbearing, greater spacing between pregnancies, and fewer children.[1]

While in effect, only a minority of China's population were subjected to the one-child policy. There were exemptions for couples who were both single offspring in families; couples who had a child with disabilities; certain ethnic minorities; families whose first child was a girl; and rural couples. Seventy percent of China's population lives in rural areas.

The one-child policy primarily affected urban and government workers. This policy became a two-child policy on November 15, 2013.

There have been persistent rumors alleging State-enforced abortions and sterilizations in China. In April 2012 Chinese dissident, Chen Guang-cheng, escaped house arrest and sought refuge in the U.S. Embassy in Beijing. He alleged to have documented 7,000 cases of forced abortions in Shantung Province. In May 2012 he was granted asylum in the United States and planned to study law at New York University.

China's fertility rate has stabilized around 1.7 percent because of a combination of factors ranging from the government's family-planning campaign to changing norms regarding desirable family size. Nearly nine out of ten married Chinese women use contraception compared to one out of three in most developing countries. The preferred methods of choice are long-term approaches—intrauterine devices and sterilization.[2]

The one-child policy may have reduced China's population by 100 million to 400 million, but China's population over sixty, currently at 35 percent, will double by 2053 with just 52 percent of the population of working age.[3]

India, with a current population of 1.15 billion people will surpass China's by 2030 when it is estimated to have 1.53 billion. India has attempted a variety of approaches to reducing growth, ranging from incentives for vasectomies and tubal ligations, government-enforced sterilization, and financial remuneration. Recognizing the relationship between poverty and high population growth as far back as 1940, the Indian government stated the need for the state to adopt family-planning policies that limited the number of children. In 1951 it embarked upon a national family-planning project. The first of several five-year plans, it sought to reduce the birth rate from 41 per 1,000 to 25 per 1,000 by the 1970s. In 1966, the Department of Family Planning (now called Family Welfare), was established in the Ministry of Health. It funded 100 percent of state-sponsored family-planning programs. In 1976 the National Population Policy introduced the study of population problems into school curricula under the Fifth Five Year Plan (1974–1978) with limited success.

In the 1980s family-planning programs were implemented through state governments with funds from the central government. By 1991 India had more than 150,000 public health facilities offering family planning services. But as in China, the preference for male heirs among rural parents proved a formidable obstacle to curbing population growth. Studies revealed that 72 percent of rural parents and 53 percent of urban couples preferred having more than one son.[4]

Neither country has been able to reverse overall growth for a variety of reasons. Cultural norms that support large families and the desire for male heirs are important. But most significantly, these nations already possess a massive population base. Even small increases yield relatively large numbers of people. For example, China's current population growth rate of 0.5 percent will lead to a doubling of its population in 105 years, and India's rate of growth of 1.34 will see a doubling of its population in fifty-two years.

An unfortunate unintended consequence of population control policies in these two countries has been the decline in female births and a dramatic increase in the sex ratio (the number of males born compared to females): China's 1.13 and India's 1.12, compared to the U.S. 1.04 and the United Kingdom's 1.05.[5]

The so-called demographic transition, that is, the shift from high to low birth and death rates as a country moves from agrarian to industrial pursuits and improvements in sanitation and health care are realized, has occurred most notably in Europe. That region will experience a reduction in population growth from a peak of 731 million around 2007 to 664 million by the middle of this century.[6]

CHANGING COMPOSITION OF THE POPULATION

A common assumption about demographic change has been the presumed salutary effect that higher living standards and technological innovations have had in decreasing population growth. Demographic trends indicate that population growth, if it occurs in Western nations, will be the result of increases in immigration. In fact, most of the 2.3 billion increase in the world's population over the next four decades will occur in developing nations.[7] The decline in Europe's population would be even more drastic (fifty million less) if not for an annual inflow of 800,000 immigrants, mostly from developing nations.

The UN predicts that fertility levels will continue to decline in developing nations (the number of countries with high fertility of five or more children per woman dropped from fifty-nine countries in 1990–1995 to twenty-seven in 2005–2010, and their share of the world's population dropped from 13 percent to 9 percent). Net international migration from less developed to more developed countries is projected to be ninety-six million by 2050. Ironically, these developed countries will experience an excess of deaths over births of fifty-eight million people, amounting to a net population growth of thirty-eight million.

The population increase in developed countries is relatively small compared to the existing base. We may expect increasing social conflict from the infusion of immigrants from developing nations with different cultural backgrounds. This supposition is bolstered by the fact that the major recipients of immigrants between 2010 and 2050 will be the following countries with *annual net* immigration: United States, 1.1 million; Canada, 214,000; United Kingdom, 174,000; Spain, 170,000; Italy, 159,000; Germany, 110,000; Australia, 100,000; and France, 100,000. All are predominantly light-skinned populations, whereas the major exporters of population annually will be Mexico, 334,000; China, 309,000; India, 253,000; Philippines, 175,000; Pakistan, 161,000; Indonesia, 156,000; and Bangladesh, 148,000.[8]

While much is said and written about the supposed wave of dark-skinned migrants sweeping across the borders of Western nations, a relatively small number of people annually emigrate outside of their country. According to the United Nations, fewer than seventy million people moved from developing to developed countries in 2009. However, there were 740 million internal migrants who comprised the bulk of the people moving in the world.[9]

Fear, Hate, and Anti-Immigration Sentiment

The movement of people from different cultural backgrounds and ethnicities into heretofore homogenous monoethnic societies can pose a challenge to individuals and society. It can even lead to tragedies like that in July 2011 in Oslo and Utoya Island in Norway. A deranged, self-styled, anti-immigration white supremacist, Anders Breivik, murdered seventy-seven people, mostly youths, who were attending a week-long camp on leadership and multiculturalism.

Violent reactions like this are rare, but resentment toward outsiders (immigrants, especially dark-skinned ones), and hostility toward Muslims in the aftermath of the tragic events of 9/11 and other Muslim terrorist attacks, have heightened antipathy toward ethnic minorities. Victims include people who are mistaken for Muslims (e.g., Sikhs and Hindus, especially in the West). In the United States, the FBI recorded a dramatic increase in hate crimes directed toward Muslims in the wake of 9/11. Still, nearly three-quarters of religiously motivated hate crimes in the United States are directed at Jews.[10]

No doubt, plans to build a mosque in the vicinity of the attack on the World Trade Center (otherwise known as "Ground Zero" in New York City) and the intemperate remarks of some politicians (e.g., U.S. Congressman Peter King of New York held Congressional hearings on the purported radicalization of Muslims in 2011) stoked the flames of anti-Islamic sentiment in the United States and other Western nations. The search for would-be terrorists and home-grown varieties of disillusioned Muslims has had mixed results. Terrorist attacks in the United Kingdom spurred similar investigations in Germany, the Netherlands, and other Western nations.

The inflammatory rhetoric of politicians and fear mongers has to be tempered with the commitment of democratic nations to freedom of speech and assembly. The line dividing the good and bad becomes blurred, as in the use of state-sanctioned torture during the recent Bush administration. Governments must reach an accommodation with immigrants and reject extremist exclusionary pressures that threaten the core values of their legitimacy. Otherwise, to use Richard Widmark's words, when urged to go lightly on Nazi judges on trial in the film *Judgment at Nuremberg*, "Why did we fight? What was it all about?"[11]

In the United States, a number of anti-immigrant organizations, ostensibly created to rectify inequities in immigration, have unleashed blatant attacks on illegal immigrants. This has increased tension between indigenous whites and Latinos. The net result of such activities has been to create animosity toward immigrants and increase the number of hate crimes perpetrated against people of color and religious minorities.

Perhaps the best-known and most vociferous anti-immigration organization in the United States is the Federation for American Immigration Reform (FAIR). It was created as "a national, nonprofit, public interest, membership organization of concerned citizens who share a common belief that our nation's immigration policies must be reformed to serve the national interest." Its founder, John Tanton, once observed, "I've come to the point of view that for the European-American society and culture to persist requires a European-American majority, and a clear one at that." The Southern Poverty Law Center designated FAIR as a hate group in 2007.[12]

Such rhetoric in the United States, one of the world's most pluralistic countries, is distressing. But remarks by English Prime Minister David Cameron in a 2011 speech are more disturbing. Reversing decades of that nation's multicultural policy, he criticized Britain and other European nations' "hands-off tolerance." This encouraged Muslims and other immigrant groups to live separate lives and resist assimilation. Fearing that such policies create a climate conducive to extremism and terrorism, he warned, "Europe needs to wake up to what is happening in our own countries."[13] Cameron's reaction to recent terrorist incidents in the United Kingdom demonstrates the insidious effects that immigration can have on society by creating an environment of fear, apprehension, and hostility toward "the other."

When immigrants are isolated and ostracized, some may feel compelled to retaliate. Far more attacks are perpetrated on immigrants around the world than they commit in acts of terrorism. The worldwide transmission of individuals and ideas through travel and telecommunications is transforming, and in some peoples' minds, undermining societies. The Council of Europe's European Commission against Racism report in 2011 noted that racist incidents were becoming more frequent. Police in the forty-seven member states were disproportionately targeting minorities such as Gypsies and asylum seekers. The report noted that severe levels of prejudice were apparent against Muslims and racist, xenophobic media reports contributed to the prejudicial climate. A high level of racial profiling was also found.

The English paper, the *Guardian*, reported a study by London School of Economics professors that blacks were 26.6 times, and Asians 6.3

times, more likely to be stopped and searched by police than whites.[14] Reports by Amnesty International and the American Civil Liberties Union indicate that racial profiling of minorities in the United States is also pervasive.[15]

In its 2010 annual report, the Council of Europe noted the continuation of anti-immigrant and Islamophobic attitudes and behavior in its member states:

> Special hostility is reserved for *refugees and asylum-seekers* because of perceptions concerning reliance on welfare benefits and competition for jobs. Quite often, religion adds another dimension to the negative climate of opinion, ECRI (European Commission against Racism and Intolerance) has, as a result, found persisting problems of prejudice against *Muslims*, often expressed in debates about "values." Islamophobia inevitably materialises in everyday life and in the contacts with authorities.[16]

WHY PEOPLE MIGRATE

In our increasingly diverse and mobile world people choose to leave their homeland for a variety of reasons. The search for a better life that includes religious, political, and economic freedom is often an important factor. Three-fourths of international migrants go to countries with higher levels of human development than their own.

Yet, poverty inhibits mobility. The United Nations found that people in poorer countries are much less mobile than people in more affluent places. For example, less than 1 percent of Africans have moved to Europe. This is an insignificant number when compared to the total European population, but the number can be physically and psychologically magnified if immigrants cluster in specific areas.

This is precisely what happened in the United States at the turn of the twentieth century. Newly arrived immigrants formed insular ethnic communities in cities such as New York and Chicago. Today, it is happening in many European countries. For example, 13 percent of Amsterdam's population is Muslim while only 5.8 percent of the total Dutch population is. Although 3.6 percent of the German population is Muslim, the city of Cologne has a Muslim population of 12 percent. Denmark, with a total Muslim population of 5 percent, has a Muslim population of nearly 13 percent in Copenhagen. Sixty percent of the foreign immigrants in France are concentrated around Paris, Lyon, and Marseille.[17]

UN demographers predict a leveling off of world population growth based on a variety of indicators. Fertility rates have been falling in less developed countries. The number of nations with high fertility (women having five or more children) is dropping by half. On the other hand, all forty-five developed countries having at least 100,000 in population in

2009 had below replacement fertility in 2010. Interestingly, from 2005–2010, the seventy-six countries with below replacement fertility accounted for nearly half (47 percent) of the world's population. Among these nations are China, Brazil, Vietnam, Iran, Thailand, and the Republic of Korea.[18]

The Arab Spring of 2011 provides a fascinating preview of what our world might look like as a result of unbridled population growth and unresponsive tyrannical governments. Forty-five of the fifty countries with population growth rates of 2 percent or more in 2011 were in Africa or the Middle East. This includes nine of the ten countries with the highest population growth rates, ranging from annual growth of 4.31 percent for number one, Zimbabwe, to Zambia with an annual growth rate of 3.062. See table 4.1.

At a 1 percent annual rate of growth, a population doubles in size in seventy years. A 2 percent annual growth rate causes a doubling in thirty-five years. At a rate of 3 percent (e.g., Niger, Uganda, Burundi, the Gaza Strip, United Arab Emirates, Ethiopia, Burkina Faso, and Zambia), the population doubles in just eighteen years. At over 4 percent, Zimbabwe will see its population double in less than nine years.

Just looking at a country's population doesn't tell the whole story. Most of the nations with high fertility rates (the ratio of live births in an area compared to the population of that area) and high population growth rates also have high mortality rates. This is often from infectious and communicable diseases, unsanitary living conditions, and poor health care. For example, the world infant mortality rate, which is the number of deaths in the first year of birth per 1,000 live births, is forty-six. However, the rate in the "more developed" regions of the world (e.g., North America and Western Europe) is 6 per 1,000. But the rate in the "least developed" regions of the world is 80 per 1,000 (e.g., Angola, Benin, Ethiopia).

If we compare these regions in life expectancy, we again find glaring disparities. The world's life expectancy stands at 67.9 years. People living in the "more" regions can expect to live 76.9 years, compared to 65.9 years in the "less developed" countries and only 56.9 years in the "least developed" areas.

POPULATION GROWTH AND UNEMPLOYMENT

The pattern that emerges is one of high birth rates, high infant mortality, and lower life expectancy. These combine to perpetuate poverty and unemployment in less developed countries predominantly in Africa and Asia. The plight of youthful workers (aged fifteen to twenty-four) in 2010 is illustrative of these trends. Worldwide youth unemployment was estimated to be 77.7 million people or 12.6 percent of the working youth age

Table 4.1. Population Growth Rate by Country and Year

Rank	Country	Percent Annual Growth	Year
1	Zimbabwe	4.31	2011
2	Niger	3.643	2011
3	Uganda	3.576	2011
4	Turks & Caicos Islands	3.485	2011
5	Burundi	3.462	2011
6	Gaza Strip	3.422	2008
7	United Arab Emirates	3.282	2011
8	Ethiopia	3.194	2011
9	Burkina Faso	3.085	2011
10	Zambia	3.062	2011
11	Madagascar	2.973	2011
12	Benin	2.911	2011
13	Western Sarah	2.868	2008
14	Republic of Congo	2.835	2011
15	Bahrain	2.814	2011
16	Rwanda	2.792	2011
17	Malawi	2.763	2011
18	Togo	2.762	2011
19	Comoros	2.696	2011
20	Liberia	2.663	2011
21	Yemen	2.647	2011
22	Guinea	2.645	2011
23	Equatorial Guinea	2.641	2011
24	Democratic Rep. of Congo	2.614	2011
25	Mali	2.610	2011
26	Senegal	2.557	2011
27	Sudan	2.484	2011
28	Eritrea	2.472	2011
29	Kenya	2.462	2011
30	Mozambique	2.444	2011
31	Iraq	2.399	2011
32	Gambia	2.396	2011
33	Afghanistan	2.375	2011

34	Mauritania	2.349	2011
35	Cayman Islands	2.287	2011
36	Sierra Leone	2.249	2011
37	Djibouti	2.237	2011
38	West Bank	2.225	2008
39	Solomon Islands	2.220	2011
40	Anguilla	2.173	2011
41	Central African Rep.	2.146	2011
42	Cameroon	2.121	2011
43	Cote d'Ivoire	2.078	2011
44	Libya	2.064	2011
45	Belize	2.056	2011
46	Sao Tome' & Principe	2.052	2011
47	Angola	2.034	2011
48	Oman	2.023	2011
49	Chad	2.009	2011
50	Tanzania	2.002	2011

Source: NationMaster.com. (See http://www.nationmast er.com/graph/peo_pop_ gro_rat-people-population-growth-rate.)

population. But this figure ignored the large number of discouraged youth no longer seeking employment—a figure estimated by the United Nations at nearly two million in fifty-six reporting countries.

Interestingly, the Middle East had one of the highest regional unemployment rates in the world—10.3 percent, with a youth unemployment rate three times the adult. North Africa, another area in turmoil, with 9.8 percent unemployment, posted a 23.6 percent unemployment rate for active young people in 2010. Sub-Saharan Africa's rate of 8 percent was also higher than most regions of the world.

The continuing economic challenges faced by the twenty-seven countries in the European Union created a general unemployment level of 12 percent in 2013. Youth unemployment averaged 18 percent and over 50 percent in Greece and Spain. Such numbers no doubt contributed to increased social unrest in these developed nations.

Table 4.2 presents information about the percentage of youth and their level of unemployment in the Middle East region (excluding Israel) in 2010. With average youth (ages fifteen to twenty-four) unemployment ranging up to 46 and 45 percent in Algeria and Iraq respectively, it is no small wonder that the restlessness and enthusiasm of that generation boiled over into the turmoil of the 2011 Arab Spring.

The high unemployment rates for black and Latino youth in the United States demonstrates the persistence of uneven opportunities and systemic/institutional racism as described by sociologist Joe Feagin in his book *Racist America*.[19] See table 4.2.

Table 4.2. Percentage of Youth and Youth Unemployment by Middle Eastern Country, 2010

Country	Percent Youth (15–29)	Percent Unemployment (15–24)
Iran	34	20.4
Iraq	28	45.4
Syria	31	6.5
Jordan	30	22.2
Kuwait	25	5.3
Saudi Arabia	28	16.3
Qatar	34	17.0
Yemen	30	18.7
Oman	31	19.7
United Arab Emirates	27	7.6
West Bank Gaza	27	37.0
Lebanon	27	17.4
Egypt	29	21.7
Libya	28	27.4
Tunisia	29	27.3
Algeria	31	45.6
Morocco	29	18.3
Bahrain	28	20.7
United States	21 (ages 16–24)	18.1
—Whites	16	15.9
—Asians	1	15.3
—Blacks	3	31.0
—Hispanics	4	20.1

Sources: Samantha Constant and Mary Kraetsch, "Taking Stock of the Youth Challenge in the Middle East: New Data and Questions," Brookings Institute, June, 2010, accessed January 4, 2012, http://www.brookings.edu/articles/2010/06_middle_east_youth.aspx?sc_lang=en. "Employment and Unemployment Among Youth Summary," Bureau of Labor Statistics, U.S. Department of Labor, August 24, 2011, http://bls.gov/news.release/youth.nr0.htm.

While the 2007–2009 recession increased unemployment around the world, it was especially hard on developed nations. Unemployment rose and persisted while joblessness declined in other regions of the world. The 2010 world unemployment rate of 6.2 percent was significantly lower than the rate in some of the developed economies, which have since experienced even higher levels of unemployment (e.g., the European Union). With the exception of the Middle East, these figures were significantly higher than other regions of the world: East Asia (4.1 percent), Southeast Asia and the Pacific (5.1 percent), South Asia (4.3 percent), and Latin America and the Caribbean (7.7 percent).

These statistics only give a partial view of the employment picture. Worldwide, 205 million people were unemployed in 2010, with 1.7 million fewer youth in the labor force. Even more startling is the fact that 1.2 billion people worked for less than $2 a day in 2009. In Sub-Saharan Africa, three-fourths of the workers fell into this category. [20]

Table 4.3 compares the ten nations with the highest and lowest population growth rates on several indicators of quality of life. With a couple of exceptions, there is a strong correlation between the rate of population growth, life expectancy, and infant mortality. We have already linked these conditions to poverty and unemployment. [21]

Table 4.3. Comparison of Highest and Lowest Birth Growth Countries, 2011

Highest	Population Growth Rate (%)	Infant Mortality Rate (Deaths/1,000 Live Births)	Life Expectancy (years)
Zimbabwe	4.31	59	46.6
Niger	3.64	96	53.1
Uganda	3.58	79	52.2
Burundi	3.46	101	48.8
United Arab Emirates	3.28	7	75.9
Ethiopia	3.19	72	57.2
Burkina Faso	3.08	79	48.8
Zambia	3.06	95	46.9
Benin	2.91	85	54.6
Rep. of Congo	2.83	116	56.0

Lowest	Population Growth Rate (%)	Infant Mortality Rate (Deaths/1,000 Live Births)	Life Expectancy (years)
Bulgaria	−0.78	10	72.7
Estonia	−0.64	5	73.9
Ukraine	−0.62	13	67.5

Latvia	−0.60	8	72.3
Russia	−0.47	11	67.7
Serbia/Montenegro	−0.47	10	74.0
Guyana	−0.44	42	—
South Africa	−0.38	55	51.2
Belarus	−0.36	7	69.4
Georgia	−0.33	29	73.1
United States	0.96	7	78.0
United Kingdom	0.56	5	80.0
France	0.5	4	81.7
Germany	−0.21	4	79.8
Sweden	0.16	3	80.9
China	0.49	22	73.8
India	1.34	53	64.2
European Union	0.1	5.6	78.8
World	1.0	46	67.2

Sources: "Population Growth Rates by Country," Nationmaster.com, http://www.nationmaster.com/graph/peo_pop_gro_rat-people-population-growth-rate; World Population Prospects "The 2010 Revision," File 6-1: Infant Mortality (Both Sexes Combined) by Major Area, Region and Country, 1950–2010, and File 5-1: Life Expectancy at Birth (Both Sexes Combined) by Major Area, Region and Country, 1950–2100, Department of Economic and Social Affairs, Population Division (Geneva: United Nations, 2011), http://esa.un.org/wpp/sorting-Tables/tab-sorting_mortality.htm.

UNDERSTANDING THE IMPLICATIONS OF IMMIGRATION

What do these statistics mean for our discussion? First, these are projections and subject to change. While based on concrete trend analyses, the suppositions are conjectural. The demographic transition is not an immutable, inviolable iron law. Social life is influenced by many factors, often simultaneously. Rarely can we say that A is the sole cause of B. Determining the many forces that affect our behavior, what is referred to as multiple causality, is what keeps social scientists awake at night. The complexity of social systems and the myriad stimuli that impinge on people are not amenable to definitive calculations of the kind utilized by physical scientists.

In human relations, 2 + 2 does not always equal 4. For example, one might conclude from the previous discussion that there would be a high inverse correlation between population growth rates and per capita income and that the negative effects of population growth on infant mortal-

ity and life expectancy would lower income in nations with high population growth rates. Yet, table 4.4 indicates a number of anomalies. For
example, countries with low population growth rates such as Estonia,
Guyana, South Africa, and Georgia have *low* per capita income, while the
United Arab Emirates (UAE), with a high population growth rate, has the
highest per capita income among nations listed.

This demonstrates that correlation does not prove causation. In this
case there are other factors, or intervening variables, that influence the
results in the table. For example, the impact and disbursement of natural
resources (oil revenues) in the UAE[22] and the struggling economies and
governments of the countries in the former Soviet Union: Ukraine and
Estonia. The situation of South Africa and Guyana is complicated in the
former by high mortality associated with HIV infections and in the latter
by the residual effects of hundreds of years of colonization by the Dutch
and British.

It is not just the imprecision of our attempts to codify and predict
human behavior that complicates our efforts to gauge future demographic trends. Natural phenomena, e.g., drought, pestilence, earth quakes,
and floods wreak havoc on our best estimates, driving planners back to
their computers to recalculate their projections.

IMMIGRATION ANXIETY

An even more perplexing and confounding element in our attempt to
predict demographic trends is human variability. It is the penchant for
people to behave unpredictably in social situations. This happens for a
variety of reasons. Different learning experiences and variations in people's backgrounds influence their perception of social reality. Social and
cultural norms also define what may be acceptable responses in given
situations.

In relation to our discussion, this last caveat is, perhaps, most significant. Culture has a dramatic impact on peoples' values regarding family
size *and* their acceptability and subsequent rate of assimilation into host
societies after immigration. The fact remains that developed nations,
which are preponderantly white, will continue to be recipients of large
numbers of immigrants of color from developing nations. This phenomenon has two important effects. First, declining replacement rates in developed nations will necessitate the importation of labor to fill job vacancies
left open by declining birth rates.

Second, the introduction of large numbers of people from other cultures may precipitate, as in the United States and Western Europe, resentment, frustration, fear, and anger on the part of indigenous populations.[23] In the United States nativistic groups, such as the Minutemen,
have been "patrolling" borders in Southwestern states (e.g., Arizona,

Table 4.4. Per Capita Income and Population Growth Rates

High	Population Growth Rates (2006–2010)	Per Capita Income (USD for 2008)
Zimbabwe	4.31	314
Niger	3.64	354
Uganda	3.58	500
Burundi	3.46	138
UAE	3.28	63,966
Ethiopia	3.19	319
Burkina Faso	3.08	522
Zambia	3.06	1,144
Benin	2.91	767
Rep. of Congo	2.83	2,934
Low	**Population Growth Rates (2006–2010)**	**Per Capita Income (USD for 2008)**
Bulgaria	−0.78	6,573
Estonia	−0.64	17,298
Ukraine	−0.62	3,921
Latvia	−0.60	14,956
Russia	−0.47	11,858
Serbia/Mont.	−0.47	6,871
Guyana	−0.44	1,543
South Africa	−0.38	5,566
Belarus	−0.36	6,230
Georgia	−0.33	2,970
United States	0.96	45,230
United Kingdom	0.56	43,544
France	0.50	44,675
Germany	−0.21	44,363
Sweden	0.16	52,035
China	0.49	3,292
India	1.34	1,061

Source: "Indicators on Income and Economic Activity," United Nations, Department of Economic and Social Affairs, June 2011, http://unstats.un.org/unsd/demographic/products/socind/inc-eco.htm.

New Mexico, California) for more than a decade, ostensibly protecting American values and society from illegal "alien" immigrants disproportionately from Mexico. The Southern Poverty Law Center (SPLC)[24] lists 319 hate groups that focus on immigrants, such as the Minuteman Civil Defense Corps, Minuteman Project, and the Federation of Immigration Reform and Enforcement Coalition.[25]

The SPLC has documented the stigmatization and widespread abuse of people who have been intercepted by such self-styled vigilantes and survivalist militias. They are obsessed with preserving American values and culture from invading "hordes" of brown and black people. The founders of white supremacist organizations, like William Daniel Johnson of the American Third Position (A3P) (recently renamed the American Freedom Party), barely conceal their contempt for dark-skinned immigrants and the fear of possible cultural contamination. "The A3P will restore America to its former glory," states the party, while white supremacists' march to the racist slogan, "We must secure the existence of our people and a future for White children."[26] Presumably, whiteness equates with moral, physical, and psychological superiority, as if whites in America had nothing to do with the genocide of Native Americans, slavery, and the perfidious business transactions that led to the near collapse of the nation's (and world's) economic system in 2008.

The protests of some Tea Party racists fan the flames of ethnocentrism.[27] So, too, do the actions of state governments such as Arizona, Alabama, Utah, and Georgia, which passed constitutionally questionable restrictive immigration legislation that allows racial profiling of assumed illegal immigrants. In October 2011 Alabama's anti-immigration law, considered the toughest in the nation, was implemented. It allows authorities to question people suspected of being in the country illegally. They can be held without bond. Public school children can also be screened to determine their immigration status.

Farmers began complaining that their crops were rotting in the fields because of a labor shortage related to the new law. A hotline established by the Southern Poverty Law Center to receive complaints related to the law logged 4,200 calls in the first few months alleging the bullying and harassing of Latino children in school and widespread fear among Latino families. The U.S. Department of Justice asked the Eleventh Circuit Court of Appeals in Atlanta on October 7, 2011, to block implementation of the law on the ground that it "is likely to expose persons lawfully in the United States, including school children, to new difficulties in routine dealings."[28] On October 29, 2013, a coalition of civil rights groups announced an agreement with the state that permanently blocks key provisions of the law that led to racial profiling.

On June 25, 2012, the U.S. Supreme Court struck down three of the four key provisions of Arizona's similarly harsh immigration law (warrantless arrests of people suspected of being deportable, making it a state crime for immigrants to seek or hold jobs without proper documents, and punishment for immigrants failing to register with the federal government). It did uphold the law's requirement to determine the immigration status of people stopped by police or arrested if they suspect they are in the country illegally.[29]

What's Behind the Immigration Backlash?

Rabid anti-immigration rhetoric of nativists and white supremacists in the United States and around the globe is nothing new. As people became mobile in the nineteenth and twentieth centuries through rail, automotive, and air transportation, large numbers of them began to move across porous borders. Natural impediments to mobility that took our ancestors thousands of years to travail, like mountains, deserts, and oceans, became accessible and surmounted within weeks, days, even hours. Now cultures as well as borders were being transcended. Ethnic groups and ruling elites who had maintained hegemony over their domain were now interacting with people whose cultures were strikingly different from their own. Language, customs, dress, food, and religious beliefs were thrust into heretofore closed societies.

Three fears have traditionally arisen among indigenous-receiving cultures throughout the millennia. First, and perhaps most obvious, has been the fear that immigration would lead to cultural contamination. The intrusion of customs and beliefs brought by immigrants has traditionally been perceived by some indigenous people as tantamount to an invasion of hostile ideologies. They are viewed as pernicious and destructive of the host culture, threatening the stability of the society.

Second, host societies not only fear, but resent, the intrusion of immigrants. They are perceived as competitors vying for scarce resources, straining economic, health, and other social services, and adversely affecting the labor market. It is assumed they take jobs ordinarily filled by indigenous workers and drive down wages by flooding the labor force with low-skilled and semi-skilled workers.

Finally, and most insidiously, there are fears arising from sexual competition and the purported degradation of the indigenous "superior" white culture. These concerns emanate from the ethnocentric belief that immigrant stock is inferior to indigenous genetic lines. More to the point is the threat posed by immigrant males to indigenous male hegemony over females. Competition for mates has often led to the social and cultural stigmatization of immigrants. They are depicted as undesirable, unattractive, even subhuman. This effort, at times subliminal, is to culturally emasculate potential sexual competitors. We now turn to a discussion about the veracity of these assumptions.

The Truth about Immigration

Fears about the intrusion of different cultures into dominant host societies have been expressed for centuries. Much of the rhetoric denouncing supposed negative effects of this phenomenon have proven baseless. Research shows the positive contributions immigrants have made and continue to make to host societies. Immigrants leave their native lands for a variety of reasons. Political or religious persecution, economic hardship, wanderlust and the search for new experiences or security unavailable at home influence their decisions. Immigrants transmit material (dress, art, architecture, foods) and nonmaterial culture (religion, ideas, traditions, and behavior patterns such as childrearing) to their host nation.

It is absurd to conclude, as some neo-eugenicists and racists contend, that immigrants are engaged in a covert war to control North America or Europe.[30] Or, that the contemporary movement of Muslims into Western societies is part of a calculated plot to conquer these nations by infusing their societies with Shariah law. Or, that the influx of Mexican immigrants into the United States is part of an annexation plan to create a nation called Aztlan. This myth contends Mexico will reclaim the southwestern territory lost in the Mexican-American War that was ceded to the United States in the 1848 Treaty of Guadalupe-Hildago.[31] There is no substantive body of evidence proving the veracity of such plots. In fact, immigration is a process that exchanges values and behaviors in both directions.

Contrary to popular mythology, roughly 3 percent of the world's population is composed of international immigrants. Both immigrants and the dominant host population transmit and share cultural information during the process of assimilation. Cultural exchange between immigrants and host nations actually threatens to weaken traditional immigrant values. For example, Muslim culture in the West has been eroding in recent years.[32] In fact, a European Social Survey conducted in 2010 by Heikki Ervasti of the University of Turku in Finland, found that the number of Muslim immigrants going to mosques in Europe dropped significantly. After living on that continent, attendance declined from 60.5 percent regularly attending who lived there less than a year to 48.8 percent for Muslim immigrants residing in Europe for a year or more, *and more than half in this category reported that they rarely or never go.*[33]

Furthermore, the percentage of Muslims in historically white Western European nations is relatively small: 5.8 percent in the Netherlands, 3 percent in Sweden, 4.2 percent in Switzerland, 2.3 percent in Spain, 1.4 percent in Italy, 9 percent in France, 5 percent in Denmark, 4 percent in Belgium, 4.1 percent in Austria, 3 percent in Norway. In 2010, there were 44.1 million Muslims in Europe, excluding Turkey, with 16 million in the European Community.

The PEW Forum on Religion and Public Life estimated that the percentage of Muslims residing in Europe would increase to 8 percent by 2030.[34] The recent murder of seventy-seven people in Norway by white supremacist Anders Behring Breivik, who feared the Islamization of his country, reveals the hysteria among some members of that movement.[35] In light of the facts, such sentiments are revealed as superficial and all the more tragic. At present rates of growth, Muslims will constitute between 4 and 11 percent of the Norwegian population by 2060.

Nevertheless, the presence of Muslims in Western countries has created a legal backlash aimed at extirpating Muslim traditions such as the wearing of head (*hijab*) and full body covering (*burqa*) by some Muslim women.[36]

The fact that some Muslims choose (or are relegated) to live in cloistered ghetto-like enclaves in England, France, the Netherlands, and Germany, or Dearborn, Michigan, may be a demonstration of their attempt to maintain their customs and traditions in the face of the overwhelming pervasiveness of dominant secular, Western values. Living in tight-knit communities eases the trauma of immigration. It provides safety, security, and familiarity with values and traditions from the country left behind. It helps to maintain stability in the face of change as the group wrestles with the challenge of being assimilated.

Fear of change can lead to anomie and dysfunction. Rather than castigating immigrants and stereotyping these enclaves, we should be thankful for their existence and the stabilizing role they play in assisting people in their transition into Western society.

One of the complaints of white supremacists and anti-immigrationists has been the supposed reluctance of new immigrants to learn the host country's language. In the United States, Latinos have been singled out as unwilling to accommodate to American society and learn English. Yet, research indicates the opposite.

In a survey of Latinos, the PEW Hispanic Center found, "Hispanics by a large margin believe that immigrants have to speak English to be a part of American society and even more so that English should be taught to the children of immigrants." Further, the report concluded, "The endorsement of the English language, both for immigrants and for their children, is strong among all Hispanics regardless of income, party affiliation, fluency in English or how long they have lived in the United States."[37] Another PEW survey found that *nearly all* (88–94 percent) of Hispanic adults born in the United States to immigrant parents were fluent in English, using it at home and work.[38]

The rhetoric surrounding Latino immigration heated up in the United States in 2013–2014. A possible compromise between Republicans and Democrats to allow illegal immigrants a path for citizenship in the United States will be related to the fact that the Republican Presidential candidate in 2012, Mitt Romney, received only 29 percent of the Latino vote.

The Grand Old Party recognizes the need to reshape its image to appeal to the growing Latino segment of the electorate.

No doubt immigrant ethnic groups assimilate at different rates into Western societies. Obviously, individuals from countries with vastly different norms, cultures, and languages from the host nation will assimilate more slowly than people originating from countries with more similar traditions.

There are enclaves of immigrants and their descendants who choose not to assimilate into Western societies. They reject the dominant secular value system, or prefer to maintain their traditional lifestyles. The fact that people immigrate to the West and, for the most part, assimilate into the societies they choose to live in, undercuts racist assumptions about the motivation for immigration and the effects of the immigrants on the dominant host culture.

The act of leaving one's home is evidence of an immigrant's desire to alter his/her lifestyle and life chances. Not all members of an immigrant's family may embrace the move to a different culture. But it is the height of naiveté to assume that immigrants arriving in Western nations are oblivious to the secular nature of host countries or that they do not expect to reach an accommodation with the dominant culture. Equally preposterous is the supposition that they did not immigrate for the purpose of taking the opportunity to benefit from that culture.

Certainly, there have been negative reactions among some immigrants to the "excesses" of Western materialism (e.g., styles of dress, religiosity, relaxed sexual mores, the intrusion of the media into interpersonal relations, political activity, and economic [work] relationships). Some people have attempted to steadfastly cling to their traditional roots. Others have become radicalized in their disdain for contemporary Western values. But the overwhelming majority of immigrants entering Western societies make their pilgrimages in search of better lives. They understand and desire to embrace and emulate the values of the host society.

Knowing the facts about the motivation for immigration helps demythologize another widely alleged fallacy about immigrants—their supposed low work ethic. Coupled with this assertion is the belief that immigrants take jobs from the indigenous population—that they hold primarily low-level, unskilled jobs and drive down wages by accepting meager compensation. All of these assumptions are false.

The allegation that immigrants come to Western nations because they have a low work ethic and want generous welfare benefits (e.g., health, education, and living assistance such as housing and food) is a malicious distortion of the facts. It is designed to promote anti-immigrant xenophobia.

Labor economists hold different perspectives on the percentage of native workers displaced by immigrant labor. There is general agreement that the large increase in the number of undocumented immigrants to the

United States between 1990 and 2007 *did not* lead to higher unemployment in the United States. Harvard professor, George Bjoras, contends that illegal immigration increases unemployment and depresses wages, while Berkeley economist, David Card and Robert J. La Londe of the University of Chicago believe there is a negligible effect, as does Jeffrey Passel, a senior research associate at the PEW Hispanic Center.

Research indicates that illegal immigration may depress wages at the lowest level of employment. Those most adversely affected may be the most recent immigrants. Immigration helps the economy by creating value in other areas (e.g., spending on goods and services such as food, housing, and transportation). The low wages that many illegal immigrants earn also helps to bring down the cost of some products such as food.

A 2007 PEW Hispanic Center analysis at the height of illegal Mexican immigration into the United States found that there were eight million undocumented Hispanic immigrants in the U.S. labor force, filling a wide variety of positions: 20 percent of construction jobs, 17 percent of positions in the leisure and hospitality fields, 14 percent of manufacturing jobs, and 11 percent of workers in wholesale and retail jobs.

A Congressional Budget Office study concluded that the proposed immigration bill of 2013 would actually cut the federal deficit by $1 trillion over the next two decades by adding ten million people to the tax-paying roles.[39]

While the most recent wave of illegal immigrants to the United States from Mexico and Central and South America may initially have low levels of education, past experience indicates second and third generations will not only assimilate into the larger society but, like the children of former immigrants, make major contributions.

William Wulf, president of the National Academy of Engineers, reminded Congress of the important contribution immigrants have made to the nation's intellectual establishment: 37 percent of PhD scientists and engineers, 45 percent of all physicists, and over 50 percent of all engineers in the United States are foreign born. A quarter of the engineering faculty at universities around the United States are also foreign born. Between 1990 and 2004, a third of all Nobel Prize winners in the United States were foreign-born scientists. A study by the Partnership for a New American Economy, a nonprofit organization cofounded by former New York City Mayor Michael Bloomberg found that foreign-born nationals played a role in 75 percent of the patents at the nation's top research universities.[40]

The low population growth rate in the United States means that the country, like other Western nations, is running out of youthful indigenous workers. The annual growth of our labor force is slightly more than half a percent (0.6). By 2050 the labor force is projected to be nearly 195 million workers. Our aging population will push the need for immigrant labor to fill the job openings because a quarter of the labor force will be over fifty-five at that time. By 2050 white, non-Hispanics will comprise just half (51.4 percent) of the labor force, blacks—14 percent, Asians—8.3 percent, and Latinos—23.2 percent. [41]

Immigration already accounts for 40 percent of the growth in the U.S. population. Despite the sluggish growth of jobs during and after the recession in 2007–2009 in the U.S. labor force, we will need to import millions of workers over the next decades to fill needed positions if our economy is to grow and prosper. A premium will be placed on jobs requiring higher education. But the demand for low-paying service jobs will remain high as long as current political policies continue to foster the exploitation of low educated native and immigrant workers in such industries as hospitality, agriculture, food preparation, and care of the elderly.

The 2007–2009 recession demonstrated the fallacy of the anti-immigrationists' argument that immigrants enter the United States for the purpose of obtaining public assistance. As the recession worsened, the number of immigrants declined precipitously. The PEW Hispanic Center documented a 60 percent decline in the number of Mexicans between 2006 and 2010 (from one million to 404,000 annually). This phenomenon was also affected by increased border enforcement in the United States and stronger economic growth in Mexico. [42]

Another report of the PEW Center revealed that Hispanic immigrants (especially those from Mexico) were declining precipitously in the wake of the 2007–2010 economic downturn in the United States. The U.S. birthrate of 63.2 in 2011 was the lowest ever recorded (the number of births per 1,000 women ages fifteen to forty-four). It fell 23 percent for Mexican immigrants during this time. Nevertheless, the PEW Center predicts that immigrants arriving in the United States since 2005 and their descendants will account for 82 percent of the U.S. population growth by 2050. [43]

Contrary to the assumption that immigrants are a drain on the U.S. economy, research indicates that states and the nation receive a substantial net gain from their presence. Immigrants pay taxes (estimated at over $90 billion a year), spend money, and stimulate the economy. It is estimated they will contribute nearly half a trillion dollars to the Social Security Trust Fund between 1998 and 2022. Economist Francine Lipman estimated that the government collected $7 billion in Social Security taxes in 2003 from 7.5 million workers with mismatched Social Security numbers, presumably belonging to illegal immigrants. They will not be able to benefit from their contributions.

Another vicious stereotype about contemporary legal and illegal immigrants in the United States, particularly Latinos, is the allegation that they have high crime rates. This argument is absurd when one considers the sacrifice immigrants make in their attempt to enter the United States. After risking their lives and finances, why would they engage in behavior that would draw attention to them that might eventuate in their deportation? In fact, studies confirm that immigrants have lower crime rates than indigenous citizens, but their crime rate increases the longer they reside in the United States.[44]

Looking at the positive effects of immigration, the United Nations Development Programme concluded, "The unprecedented flows of ideas across countries in recent times—ranging from health-saving techniques to political ideals and to productive practices—have been transformative."[45] Yet, a cascade of anti-immigrant rhetoric continues to inundate Western nations with fear-mongering diatribes, brimming with misinformation and hate. We now turn to a discussion about why this is occurring.

SUMMING UP

- Social unrest around the world is related to high population growth and poor educational and work opportunities.
- Places with low population growth (e.g., Europe, Japan and North America) will need immigrants to fill jobs so their economies thrive.
- Anti-immigrant sentiment around the world is fueled by ignorance, hate, and fear of social change.
- People migrate in search of better lives for themselves and their families.
- Immigrants seek to assimilate into their new culture by learning the language, improving their education, and getting jobs.

NOTES

1. Therese Hesketh, Li Lu, and Zhu Wei Xing, "The Effect of China's One-Child Family Policy aAfter 25 Years," *New England Journal of Medicine,* 353 (September 15, 2005): 1171–1176.

2. Ibid.

3. Ed Flanagan, "Chinese Say One Child Is Enough as Beijing Weighs End of Policy," *NBC News,* November 1, 2012, http://behindthewall.nbcnews.com/_news/2012/11/01/14856974.

4. "Country Studies," http://www.country-studies.com/india/population-and-family-planning-policy.html; "National Population Policy of India," http://www.indiaonlinepages.com/population/indian-population-policy.html; "Population Growth Rate Top 100," http://www.indexmundi.com/g/r.aspx?+=100&v=24.

5. For more information, see U.S. central Intelligence Agency, "Field Listing: Sex Ratio," *The World Factbook,* https://www.cia.gov/library/publications/the-world-factbook/fields/2018.html.

6. For a discussion of this, see Joseph Chamie, "Fewer Babies Pose Difficult Challenges for Europe," *Global Envision,* http://www.globalvision.org/library/8/1776/.

7. United Nations Department of Economic and Social Affairs, Population Division, "World Population Prospects, the 2008 Revision," Highlights, Working Paper No. ESA/P/wp.210, 2009.

8. United Nations, "World Population Prospects, the 2008 Revision."

9. "Overcoming Barriers: Human Mobility and Development," Human Development Report, (New York: United Nations Development Programme, 2009), http://hdr.undp.org/en/media/HDR_2009_EN_complete.pdf.

10. The Southern Poverty Law Center recently detailed a list of the most rabid anti-Muslim Islamophobes in the United States. For more information on the number and types of hate crimes, see the Uniform Crime Report of the FBI Hate Crime Statistics at http://www.fbi.gov/news/stories/2010/november/hate_112210/hate_112210. For an analysis of anti-Muslim activities, see Robert Steinback, "Jihad against Islam," *Intelligence Report*, Southern Poverty Law Center, no. 142 (Summer 2011): 15–24.

11. For an in-depth look at one Islamophobe, David Yerushalmi, see Andrea Elliott, "Behind an Anti-Shariah Push," *New York Times*, July 31, 2011, 1, 16.

12. FAIR's website is http://www.fairus.org/site/PageNavigator/about.html. Even more strident views and activities can be found among anti-immigrant vigilante groups such as the Minuteman organization. See http://www.minutemanhq.com/hq/.

13. John F. Burns, "Prime Minister Criticizes British 'Multiculturalism' as Allowing Extremism," *New York Times*, Sunday, February 6, 2011, International Section, 6.

14. "State of the World's Minorities and Indigenous Peoples 2011—UK," Refworld, Minority Rights Group International, July 6, 2011, http://www.unhcr.org/refworld/docid/4e16d35bc.html.

15. Amnesty International USA, "Threat and Humiliation: Racial Profiling, National Security, and Human Rights in the United States" (New York: Amnesty International USA, 2004), http://www.amnestyusa.org/pdfs/rp_report.pdf; American Civil Liberties Union, "Campaign Against Racial Profiling," http://www.aclu.org/racial-justice/racial-profiling.

16. European Commission against Racism and Intolerance, "Annual Report on ECRI's Activities, January 1–December 31, 2010" (Strasbourg: ECRI, 2012), http://www.coe.int/t/dghl/monitoring/ecri/activities/Annual_Reports/Annual%20report%202011.pdf.

17. These statistics come from "Islam in Europe," at http://islamineurope.blogspot.com/2007/11/muslim-population-in-european-cities.html and http://www.immigration.gouv.fr/IMG/pdf/IM10popetrangere06.pdf.

18. United Nations, "World Population Prospects, the 2008 Revisions."

19. Joe Feagin, *Racist America: Roots, Current Realities and Future Reparations*, 2nd ed. (New York: Routledge, 2010).

20. "Global Employment Trends, 2011: The Challenge of a Jobs Recovery," International Labor Office (Geneva, Switzerland: United Nations, 2011).

21. For further information, see "World Population Prospects: The 2010 Revision, File 6-1: Infant Mortality (Both Sexes Combined) by Major Area, Region and Country, 1950–2100," and File 5-1 "Life Expectancy and Birth (Both Sexes Combined) by Major Area, Region and Country, 1950–2100," United Nations, Department of Economic and Social Affairs, Population Division, 2011.

22. See, for example, Mohamed Shihab, "Economic Development in the UAE," http://www.uaeinteract.com/uaeint_misc/pdf/perspectives/12.pdf.

23. See Kenan Malik, *The Meaning of Race: Race, History, and Culture in Western Society* (New York: New York University Press, 1996), for a discussion of Western European hostility toward immigrants of color as immigration began to increase in Great Britain and Europe.

24. "Attacking the Constitution: State Legislators for Legal Immigration and the Anti-Immigrant Movement," March 20, 2011, http://www.splcenter.org/get-informed/publications/attacking-the-constitution-slli-and-the-anti-immigrant-movement, and "'Nativist Extreme' Groups 2010."

25. For a state by state listing, to go http://www.splcenter.org/get-informed/intelligence-report/browse-all-issues/2011/spring/the-year-in-nativism/nativist-extremists.

26. *Intelligence Report*, Southern Poverty Law Center, 138, Summer, 2010: 43, 48.

27. The NAACP adopted a resolution on July 13, 2010, condemning racism among segments of the anti–Big Government Tea Party, and in September of that year they launched a website to track racist behavior in the Tea Party movement.

28. "Justice Department Asks Appeals Court to Block Alabama's Immigration Law," *Fox News*,http://www.foxnews.com/politics/2011/10/07/justice-department-asks-appeals-court-to-block-alabamas-immigration-law/. By mid-July, 2010, eight states had filed amicus briefs supporting Arizona's punitive immigration law—Alabama, Florida, Nebraska, Pennsylvania, South Carolina, South Dakota, Texas, and Virginia. See Robbie Brown, "Georgia Gives Police Added Power to Seek Out Illegal Immigrants," *New York Times*, May 13, 2011,http://www.nytimes.com/2011/05/14/us/14georgia.html, and Josh Loftin, "Utah Immigration Law Joins Arizona Measure—In Court," *Huffington Post*,http://www.huffingtonpost.com/2011/05/11/utah-immigration-law-_n_860572.html.

29. Adam Liptak, "Court Splits Immigration Law Verdicts; Upholds Hotly Debated Centerpiece, 8–0," *New York Times*, June 26, 2012, A1, A12.

30. See Peter Brimley, *Alien Nation*, and his website, VDARE [http://vdare.com], named after the supposedly first white child born in the Virginia settlement, Virginia Dare, for more information on this point. Ironically, Brimley immigrated to the United States from England and is committed to preventing others [read "nonwhites"] from following in his footsteps. See also the Minuteman HQ website for more "facts" about the "immigration crisis" at http://www.minutemanhq.com/hq/.

31. Also see the posting of George W. on June 1, 2010, on the Patriot Action Network at http://www.patriotactionnetwork.com/profiles/blogs/what-is-la-raza-la-reconquista.

32. For a discussion of this phenomenon in Belgium, see Herman De Ley, "Humanists and Muslims in Belgian Secular Society," http://www.flw.ugent.be/cie/CIE/deley10.htm; in Spain, "EU Muslims Go the Mosque Less Often," http://www.allah.eu/general/eu-muslims-go-to-mosque-less-often.html; and conference papers on "European Muslims and the Secular State in a Comparative Perspective," in "Islam, Citizenship, and the Dynamics of European Integration," edited by Jocelyne Cesari, June 30 and July 1, 2003, http://www.arabphilosophers.com/English/discourse/east-west/Secularization/Final_ICDEI_Symposium.pdf.

33. http://.www.allah.eu/general/eu-muslims-go-to-mosque-less-often-html.

34. "The Future of the Global Muslim Population," The PEW Forum on Religion and Public Life, January 27, 2011, http://www.pewforum.org/future-of-the-global-muslim-population.

35. For a glimpse of Brevik's personality, see Richard Orange, "Anders Behring Brevik Psychiatric Report Reveals 'Kindergarten' Prison Life," *Telegraph*, January 15, 2012, http://www.Telegraph.co.uk/news/europe/norway/9016174/Anders-Behring-Brevik-psychiatric-report-reveals-kindergarten-prison-life.html. On August 23, 2012, an unrepentant Brevik was sentenced by a Norwegian court to twenty-one years in prison for these murders. Norway does not have the death penalty.

36. Turkey also bans such dress. For a summary of this controversy, see "Islamic Dress in Europe," at http://en.wikipedia.org/wiki/islamic_dress_controversy_in_Europe#Belgium.

37. PEW Hispanic Center, "Fact Sheets" June 7, 2006, http://pewhispanic.org/files/factsheets/20.pdf.

38. PEW Hispanic Center, "English Usage among Hispanics in the United States," November 29, 2007, http://pewhispanic.org/reports/report.php?reportID=82.

39. "Immigration Bill Would Cut Deficit," *Tampa Bay Times*, June 19, 2013, 2A.

40. Testimony of William A. Wulf, "The Importance of Foreign-born Scientists and Engineers to the Security of the United States," Subcommittee on the Judiciary, U.S.

House of Representatives, September 15, 2005. See Andrew Martin, "Immigrants are Crucial to Innovation, Study Says," *New York Times*, June 26, 2012, B6, for a review of the report and "Immigration and Innovation: The Impact of Immigrant Inventors and Business Leaders on American Prosperity," Partnership for a New American Economy, which notes that over one recent decade, immigrants founded ventures that created 450,000 jobs with a market capitalization estimated at $500 billion. Five additional jobs are created for every high-skilled visa (H1B) recipient. Go to http://www. renewoureconomy.org/sites/all/themes/pnae/img/ir (accessed June 28, 2012).

41. Mitra Toossi, "A New Look at Long-Term Labor Force Projections to 2050," *Monthly Labor Review*, November 2006, 19–39.

42. "The Mexican-American Boom: Births Overtake Immigration," PEW Hispanic Center, July 14, 2011, http://pewhispanic.org/reports/report.php?ReportID=144. See also the PEW Research Center Report by Jeffrey Passel, D'Vera Cohen and Ana Gonzalez-Barrera, "Net Imgration from Mexico Falls to Zero and Perhaps Less," April 23, 2012.

43. Gretchen Livingston and D'Vera Cohn, "U.S. Birth Rate Falls to a Record Low; Decline is Greatest among Immigrants," PEW Research Center, November 29, 2012, http://www.pewsocialtrends.org/2012/11/29/u-s-birth-rate--fal.

44. Andrew Karmen, *Murder Mystery* (New York: New York University Press, 2000); Robert J. Sampson, Jeffrey D. Morenoff, and Stephen Raudenbush, "Social Anatomy of Racial and Ethnic Disparities in Violence," *American Journal of Public Health* 95, no. 2 (2005): 224–232; Alejandro Portes and Ruben G. Rumbaut, *Immigrant America: A Portrait*, 3rd ed. (Berkeley: University of California Press). Information for this discussion of immigration was drawn from Roger Lowenstein, "The Immigration Equation," *New York Times*, July 9, 2006, 38–43, 69–71; Daniel Altman, "Shattering Stereotypes about Immigrant Workers," *New York Times*, June 3, 2007, Business Section, 4, http://www.nytimes.com/2007/06/03/business/yourmoney/03view.html; Yoji Cole, "Debunking 10 Myths about Immigrants," *Diversity Inc.*, September 2007, 51–54, http://www.diversityinc-digital.com/diversityincmedia/200709?pg=52; Appendix B, "Immigration Myths," Southern Poverty Law Center, April 4, 2009, http://www.splcenter.org/publications/under-siege-life-low-income-latinos-south/appendix; "10 Myths about Immigration," *Teaching Tolerance*, Southern Poverty Law Center, 39 (Spring 2011), http://www.tolerance.org/magazine/number-39–spring-2011/10–myths-about-immigration; "Top 10 Immigration Myths and Facts," National Immigration Forum, June 2003, http://www.immigrationforum.org/images/uploads/mythsandFacts.pdf; PEW Hispanic Center Reports, http://pewhispanic.org/.

45. United Nations Development Programme, *Human Development Report 2010: The Real Wealth of Nations: Pathways to Human Development* (New York: Palgrave McMillan, 2010).

FIVE

Why We Fear and Loathe "the Other"

As we ascend the social ladder, viciousness wears a thicker mask.
                                                      —Erich Fromm

*Our classrooms should not be battlegrounds where power and privilege perpetu-
ate the social inequality of society. Preconceptions about students must be left
outside to wither away like dying weeds.*

THE LINK BETWEEN WEALTH AND HATE

The twenty-first century will become known as the Age of Encounter as
people move in and out of their homelands and telecommunications cata-
pults cultures into one another on an unprecedented scale. Encounters
from migration and immigration have occurred throughout human history. In recent times, the United States experienced many large waves of
immigrants in the late nineteenth and early twentieth centuries. Then
nearly 15 percent of the population was composed of new immigrants,
compared to slightly more than 11 percent today.

The difference today is the higher mobility of the world's population
and the wholesale diffusion of ideas. The dispersal of people and cultures
is resurrecting stereotypes and precipitating hateful acts that threaten the
security and integrity of societies around the world. The same racist arguments and xenophobic sentiments about immigrants are resurfacing.
We hear the familiar refrain about the sanctity of the homeland and the
threat to established values posed by strangers.

The early eugenics movement heightened fears about immigrants
through a misapplication of Darwin's concept of natural selection to humans. The public was led to believe that some people (notably dark-
skinned people of African descent, Asians, and indigenous peoples such

as Indians) and ethnic groups (Eastern Europeans, Jews, Slavs, Poles, and Gypsies) were genetically inferior to white, European, Anglo Saxon, Aryan stock.

Influenced by the writing of the English sociologist Herbert Spencer (*The Social Organism*, 1860) and his counterparts in the United States (e.g., William Graham Sumner at Yale University), the poor and dispossessed were depicted as biologically inferior. Popular conceptions of America as "the land of the free and the home of the brave," where "the streets are paved with gold" and anyone can achieve fame and fortune through hard work, were bolstered by the Protestant work ethic. This meritocratic paradise stereotyped the socially and physically disadvantaged as less competent. They lacked the motivation to compete through a combination of social, psychological and biological flaws that made them undesirable.

Linking poverty and social inequality to human inadequacy, the Social Darwinist movement provided the underpinning for unfettered capitalism and racism. These two weaknesses continue to plague developed countries as they struggle to become inclusive and wrestle with the perplexing social issues of poverty and social pathologies, such as crime, mental illness, and substance abuse.

Social Darwinist beliefs still resonate with the public in Western, white-dominated societies, despite the increase in wealth disparity and the declining middle class. They find expression in the persistence of "the myth of meritocracy"—the popular belief that hard work and individual initiative inevitably lead to success. The pernicious side of this assumption lies in the stigmatization of the poor, minorities, and immigrants as social misfits. They are depicted as biologically incapable of competing with the supposedly superior white Anglo population. In one sweeping assumption, dark-skinned people, minorities, and the poor are labeled as genetically inferior. They become social outcasts, while the conniving excesses of capitalists are rationalized as good business practices.

Belief in the myth of meritocracy is reinforced by linking it with people who exemplify the socially desirable behavior. The net effect of this tactic is to deflect criticism from deficiencies in social institutions to deficiencies in individuals. Essentially, the public began blaming the victims of society's institutional inadequacies for their inability to lead prosperous lives.[1] Ethnic minorities and dark-skinned individuals, victims of discrimination from the legacy of slavery, colonialism, and stereotypes, became targets of racists who focused on the prevalence of social pathology among them.

Fear of economic competition is uppermost in the minds of white middle- and working-class individuals. Upward mobility by immigrants, indigenous people, and people of color, who have been excluded from full participation in society, threatens their social and economic status. In a system predicated on using, consuming, and disposing social status and the welfare of oneself and family are perceived as imperiled by the threat of upward movement of people previously restricted from competing. When work is used as a method for obtaining materialistic ends, the ethos of society focuses on gaining access to increasingly scarce resources before competitors.

This phenomenon is a perversion of Marx's concept of class warfare. Now the classes are oblivious to the underlying ideological sentiments and institutional structures that perpetuate the divisions and animosities among them. It is the modern-day equivalent of hamsters running mindlessly on treadmills. We are like Skinner's dancing chickens, rewarded with scraps for fulfilling routinized, repetitive activities. Anyone, or any group, that threatens the stimulus response system that provides gratification of materialist needs (encouraged through the media and advertising) is perceived as a threat. By invoking Social Darwinist philosophy, prejudice and discrimination are justified, even legitimized, by blaming the victims for their adverse social condition.

The personification of this dilemma can be apprehended in data on disparities in salaries and wealth in the United States. In April 2011, the *New York Times* published the 2010 compensation of the 200 chief executives at 199 public companies with annual revenue of at least $7 billion. The highest paid was Phillippe Dauman of Viacom at $84.5 million. All but four earned at least $1 million. The four laggards, each independently wealthy, were the late Steven Jobs of Apple, Vikram Pandit formerly of Citigroup, John Mackey of Whole Foods Markets, and Warren Buffett of Berkshire Hathaway.

Even more disconcerting was a report by the Washington-based Institute for Policy Studies that revealed twenty-five of the top one hundred highest paid corporate CEOs in the United States received more compensation than their companies paid in income tax in 2010! Their earnings averaged $16.7 million, and their companies averaged $307 million in tax refunds.[2]

Of the two hundred CEOs, there were only eight women, two African-Americans, and five Asians. Only ten individuals earned less than $3 million and ninety earned at least $10 million.[3] As of January 2012, there were only four African-American CEOs in the Fortune 500 corporations (0.8 percent), nine Asians (1.8 percent), five Latinos (1 percent), and eighteen women (3.6 percent).[4] All the rest were white males, earning an average 275 times more than the average nonmanagerial worker.

The disparity in wealth between whites, blacks, and Hispanics in the United States has risen to record highs according to a PEW Research Center analysis. The median net worth of white households decreased by 16 percent between 2005 and 2009, but African-American household worth declined by 53 percent and Hispanic families dropped 66 percent. In 2009, the median net worth of white households in the United States was $113,000 compared to $6,325 for Latinos and $5,677 for African-Americans.[5]

Tough economic times place stress on individuals and families of all ethnicities, but the burden is not equally spread. While the economic elite manage to survive and thrive even during recessions (the wealthiest ten percent of the U.S. population receives almost half of the pretax income in the country), the majority is left to scramble in an increasingly competitive frenzy for survival. It is not coincidental that the Southern Poverty Law Center has noted a 66 percent increase in the number of hate groups in the United States in the last decade.

GENES AND INTELLIGENCE: THE SEARCH FOR INFERIORITY

Linking biology to social pathology enabled racists and eugenicists to peddle their apologia for a socially dysfunctional society by putting the onus for failure squarely on the victims of society's dysfunctional institutions. The testing of over one million military recruits in World War I in the United States, using the Alpha and Beta intelligence inventories was, perhaps, a high point of the eugenics movement—a movement that culminated in Nazi fanaticism and the infamous Nuremberg Laws that sought to prevent sexual relations between Jews and Aryans.[6]

Taking a cue from twentieth-century eugenics, contemporary ethnocentrism found in the United States and European countries depicts individuals from non-Anglo/Aryan ethnicities and cultures as undesirable. This is, however, a monumental paradox. It comes from hundreds of years of domination and exploitation of indigenous people in developing nations by white Europeans in their quest for power, influence, and natural resources.

Imperialist nations stigmatized darker-skinned people as inferior and impeded their social, cultural, and political development. This created a self-fulfilling rationalization. The enforced backwardness of indigenous people was taken as prima facie evidence of their inferiority.

The prospect of an infusion of reputedly inferior immigrant stock into the gene pool of Western nations has been the theme of some social scientists, philosophers, politicians, and even religious leaders for centuries. The foundation of scientific racism was laid by the French aristocrat Comte Arthur de Gobineau in his 1853 statement of Aryan supremacy, *An Essay on the Inequality of the Human Races*. Gobineau's ideas influenced, among others, the German composer Richard Wagner. They became fashionable in Europe and America after a series of revolutions spread across the European continent in 1848, sending waves of immigrants from eastern and southern Europe after better lives in the United States.

Ironically, some European immigrants who were discriminated against were as white as the people in the host countries. In an effort to reject their entreaties for fairness, ethnocentric ideologies were concocted that stereotyped immigrants as culturally, morally, and intellectually inferior to Nordics (i.e., Aryans and white Anglo-Saxons). The writing of the eminent scientist Louis Agassiz, who was Swiss-born and became a U.S. naturalized citizen in the mid-1800s, also fed into racist ethnocentric stereotypes about immigrants and dark-skinned people. Agassiz even rejected Darwin's position on evolution, preferring a polygenetic thesis of human origination (multiple sites) over Darwin's monogenetic position (single place of origin).

Agassiz, and some contemporary white supremacists, believed that varieties of humans originated in different locations around the planet. This was a convenient rationalization for apparent differences in social, political, and scientific development. It avoided the negative effects of centuries of imperialism and colonization.[7] It was only a short step from there to attribute social dysfunctions such as poverty, crime, and mental illness to individual genetic deficiencies. This fallacy posed serious consequences for the poor and dispossessed, as well as cultural minorities. Embraced by the eugenics movement, it eventuated in state-enforced sterilization.

The infamous studies of supposedly hereditary genetic inferiority described in the landmark cases of *The Jukes* by Robert Dugdale (1877) and the *Kallikak Family* by Henry Goddard (1912) provided the "scientific" justification for legal sterilization in the United States. From the latter part of the nineteenth century to the mid-1970s, over 60,000 people, mostly minority, poor, developmentally disabled, and mentally ill individuals, as well as young girls and women who were runaways, were subjected to mandatory sterilization. Thirty states had such laws.

Even the eminent Supreme Court Justice Oliver Wendell Holmes was convinced of the rectitude of legally enforced sterilization. In the classic case *Buck v. Bell* that upheld a Virginia law that sterilized a young, supposedly mentally retarded woman, Holmes concluded, "Three generations of imbeciles are enough."[8] State-enforced sterilizations reached their zenith in Nazi Germany. Over 400,000 people were forcibly sterilized, and 70,000 developmentally disabled people were murdered under the infamous T-4 program to hygienically cleanse the "master race" of biologically inferior specimens.

Hatemongering and fear were fanned by the writing of eugenicists like Madison Grant,[9] Houston Stewart Chamberlain,[10] and Lothrop Stoddard.[11] American scientists such as Louis Terman, Henry Goddard, and Robert Yerkes were avid eugenicists, influencing public policy on intelligence testing in schools and the military.

THE FEAR OF SEXUAL COMPETITION AND CULTURAL DEGRADATION

Rivalry for jobs and a piece of the good life may enervate some racists and xenophobes in the United States and abroad. Another fear is the possibility of competition for white women by dark-skinned men. Some racists also feared that miscegenation could lead to the intellectual and cultural degradation of the white race. For hundreds of years white males have maintained sexual dominance over light and dark-skinned women around the world. Like conquering explorers, they not only subjugated foreign lands, they controlled and exploited indigenous women.

This practice reached the height of hypocrisy in the United States. White male slaveholders took sexual advantage of black females while enforcing codes and laws that forbade miscegenation. Often the offspring of such liaisons were relegated to second-class status. At times they were given preferential treatment on plantations but rarely treated as equals alongside the "legitimate" white offspring of male plantation owners. [12]

If black women were satisfactory sexual partners for white males and black wet nurses for white babies, why were blacks held in low regard and prevented from full participation in society? No doubt fear of competition from blacks in the labor force and the bedroom played a role in this dynamic. Stereotypes about the animal-like behavior of dark-skinned indigenous people were propounded to dehumanize and relegate them to subordinate social status.

The same stereotypes and derogatory sentiments are expressed today in the diatribes and xenophobic lexicon of white supremacists. They proclaim their commitment to preserving the white culture of the United States and the Western world for white children—the infamous fourteen words "We must secure the existence of our people and a future for white children." But it's ok to have a sexual liaison with a woman of color—surreptitiously.

White male fears of sexual competition from dark-skinned men emanates from the very stereotypes they created to dominate and subordinate them. Early Western travelers to Africa and the Americas often grossly exaggerated physical characteristics of dark-skinned people, depicting them as primitive and animal-like. Noses, breasts, buttocks, and genitals were distorted by ethnocentric explorers. When they were not exoticized they were caricatured as simians. At times they were kidnapped and transported to explorers' homelands, where they were displayed for the gawking eyes of highbrow society in theaters and museums.

One of the most notorious examples of this practice was the case of Sarah Baartman, a teenage woman from South Africa. Nicknamed the "Hottentot Venus," she was put on display in England and France in the nineteenth century. After her death in 1815, at the age of twenty-five, her skeleton, brain, and genitals were preserved in bottles and displayed in French museums for 160 years. They were returned to her native land at the request of Nelson Mandela in 1994.

Such atavistic stereotypes are resistant to change. Today, Canadian psychologist and transplanted Englishman J. Philippe Rushton contends there is an inverse correlation between the size of blacks' penises and their intellectual ability. Despite being ostracized by his intellectual colleagues, he continues to distribute his books and papers to a receptive segment of the population.[13]

THE END OF WHITENESS?

A news report in 2007 predicted that redheads were a dying breed and would become extinct by 2060. Other reports claimed that blondes would disappear by 2202. You can imagine the angst such prognostications caused white supremacists. From nineteenth-century "scientific racists," to twentieth-century eugenicists, white supremacists, and contemporary intellectual elitists, multiculturalism has become the bane of their existence. They liken it to the mongrelization and demise of the white race and the end to Aryan supremacy.[14]

The picture they paint of the destruction of the master race is laced with paranoia and hysteria. Hordes of immigrants and dark-skinned people from developing countries are said to be infecting white societies with crime, disease, alien religions and cultures and, most dreaded of all, inferior genes. This situation will supposedly degrade the genetic pool of superior whites, leading to decadence and societal disaster. Just as the news reports about the demise of redheads and blondes were misapplications of science,[15] so, too, have claims about the genetic superiority of the white race proven spurious. Humankind has paid a high price for the persistent belief that one racial or ethnic group is superior to another. This theme has emerged throughout history and intrudes into the human psyche like a worm boring into the heart of an apple.

Our discussion on the origin of our species revealed that all humans have nearly identical DNA. From a biological perspective, there is only one human race, *Homo sapiens*. The many variations in skin color, height, weight, and the shape of the nose, ears, lips, color and texture of one's hair are genetic variations that arose over eons. As discussed in chapter 2, they have a negligible effect on intellectual and athletic achievement. The fact that groups of people have different outward appearances is the result of genetic variations and mutations and the isolation of some groups that allowed them to evolve in a closed environment.

The basic underlying organizational systems of all humans are identical. We all eat; breathe air; and have blood, tissues, organs and bones, and we can exchange these because we are all of the same human species.

Because some groups developed in isolation from others their beliefs, attitudes and behavior may differ. They may, as in the case of Jews, who lived endogenously for thousands of years, share some common genes and diseases (e.g., Tay-Sachs disease found among Askhenazi Jews of Eastern Europe). But essentially, all humans are related. Differences in appearances are ephemeral and insignificant.

Cultural differences among groups of people are a more significant and interesting phenomenon. They affect how people conduct their lives and form the basis of ethnic groups with their shared attitudes, beliefs, and behaviors. While humans are all members of the same race, there are countless ethnicities. The problems mankind faces today are linked to the difficulties people have encountering members of different ethnic groups.

Nevertheless, the mixing of ethnicities through immigration and migration facilitated through mass transportation and telecommunications has increased opportunities for miscegenation on an unprecedented scale. Looking at census data in the United States demonstrates the trend. Prior to the 2000 census, respondents were forced to select just one racial/ethnic identity (e.g., black, white, American Indian, Japanese, Korean, Chinese, Filipino, Hawaiian or "other"). Biracial people were forced to select the latter category or make a choice that negated half of their parentage.

In 2000, the census Bureau allowed people to select multiple groups. Seven million Americans (2.4 percent of the population), claimed more than one racial/ethnic group. Between 2000 and 2010 the mixed-race/ethnicity population of the country grew by 35 percent.

A PEW Research Center report on intermarriage or "marrying out" of one's racial/ethnic group reported that, in 2010, 15.1 percent of newlyweds married out, more than twice as many as thirty years ago. Black men marry someone from a different racial/ethnic group almost three times more often than black women, and Asian women do so twice as often as Asian men. Black Hispanics and American Indians have the highest rates of intermarriage. American Indians marry a white person as often as another Indian. The rate of intermarriage among Asians and white Hispanics has remained static or even decreased slightly since 1980.

For every 1,000 married white people, fifty-three men and forty-four women married outside their ethnic group in 2009. Just three white men and seven white women married blacks. On the other hand, 129 black men and 58 black women married outside their group, 76 of the men and 35 of the women marrying whites. American Indians were, by far, the group with the most people crossing marital ethnic lines, but their numbers are relatively small.

Hispanics, especially black Hispanics, comprise the second largest group of interethnic marriages, and their numbers are significant. While they marry people from different ethnic groups, they tend to stay within the color line. Of every 1,000 Hispanic white men who marry, 193 marry outside their group, but 164 of them marry white women. Of the 224 Hispanic white women who marry outside of their group, 189 marry white men.

The pattern changes a bit for black Hispanic men and women, with 522 men and 524 women marrying outside of their ethnicity per 1,000: 86 men marrying white women and 91 women marrying white men. Still, the majority of both groups marry within their color group: 215 men and 279 women marrying blacks. Significantly, 151 men and 115 women married white Hispanics, staying within their ethnic group. [16]

Adding to the consternation of some whites is the fact that their share of the population of the United States and Western Europe is shrinking. The number of white children being born is falling dramatically as the population of white women ages. The median age of the white population in the United States is forty-one compared to twenty-seven for Latinos. By 2019 white children will be a minority in the nation. The population of white children fell by 10 percent (4.3 million) between 2000 and 2010, while the population of Asian and Latino children grew by 38 percent (5.5 million) during the same time period. Interestingly, the number of African-American children also fell by 2 percent.

Minorities now comprise 46.5 percent of the population under eighteen in the United States. Almost 100 percent of the population increase in the nation's largest metropolitan areas between 2000 and 2010 was because of minority growth, primarily Asians and Latinos. Whites are projected to become a minority in the country by 2041. The number of whites grew by just 1.2 percent since 1990, compared to a 43 percent increase among Latinos. [17]

The evidence is incontrovertible. By 2050 the population of the United States will reach 439 million, and over half will be ethnic minorities. Non-Hispanic, single-race whites will number 203.3 million (46 percent of the population). Nearly one in three people will be Latino (132.8 million), and 15 percent (65.7 million) will be black. The Asian population will rise to 40.6 million (9.2 percent of the population), and 62 percent of the nation's children will be ethnic minorities. [18] In light of these numbers, it is no coincidence that Latinos are bearing the brunt of the wrath of white supremacists.

Looking abroad, the nonwhite percentage of the population in Western European nations has been growing, but it is still a relatively small part of the general population, with the exception of the Netherlands, as can be seen in table 5.1. The culturally diverse European Union (EU), consisting of twenty-seven nations, had a population of 502.5 million as of January 2011, with only 6.3 percent (31.4 million) of its population born outside of an EU state.

As we noted earlier, the net population gain from nonwhite immigration in Western European countries will take decades to have a significant impact on the composition of the population. Nevertheless, in time, there will be changes in the color and culture of heretofore predominantly white nations.

The question is whether this situation is cause for rejoicing or hand-wringing. The outcome depends on one's perspective. One doesn't have to be a member of a minority group or fatalist to recognize the inevitable demographic changes that are occurring around the globe. White supremacists play on the fears of other whites and their feelings of racial superiority by warning of the impending doom ushered in with the increase of the nonwhite and Latino population.

Dire warnings about the official language of the United States being changed to Spanish in the creation of a North American Aztlan, a Muslim Eurabia, an increase in the level of crime, widespread unemployment, lower wages among whites, and a lowering in the level of intelligence are expressed to shock and raise money and resources from whites by preying on their fears.

The population of white-dominated societies is aging and shrinking. But Western nations are in need of immigrants if they are going to be able to fill the jobs necessary to make them competitive in the global society of the twenty-first century and beyond. There is one caveat, however. They must recognize that all residents should be given opportunities to develop their human potentialities.

Equality of educational and occupational opportunities must become the cornerstone of Western societies, or they risk becoming stagnant shells of their former selves. Allowing prejudice and discrimination to perpetuate social inequality disqualifies large segments of society from utilizing their talents (people of color, women, differently abled, religious and ethnic minorities, LGBTs). It deprives society of the contributions these groups could make socially, culturally and economically, and will relegate these nations to an inferior status in an increasingly competitive world.

One other point should be made: Dating and sexual activity is a matter of personal choice and consensual. Social and cultural norms have been modified over the years. Greater interaction among ethnic groups and whites has been occurring. Unlike previous times in the United States, there are no laws mandating separation of ethnicities, forcing people into social relationships against their wills. Such decisions are, as they should be, an individual, personal matter. In light of these considerations the racist rants of white supremacists are revealed as anti-intellectual hypocritical diatribes. No one is preventing them and their families from observing the magical fourteen words. The end result is destined to be a pluralist planet facilitated by the merging of mankind.

Finally, we should analyze the concept of whiteness. From the perspective of popular white supremacist websites (e.g., Stormfront, Aryan Nations, National Vanguard, Imperial Klans of America), it is clear that they assume there is something genetically different and superior about "pure" white people. Modern scientific research thoroughly discredits such assumptions by demonstrating the common origins and genetic similarities of humans.

Attempts to classify people on the basis of the color of their skin are as preposterous as were Jim Crow laws in the United States, the South African apartheid system, and the Nazi Nuremberg Laws, which attempted to define the percentage of blackness and Jewishness in the population. Living in a mobile global society may seem threatening to some whites. They were reared in socially and intellectually segregated societies where beliefs about the inferiority of dark-skinned people were inculcated at an early age. Believing that whiteness is analogous to moral, physical, and intellectual superiority prevents some people from accepting the inevitable merging of mankind. The reality of this assumption is demonstrated by the increase in hate crimes against people of color around the world, and we now address this phenomenon.

HATE CRIMES AS RESISTANCE TO CHANGE

While there is no scientific proof that one group is intellectually or athletically superior to another, the theme of racial dominance persists. It is alluring, like a mental aphrodisiac—an ethnic high that enables the bearers of supposedly superior genes to believe that they are better, more capable, and destined for greatness over other mortals. It is akin to the psychological lift some religious groups obtain from believing that they are among the chosen, destined for salvation while the rest of humanity is doomed.

There is a feeling of superiority that some people get when they embrace thoughts that elevate them at the expense of others characterized as inferior and subordinate. Such views are not infrequently manifested in delusions and paranoia enveloping adherents in an ideology of the absurd. Misfits and miscreants relish the opportunity to pretend that their twisted perspective of social reality places them on the top of the ladder of humanity.

There is no dearth of groups around the world that espouse the stale rhetoric of racial superiority and hate. Ethnic and religious animosities intrude into our lives. They permeate the news with their violence and inhumanity. Now the Internet provides a medium that feeds the human frailties of hatred and prejudice. One expert estimates there may be as many as 60,000 hate websites on the World Wide Web.[19] The Southern

Table 5.1. Population of Nonwhites in Selected Countries

Country	Percent Born in Non-EU	Percent Ethnic Groups
United Kingdom	7.7	8 (includes 2% black, 4% Asian)
France	7.8	5 (includes 3.4% African, 1.2% Asian)
Netherlands	8.5	20 (includes 2.4% Indonesian, 2.2% Turkish, 2% Moroccan, 2% Surinamese and 8% Netherlands Antilles and Aruba)
Norway	—	2 (includes Pakistanis, Vietnamese, Iranians, Sri Lankans, Iraqis)
Germany	7.8	2.4 (Turkish)
Belgium	6.4	11 (includes Moroccans, Africans)
Canada	—	29 (includes East and Southeast Asians 7%, Aboriginals 5%, Chinese 4%, South Asians 4%, North American Indians 4%, East Indians 3%, Caribbean 1%, Arabs 1%)
United States	—	21 (includes blacks 12.8%, Asians 4.5%, Native Americans 1%, Hawaiians and other Pacific Islanders .18%, Mixed 1.3%, other 1.6%)

Source: "Ethnic Groups by Country," NationMaster, accessed August 26, 2011, http://www.nationmaster.com/graph/peo_eth gro-people-ethnic-groups; "Norway," http://www.axt.org.UK/antisem/countries/norway.htm#Racism; U.S. Central Intelligence Agency, "The World Factbook," 2011, https://www.cia.gov/library/publications/the-world-factbook/geos/gm.html; "Demographics of the European Union," Wikipedia, January 2011, http://en.wikipedia.org/wiki/Demographics_of_the_European_Union; "Population by Selected Ethnic Origins, by Province and Territory, 2006," Statistics Canada, www.statcan.gc.ca.

Poverty Law Center has identified over 1,000 hate groups in the United States, a 66 percent increase since 2000.

Competition for jobs and sexual partners, as well as political differences and psychological problems, motivate people to join hate groups.

Some join for the purported preservation of the "pure" native Anglo stock. In the United States the most disparaged ethnic groups are African-Americans, Latinos, Muslims, and Jews.[20]

The FBI tracks the incidents of hate crimes in the United States. In 2009, it reported there were 6,604 hate crimes involving 8,336 victims. Slightly over 4,000 of these crimes were racially motivated, along with another 1,109 ethnically motivated offenses. Almost two-thirds of the offenders were white, compared to 18.5 percent black.[21]

As depressing as these figures are, a Bureau of Justice Statistics report in 2005, based on household interviews with 20,000 people, indicated the annual number of hate crimes in the United States might be as high as 200,000![22]

Whichever statistics one chooses to accept, there can be little doubt that many people in the United States (and elsewhere around the world) perceive themselves as victims of prejudice and discrimination. Peoples' perceptions are reality for them. The human tragedy recounted in violence and injustice is, every day and everywhere, demonstrated for us on the stage of events that reflect our history.

While some whites in European nations are appalled by the influx of religious minorities and dark-skinned immigrants, the demographic equation in the United States is far more tilted toward pluralism and multiculturalism—a fact that may underlay the increase there in hate groups and hate speech online.

EUROPEAN XENOPHOBIA

Intemperate race-baiting statements and actions are not confined to the United States. They are commonplace in Western European nations such as France, Germany, Belgium, the Netherlands, England, and, most recently, Norway. Racial profiling of minority groups; banning outward manifestations of religion and culture that differ from the dominant one; strident police actions against racial and religious minorities; and restrictions on freedom of speech, press, and assembly have, and continue to be, documented in many of these nations.

A report by the Council of Europe on the way minorities are treated in Great Britain noted concerns that "racist incidents had become more frequent, police powers were exercised in a manner that disproportionately affected minority groups, and Gypsies and [Irish] Travellers still faced discrimination and asylum seekers remained in a vulnerable position." The report also noted severe levels of prejudice and discrimination against Muslims punctuated by racist, xenophobic media reports with widespread racial profiling by the police.[23]

The *Guardian* reported a study by the London School of Economics that blacks in the United Kingdom are 26.6 times, and Asians 6.3 times, more likely to be stopped and searched than whites. There were 60 searches for every 1,000 blacks compared to 1.6 for every 1,000 whites. [24]

These problems continually surface on the European continent. This led to the formation of the Council of Europe's forty-seven member nation European Commission against Racism and Intolerance (ECRI) on June 13, 2002. After surveying the negative impact that the economic recession is having on minorities in Europe, the Council concluded:

> Special hostility is reserved for *refugees and asylum-seekers* because of perceptions concerning reliance on welfare benefits and competition for jobs. Quite often, religion adds another dimension to the negative climate of opinion. ECRI has, as a result, found persisting problems of prejudice against *Muslims*, often expressed in debates about "values." Islamophobia inevitably materializes in widespread discrimination in everyday life and in contacts with authorities. [25]

Other nations around the world are also experiencing majority versus minority discrimination. After winning the right to host the 2018 World Cup of soccer, Russia was torn by ethnic violence directed toward immigrants from the North Caucasus. Thousands of youths rampaged through the streets of Moscow, beating and harassing people for days, jeopardizing the country's bid to entertain the prestigious sporting event. [26]

Recent acts of violence have occurred in China directed against the predominantly Muslim Uighurs; in Indonesia where Muslims have attacked Christians; in Sudan where northern Sudanese Muslims committed atrocities in Darfur, which is heavily populated by Christians and animists; in the former Yugoslavia, which pitted Serbs against Muslims; in Rwanda, where majority Hutus massacred Tutsis; and in Burma/Myanmar between Buddhists and Muslims. [27]

HOW HATRED SPREAD THROUGH THE WORLD

Why do people hate "the other" when there is abundant evidence that we are all related? Research on the science of the origin of languages supports the theory that Africa is our motherland. It is the place where humans and language first appeared. [28] Languages diversified as people left their ancestral home. As ethnicities and languages emerged in isolation, values of superiority and exclusivity arose.

Humans separated from interaction with other groups became ethnocentric. One of the most transcendent threats mankind faces today is fear of and contempt for people from other ethnic groups. Isolation, which protected humans from hostile groups in the past, is no longer possible or desirable in the modern world.

Geneticist Spencer Wells captured the essence of the conundrum of immigration for the ancients, and it is still relevant today:

> For most indigenous people, the rewards of becoming part of the glo-
> bal village are simply too enticing to be ignored. Decisions to leave
> ancient villages usually come down to personal choices—a perception
> that opportunity is better elsewhere, or that it has disappeared at home.
> In the end, because they cannot limit personal choices, it is a battle the
> activists are doomed to lose.[29]

But the struggle goes on as people from developing nations converge on the more advantaged societies to seek better lives.

If we are all nth generation cousins, related by the very genes that compose our bodily essence, why do humans fear, loathe, and persecute one another? The answer lies in what is essentially a superficial and ephemeral human characteristic—our appearance. In the most significant ways, biologically, we are virtually identical. Humans who dwelled together for lengthy periods evolved physical characteristics, external markers that defined them as being members of a specific genetic unit, or haplogroup. These markers helped the group adapt to its environment. Social and psychological meanings evolved in the group, forming its culture that distinguished it from other groups that may have been perceived as threats.

The origin of ethnocentrism, the belief that one's group is superior to others, lies then not only in the genetic, but also the social and psychological, manifestations of separateness. This comes from attempts to insulate, protect, defend, and promote the special attributes of a group's essence. As geographer Jared Diamond noted, "Racial classification didn't come from science but from the body's signals for differentiating attractive from unattractive sex partners, and friends from foe."[30] If we substitute the word *group* for *body*, we are able to discern the important social component of human interaction that has led to interminable conflict on our planet as groups vie for resources to sustain them.

As our Paleolithic ancestors roamed the earth they encountered other groups who were also foraging and hunting. Conflict among competing groups was not uncommon and may have led to the extinction of one of our ancestral relatives, the Neanderthals.[31]

To be sure, the struggle for survival in the Paleo and Neolithic Ages was harsh, but devoid of the modern social and political inventions associated with land, labor, and capital. These created the concept of private property. This concept not only engendered individual rights, but also injected the social and psychological dimensions of exclusivity and boundaries between and among people and societies.

The domestication of animals and farming contributed to the rise of a food surplus and, simultaneously, the concept of private property and wealth. Once humans learned how to harvest food, they prioritized property rights to protect their investment. In the context of survival, it is not surprising that strangers were often perceived as threats.

Research on the human brain reveals that it developed an early or primitive evolutionary mechanism to guard against strangers. Located in the right and left temples and the medial temporal lobe, this area encompasses the amygdala, hypothalamus, and hippocampus. They are designed to alert the organism to external threat. Reactions emanating from this area are reflexive and impulsive. They served our ancestors well; otherwise we wouldn't be here now. Nevertheless, ancients recognized the necessity for cooperating with neighbors in the struggle for survival, and religious texts are replete with varieties of the "Golden Rule."[32]

Encounters with strangers were then, as now, often perceived as potentially threatening. But the ancients did not have to labor under two important considerations that complicate contemporary human relationships: modern population pressures and large-scale immigration. These two phenomena contribute to the enormous stress and fear of change that currently grip nations and ethnic groups around the world. Population growth is leading to the depletion of natural resources such as oil and potable water. Simultaneously, interaction between heretofore relatively isolated ethnic groups is being increased through immigration, mass transportation, and telecommunications.

A biological case can be made for predisposing humans to hate based on perceived threat to the viability of the organism. But social psychological considerations far exceed such momentary stimuli in their effect on human cognition and action. Repulsion stemming from fear of bodily harm by outsiders or "others" is often transient. Hatred derived from the inculcation of values and beliefs that have been learned and internalized over a lifetime have far greater influence on one's perspective and behavior.[33]

Although the threat of physical harm wrought by individuals, groups, and even nations is ever-present in our destabilized world, humans have learned how to parry aggressive intentions. Dialogue and mediation can be used to diminish conflict, though the process can be ignored or tortuous. The conflict in the Middle East represents many of the concepts we have been discussing: arduous, tendentious, protracted, and bitterly divisive negotiations stemming from contradictory cultural (religious, technological) worldviews. The protagonists share not only biological but spiritual bonds. Other variables (competition for scarce natural resources such as land, water, and oil and entrenched geopolitical/ideological positions) complicate the situation.[34]

The Middle East epitomizes the modern human condition: in his search for peace, freedom, and justice, man is often held hostage by his penchant for materialism. When cultures collide, as in that region, conflict between values and the means for obtaining the "good life" divide the land and its inhabitants. A culture of anger, violence, and human anguish is created. Religion plays an important role in dividing societies, but, as we will see in the next chapter, it can also be an instrument for tolerance and understanding, a bridge of hope in a despairing world.

SUMMING UP

- Eugenicists and racists believe that whites are biologically superior to people of color and poor people are inferior.
- Hate groups are growing around the world because they fear competition from immigrants and people of color.
- More interracial marriages are occurring today among different ethnic groups, but the majority of people still marry within their own group.
- By 2050, population changes in the United States will mean Latinos, African Americans, Asians, Native Americans, and biracial people will become the majority.
- Hatred and fear of strangers, "the other," must be overcome for all children to receive equal educational opportunities.

NOTES

1. For a discussion of this point, see William Ryan, *Blaming the Victim* (New York: Knoph, Doubleday, 1976).

2. Sarah Anderson, Chuck Collins, Scott Klinger, and Sam Pizzigati, "Executive Excess 2011: The Massive CEO Rewards for Tax Dodging," Washington, DC, Institute for Policy Studies, August 31, 2011, http://www.ips-dc.org/reports/executive_excess_2011_the_massive_ceo_rewards_for_tax_dodging/.

3. "The Pay at the Top," *New York Times*, April 9, 2011, http://projects.nytimes.com/executive_compensation.

4. "Where's the Diversity in the Fortune 500 CEOs?" *DiversityInc.*, accessed January 5, 2012, http://diversityinc.com/diversity-facts/wheres-the-diversity-in-fortune-500–ceos/.

5. Rakesh Kochhar, Richard Fry, and Paul Taylor, "Wealth Gaps Rise to Record Highs between Whites, Blacks, and Hispanics," PEW Research Center Publications, July 26, 2011, http://www.pewsocialtrends.org/2011/07/26/wealth-gaps-rise-to-record-highs-between-whites-blacks-hispanics/.

6. For example, "The Law for the Protection of German Blood and Honor," "Reich Citizenship Law," and "The Law for the Protection of the Genetic Health of the German People." For a chart detailing the various genetic percentages of part Jews or Mischlingen, go to http://www.historyplace.com/worldwar2/timeline/nurem-laws.htm.

7. For more on this point, see Adrian Desmond and James Moore, *Darwin's Sacred Cause* (Boston: Houghton Mifflin, 2009).

8. For a review of this issue, go to http://www.inclusiondailynews. See Stephen Jay Gould's *The Mismeasure of Man* (New York: W.W. Norton, 1996) for a refutation of scientific racism. In January 2012, a North Carolina task force on the issue recommended that each of the survivors of that state's sterilization program, estimated at 1,500–2,000 people of the 7,600 subjected to the procedure, receive $50,000. See Kim Severson, "Payment Set for Those Sterilized in Program," *New York Times*, January 10, 2012, accessed January 12, 2012, http://www.nytimes.com/2012/01/11/us/north-carolina-sterilization-victims-get-restitution-decision.html.

9. Madison Grant, *The Passing of the Great Race: Or the Racial Basis of European History*, 4th ed. (New York: Charles Scribner's Sons, 1921).

10. Houston Stewart Chamberlain, *Foundations of the Nineteenth century*, trans. John Lees (London: John Lane, 1911).

11. Lothrop Stoddard, *The Revolt of Civilization: The Menace of the Underman* (New York: Charles Scribner's Sons, 1922).

12. A classic study of these inconsistencies can be found in Annette Gordon-Reed's discussion of Thomas Jefferson's children with his slave, Sally Hemings, *The Hemingses of Monticello* (New York: W.W. Norton, 2008).

13. See the "scientific" discussion of black physiology and intellect in J. Philippe Rushton, *Evolution and Behavior* (New Brunswick, Transaction Books, 1995).

14. For example, Richard Herrnstein and Charles Murray's *Bell Curve* (New York: Free Press, 1994) and their fascination with the "cognitive elite." Even the erudite magnum opus of Harvard political scientist Samuel Huntington concludes with an attack on pluralism and multiculturalism, warning of the dire threat to the U.S. civilization from such activities. Samuel P. Huntington, *The Clash of Civilizations and the Remaking of World Order* (New York: Simon & Schuster, 1996).

15. Jacob Silverman, "Are Redheads Going Extinct?" *How Stuff Works*, http://science.howstuffworks.com/environmental/life/genetic/redhead-extinction.htm.

16. Susan Saluny, "Black? White? Asian? More Young Americans Choose all of the Above," *New York Times*, January 30, 2011, 1, 20–21; Wendy Wang, "The Rise of Intermarriage," PEW Social and Demographic Trends, PEW Research Center, February 16, 2012, http://www.pewsocialtrends.org/2012/02/16/the-rise-of-intermarriage/.

17. Sabrina Tavernise, "Numbers of Children of Whites Falling Fast," *New York Times*, April 6, 2011, A14; "Minorities Led Growth in U.S. Cities," *St. Petersburg Times*, August 31, 2011, 5A.

18. "An Older and More Diverse Nation by Midcentury," *U.S. Census Bureau News*, U.S. Department of Commerce, Washington, DC, August 14, 2008.

19. Jesse Daniels, *Cyber Racism: White Supremacy and the New Attack on Civil Rights* (Lanham, MD: Rowman & Littlefield, 2009).

20. Asians are also stereotyped, but their economic and intellectual accomplishments outstrip white Americans. With average household earnings of $68,780 in 2009, compared to the national average of $50,221, and their superior educational attainment, their social status surpasses that of the other groups.

21. Federal Bureau of Investigation, "Hate Crime Statistics Report, 2009," November 22, 2011, http://www.fbi.gov/news/stories/2010/november/hate_112210/hate_112210.

22. Caroline Wolf Harlow, "Hate Crime Reported by Victims and Police," Bureau of Justice Statistics, Special Report, U.S. Department of Justice, Office of Justice Program, November 2005, NCJ 209911. In a replication of this survey conducted by the Bureau of Justice Statistics between 2003 and 2009, the annual number decreased to 148,400. Ninety percent of the reported hate crimes were motivated by racial and/or ethnic prejudice.

23. Minority Rights Group International, "State of the World's Minorities and Indigenous Peoples, 2011," July 6, 2011, http://www.unhcr.org/refworld/docid/4e16d35bc.html.

24. Ibid. The United States is also prone to such action. An Amnesty International report concluded, "Racial profiling is a serious human rights problem affecting millions of people in the United States in even the most routine aspects of their daily lives." The report noted that thirty-two million Americans reported being victims of racial profiling. See "Threat and Humiliation: Racial Profiling, National Security, and Human Rights in the United States" (New York: Amnesty International USA, October 2004).

25. European Commission against Racism and Intolerance, "Annual Report on ECRI's Activities, January 1–December 31, 2010" (Strasbourg: Council of Europe, 2012), http://www.coe.int/t/dghl/monitoring/ecri/activities/Annual_Reports/Annual%

20report%202011.pdf.

26. Simon Shuster, "Racist Violence Threatens Russia's World Cup Plans," *Time*, December 23, 2010, http://www.time.com/time/printout/0,8816,2039519,00.html.

27. For analyses of these and other cases of racial and ethnic conflict, see www. amnesty.org and www.hrw.org.

28. Quentin D. Atkinson, "Phonemic Diversity Supports a Serial Founder Effect Model of Language Expansion from Africa," *Science*, April 15, 2011, 346–349.

29. Spencer Wells, *The Journey of Man* (Princeton, NJ: Princeton University Press, 2003), 195.

30. Jared Diamond, "Race Without Color," *Discover Magazine*, November 1994, 89.

31. John Relethford, *Reflections of Our Past* (Cambridge, MA: Westview Press, 2003); Kate Wong, "Twilight of the Neandertals," *Scientific American* 301, no. 2 (2009). Until recently, it was thought that modern humans were unrelated to Neandertals, however articles in *Science Magazine*—Richard E. Green et al., "A Draft Sequence of the Neandertal Genome," 328, no. 5979 (2010): 710–722; Hernan A. Burbano, et al., "Targeted Investigation of the Neandertal Genome by Array-Based Sequence Capture," 328, no. 5979 (2010): 723–725—indicate that Neandertal DNA may be in the human genome.

32. Christianity: "And as ye would that men should do to you, do ye also to them likewise" (Luke 6:13); Confucianism: "Do not to others what you do not want them to do to you" (Analects 15:23); Hinduism: "This is the sum of duty: do not to others what would cause pain if done to you" (Mahabharata 5:1517); Islam: "None of you [truly] believes until he wishes for his brother what he wishes for himself" (number 13 of Imam, "Al-Nawawi's Forty Hadiths"); Judaism: "thou shalt love they neighbor as thy self" (Leviticus 19:18). Source: Ontario Consultants on Religious Tolerance, "The Golden Rule" (a.k.a. Ethics of Reciprocity), at http://www.religioustolerance.org/reciproc2.htm.

33. See Erich Fromm for a discussion of character conditioned hate which he suggested was the most insidious and dangerous form of hatred. Erich Fromm, *Man for Himself: An Enquiry into the Psychology of Ethics* (London: Routledge, 2002, first published 1947).

34. See Farooq Mitha for a discussion of these points in Middle East relations: "The Jordanian-Israeli Relationship: The Reality of 'Cooperation,'" *Middle East Policy* 17, no. 2 (2010): 105–126.

SIX

Fundamentalism and Religious Intolerance

Today, nowhere around the globe do religious groups that promote tolerance or reconciliation outpace or out-attract those that erect barriers against others and in which the belongers are hostile to religious strangers.

—Martin E. Marty, *When Faiths Collide*

Teachers must not allow their personal beliefs to interfere with the education of their students. Teaching about religion is acceptable and may be useful; proselytizing, however well intentioned, is legally and morally wrong.

THE FUNCTION OF RELIGION

What is the greatest mystery of mankind? It is, to borrow the title of Viktor Frankl's poignant work, "man's search for meaning."[1] It is man's attempt to understand what happens after his short time on this planet. Man's search for meaning is, in effect, as Freud observed, his struggle to cope with the unknown. If left unchecked it creates terror, hardship, and suffering.[2] Most of all, it is his attempt to know about the unknown, that vast eternity that awaits us all at the end of our lives.

To fill the void, the enormity of lifelessness, man takes "a leap of faith," as Danish existentialist philosopher Soren Kierkegaard noted.[3] Into the vacuum of knowledge left by science about death, steps religion. Its suppositions about transcendent spirituality and the prospect of life after death are promised to the faithful if they adhere to socially prescribed patterns of behavior. There is no stronger form of normative compulsion, no more powerful method of coercing individuals to accede to

115

morally sanctioned behavior than religion, because it seeks to provide answers about the "Great Mystery" that science cannot.

While science describes the biological changes that occur to the human corpse, religion addresses the spiritual, and that is where religion trumps empiricism. Scientists can measure changes in bodily structure and composition upon death, but they cannot discern or measure a soul. In his never-ending quest to prolong life and come to terms with death, man seeks solace in the possibility held out by religion that life does not end with death. It is only a transition or passing from one stage of being to another.

Now, we see the awesome power of a belief system that holds out the tantalizing promise of life beyond death for true believers. The faithful will dwell in paradise, nirvana, heaven, or even come back as a superior being endowed with wealth and fame. Disbelievers and transgressors, the infidels and heretics, who violated the laws and morals established by the faith, face the prospect of damnation, living eternally in purgatory, the Netherworld, Hell.

Man has always struggled to make sense out of the "Great Mystery." The ancients built tombs and erected monoliths to placate the forces that periodically wreaked havoc on society and took the lives of loved ones. Animal and human sacrifice was practiced in various cultures to appease the Gods/spirits that purportedly controlled nature and the fate of men and women. Before the first pyramids of ancient Egypt, more than 5,000 years ago, our ancestors built alters to mollify spirits in an attempt to infuse reason into their seemingly irrational struggle for existence.

As people coalesced into communities and societies, a moral order arose. This complemented a spiritual code of conduct that dictated behavior to promote congenial relationships and forbade actions inimical to the social order. Every religion has embedded within it a morality predicated on the assumption that the faithful will be rewarded for their convictions. They are promised rewards in the afterlife for sacrifices made during their pitiable existence, a condition that led Marx to refer to religion as "the opium of the people."

If the downtrodden, oppressed, and luckless can't make it in life, religion offers them salvation through death *provided* they subscribe to a value system and code of conduct that demonstrates their commitment to and belief in a supernatural being(s) who will reward them for their piety. What a perfect method of social control, and one so effective that billions of people adhere to it this very day. Of course, true believers may be right—there is no way of absolutely disproving their faith. And periodically we are told of "evidence" confirming it, such as miracles and the visage of gods and holy people in the oddest places, e.g., sandwiches, windows, and on the hides of animals.

The faithful come to view themselves in ethnocentric and exclusive terms. Their beliefs, values and behaviors are thought to be superior to other faiths and nonbelievers. Other faiths offer the promise of redemption, but only theirs is the true path to enlightenment and spiritual salvation. Historian Martin Marty depicts this phenomenon as pitting believers ("belongers") against "strangers," similar to a competition for the hearts and souls of the populace: "They conceive of these holy books as bringing messages that are inaccessible to all but believers."[4]

One of the puzzling contradictions about the existence and practice of religious dogma is its obsessional fear of ideas brandished by "strangers" (i.e., people of other faith traditions). Despite significant movements in the United States and other Western countries to improve communication among faiths, given a boost by the 1965 Vatican II Nostra Aetate document that formally transformed relationships between Catholics, Jews, and other non-Christian religions, some religions studiously avoid interactions with other faiths.[5]

As one who has attempted to bridge this divide through interfaith activities, the reticence of Southern Baptists to participate stands out as a glaring paradox. Despite believing in a common ancestral heritage with Jews, other Christians, and Muslims, (Abraham and Jesus), they are reluctant to engage in such activities. Many believe their way is the only valid path to salvation. Others may be fearful of interacting with people from different theological perspectives because it challenges their perception of reality and may eventuate in defections.

Numerous initiatives have been undertaken to assuage fears about competition and proselytization in interfaith activities. Apprehension among religions remains about such activities, especially among Jews, who have been a target of religious zealots and state-sponsored pogroms. Rivalry has escalated in recent years as religious denominations have become increasingly large, bureaucratized, and wealthy, especially as they come into contact with one another.

The collision among faiths around the world today is not just over religious dogma. Material benefits (land, human, and financial capital) associated with their growth have become paramount. This helps to explain the zeal with which some faith traditions, most notably Christianity and Islam, assiduously proselytize the unchurched, unaffiliated, and one another.

It was the thesis of the late Harvard political scientist Samuel Huntington that the twenty-first century would be marked by a series of increasingly acrimonious skirmishes. These would be fought between "the West and the rest" over ethnic, religious and cultural conflicts, most notably between Christianity and Islam.[6] We will revisit Huntington's pessimistic perspective on the future of mankind shortly. One cannot summarily dismiss his work that, though Islamophobic, represents an attempt to develop a grand theory of the evolution of civilizations based on social and cultural contradictions among societies.

Religion, despite creating conflicts, has had a dramatic impact on ci-
vility. In small-scale societies where people could observe one another
and scrutinize their behavior, it was powerful. Religious moral codes
promoted communal camaraderie in small-scale preindustrial societies.
Relationships among members of clans and tribes and residents of villages and towns, even small cities, were close-knit and instrumental. People knew one another and abided by the prevailing norms. Transgressors
were easily identified and punished by scolding, ridicule, gossip, or ostracism. Being banished from a preindustrial community could mean
death for the individual and the family.

Communal life in preindustrial societies strengthened the bonds
among likeminded inhabitants and helped to integrate and institutional-
ize belief systems. Magic, superstition, and religion exerted a great deal
of influence in peoples' lives as they sought to grasp the meaning of
events that shaped their existence.

HOW RELIGION DEFINES SELF: HINDUISM

The normative power of religion still prevails in rural communities
around the world. For example, the Indian caste system, closely aligned
with the Hindu religion, is over 3,000 years old. Hinduism itself is
thought to be 6,000 years old and descended from an ancient Vedic religion brought to northern India by Aryans. Hinduism has no particular
founder or universally acknowledged holy book, but the Vedas and
Upanishad are widely read.

There is no central institution that monitors or controls activity within
it. Unlike Christianity and Islam, there is no active proselytization. Also
unlike these two, diverse theological thoughts are accepted as legitimate
paths to enlightenment. "The truth is One, but different Sages call it by
different names." In fact, modern Hinduism acknowledges that it is continually evolving.

A powerful method of social control is embedded in Hinduism — rein-
carnation. The transmigration of the soul is thought to be related to the
life one lives, with good and bad deeds influencing future incarnations.
Adherents believe that the way one lives one's life, or karma, will determine your next life, with the ultimate goal of *moska*, being liberated from
samsara, or the cycle of birth, life, death, and rebirth.

A caste system composed of four central groups known as *Varnas*
evolved. This helps to reinforce social norms derived from spiritual foundations. Different parts of the body of primal man, *Purush*, are used to
designate the origin and status of individuals. The four main castes or *Jati*
are *Brahman* (high priests and educators) who sprang from the head of
Purush; *Kshatriya* (rulers and warriors) who came from his hands; *Vaishya*
(landlords and businessmen) who emerged from his loins; and *Sudra*

(peasants and workers) who came from his feet. The "untouchables" or *Harijans* are those masses of people who dwell outside the caste system. They were despised, loathed, and widely discriminated against until the government enacted legislation in 1950 prohibiting this, in part from the work of Mahatma Gandhi.

The fascinating feature of the caste system is that it ascribes social status, occupation, marriage, education, and dietary rules for members. Even the color of one's clothing is dictated: white for *Brahman*, red for *Kshatriya*, yellow for *Vaishya*, and black for *Sudra*. While modern India struggles to diminish vestiges of caste, it is still a powerful force in the 600,000 villages where 75 percent of the population lives. Nearly a quarter million of these villages have less than five hundred residents. There, individuals and family identities are known from birth, and caste traditions are enforced under the watchful eyes of village elders.

Life in the burgeoning Indian cities is another situation. The anonymity afforded by living in large social groupings provides opportunities to jettison caste formalities and restrictions. Entrenched customs and traditions yield to modern forms of social and economic interaction. In the modern social system, the emphasis is on maximizing production, consumption, and materialism. Still, millions of Indians remain chained to stultifying caste prescriptions that impede human and social progress, testifying to the normative power of religion.

HOW RELIGION AND POWER INTERACT

Caste in India and elsewhere, along with the power of religion, were eroded as societies grew, thanks to the increasing food surplus. At first, ruling elites used religion to justify their preeminent social position. Then, and even now, wealthy people were esteemed, even revered, as having been rewarded for their piety. God bestowed them with affluence and appointed them as conservators of his divine plan to utilize and dispense rewards. Their service was to humanity and reflected the "higher, greater glory" of God's will.

The relationship between the ruling elites and the clergy was solidified through reciprocal relationships that reinforced the status quo (e.g., monarchs' ability to grant perquisites to prelates in return for their imprimatur confirming the rulers' divine right to govern). Such practices were, unquestionably, a reasonable extension of prior assumptions about rewarding people for doing God's deeds.

Yet, what about the pious poor? How could one explain their predicament? The more affluent members of society were able to dismiss such contradictions through the conclusion that God rewards those "who help themselves." Obviously, individuals who were not successful had some kind of character or biological flaw. In some perspectives, they were being punished for the transgressions they or their family members had committed in this or a prior life.[7]

The normative power of religion begins to break down as society becomes larger and secular. People living in urban areas feel less constrained about adhering to religious and caste prescriptions. They pursue lifestyles at odds with, and inimical to, the sacred societies depicted by French sociologist Emile Durkheim.[8] In the rush toward materialism, people are used and consumed like objects, and just like objects they are discarded when they are no longer useful (e.g., the elderly).

It is the modern large-scale society, what sociologist Ferdinand Töinnes referred to as the *Gesellschaft* social system, in contrast to the small-scale *Gemeinschaft* entrepreneurial society, that experiences cultural, social, and scientific efflorescence.[9] In the face of man's attempt to dominate nature and provide for his creature comforts, religion, custom, and tradition are threatened. Security and stability yield to the impermanence of man's quest for materialism. Rules, codes of behavior, and adherence to religious dogma that guided and purportedly protected him for thousands of years are challenged. They begin to lose their normative compulsion and ultimately are rejected—but not by all.

The tension between religious dogma and tradition on the one hand, and the drive for materialism with its emphasis on mechanistic, instrumental relationships on the other, has set the stage for the modern clash of civilizations. It has created a competition for the hearts and souls of humanity as one great religious system competes with another to gain preeminence. The collision between religious fundamentalism and secularism is being accelerated by mass transportation and communication. Historian Martin Marty reports that studies of militant fundamentalism around the world show the pivotal role of mass media as an agent of threat and change to this movement, evoking defensive strategies and provoking offensive tactics by threatened groups.[10]

WHY RELIGIONS COLLIDE

In 2007, an attempt was made to enumerate the number of adherents to the world's religions. Table 6.1 shows that nearly half the people in the world are followers of Christianity (2.1 billion) and Islam (1.5 billion). With 900 million adherents, Hinduism accounts for 14 percent of the rest, followed by traditional Chinese religions—6 percent (e.g., Confucianism), Buddhism—6 percent, and primal-indigenous religions—6 percent. Note also the large percentage of nonreligious—16 percent.

The following discussion will focus on the three major Abrahamic religions—Judaism, Christianity, and Islam. Much of mankind's journey with spirituality has been profoundly affected by them. As Huntington demonstrated, they have been and currently are involved in an inordi-

Table 6.1.

Religion	Adherents
Christianity	2.1 billion
Islam	1.5 billion
Hinduism	900 million
Chinese Traditional	394 million
Buddhism	376 million
Primal-indigenous	300 million
African Traditional and Diasporic	100 million
Sikhism	23 million
Juche	19 million
Spiritism	15 million
Judaism	14 million
Baha'i'	7 million
Jainism	4.2 million
Shinto	4 million
Cao Dai	4 million
Zoroastrianism	2.6 million
Tenrikyo	2 million
Neo-Paganism	1 million
Rastafarianism	600,000
Scientology	500,000

Source: http://www.adherents.com/Religions_By_Adherents.html.

nate amount of conflict among themselves. All three faiths are monotheistic and trace their origin to an obscure shepherd, Abraham, who lived approximately 4,000 years ago in various locations in the Fertile Crescent.

In an attempt to understand the affinity these religions have for this man, whose life story may be more myth than reality, author Bruce Feiler interviewed theologians and scholars around the world. Who was this man who purportedly lived to 175 years? He abandoned his father at the age of seventy-five. He left his homeland and moved to Cannan, then on to Egypt. He fathered two sons who became the bedrock of Islam and Judaism. He circumcised himself at the age of ninety-nine, and exiled his first son, Ishmael. This man willingly offered one of his sons as a sacrifice to God, fought in wars, became a landowner, buried his first wife, and fathered six children past the age of one hundred?[11]

Feiler struggles to find common ground among the foundational stories of Judaism, Islam, and Christianity by comparing their versions of
the life and contributions of Abraham to their faith. In the absence of
verifiable records we are left with interesting stories stretched to justify
the theological assumptions of each tradition. Though lacking in verifi-
ability, they make for fascinating reading at the core of religious beliefs
that influence a third of the world's population.

We will not attempt to dissect the veracity of the tenets of these religious traditions that claim (in addition to the Baha'i'faith founded by Ba-
haullah in 1863) they are descendants of the Patriarch, Abraham. As Feiler colorfully shows, each faith tradition drew on his purported relationship with God and interpreted his actions to justify their own exclusive
lineage to him and the Almighty.

One of the most striking conflicts occurs between Judaic and Islamic
accounts of the near sacrifice of Abraham's son—what turns out to be a
test of his faith in the Almighty. Known among Jews as the *akedah*, the
event is assumed to involve Isaac, who became the founder of the Jewish
nation. But Muslims contend that the boy Abraham was dutifully willing
to kill was, in fact, his first born, Ishmael, who was fourteen when Isaac
was born. (According to the Bible, Abraham was eighty-five when Ishmael was born and nearly one hundred at the time of Isaac's birth.)

Aside from establishing who was the near-victim of this act, other
differences between Judaism and Islam emerge in Biblical accounts.

Each of these religions claims Abraham as the progenitor of monotheism and a pivotal figure in their faith. However, the narrative in Genesis
clearly states that both sons will form great nations, the lineage of Ishmael becoming Islam, and that of Isaac, Judaism.

The struggle between Hagar, the mother of Ishmael and a servant of
Abraham's wife, Sarah, enveloped the two families in a conflict that led
to the expulsion and exile of Hagar and Ishmael into the desert of Shur.
The friction between Sarah and Hagar originated in Sarah's infertility.
Knowing Abraham wanted children, she encouraged him to sleep with
Hagar. Under the Code of Hammurabi, existent at that time, children
from such a legal union belonged to Sarah. Upon seeing the outcome of
the relationship that she promoted, she was afflicted with an ancient case
of matchmaker's remorse. The tension emanating from this situation adversely affected Abraham's relationship with Hagar, Ishmael, and his
younger son, Isaac.

What concerns us here is the nature of relationships among these
religions as they affect prospects for coexistence and peace today. To
understand current attitudes and behavior we must take a brief look into
the historical relationships among them. Each of these Abrahamic faith
traditions attempt to legitimize the credibility of their theology through
the development of a formal story that ties them to the Patriarch. Although there are variations on this theme, the essential story depicts

Abraham as an independent thinker who rejected polytheistic idolatry for monotheism.

Another shared characteristic is their struggle to survive and thrive in the face of large numbers of nonbelievers. They were, in effect, strangers, "aliens" in their own lands. They were regarded as nonconformists and threats to the prevailing social order. At times they endured official punishment for their beliefs and practices that conflicted with the norms of their society. At others, they were unofficially excoriated, ostracized, and ridiculed. Initially, they found themselves on the fringe of established society because they threatened the modus operandi.

Social change is often greeted with fear and suspicion. The concepts promulgated by the Abrahamic faiths challenged the existing social system and cast doubt on traditional beliefs about spirituality and, most importantly, the "Great Mystery." It is one thing to challenge life as people know it. Questioning their assumptions about the Hereafter, the great unknown void that awaits us through eternity, is tampering with a more transcendent phenomenon with ramifications few people are willing to risk.

The sea change ushered in with monotheism posed a threat to established belief systems and their proponents—shaman, holy men and women, priests, elders, chiefs, monarchs. The new true believers were met with disbelief, disdain, even hostility as the struggle for the world of ideas and metaphysics cast them as threats to the established social order.

For example, Jewish resistance to Roman occupation in the year 39 C.E. occurred when Emperor Caligula declared himself a deity. When Jews refused to erect his statue in their temple in Jerusalem he exclaimed "So you are the enemies of the gods, the only people who refuse to recognize my divinity." Though he died suddenly thereafter, and the Jews in the Holy Land experienced a number of military victories against the Romans, they were crushed by Roman Legions, who killed and enslaved over 100,000 in the Galilee in 66 C.E.[12]

The struggle for theological supremacy, or triumphalism, among the Abrahamic religions left a trail of corpses throughout the Middle East and the Occident. Even before the spread of Christianity in the Holy Land, a heated rivalry existed among different sects of Jews (Sadducees, Pharisees, Essenes) over the primacy of the written word versus oral tradition and ritualistic practices.

Despite their belief in monotheism, their willingness to reach an accommodation with the Romans (the Sadducees) over the common citizens (the Pharisees) caused friction in the Sanhedrin, the governing body of Israel. For their part, the Essenes practiced ritualistic purity and separated themselves from the more secular society. The Dead Sea Scrolls were written and preserved by this sect. All three largely disintegrated when the Romans destroyed the Temple in 70 C.E.

While Christians, Jews and Muslims lived contemporaneously in the Holy Land, there was conflict among them over land and theological differences. At times, the only unifying force was their enmity toward Rome and its legions, which exerted control over commerce in the area.

In their quest for theological supremacy and control over resources in the region, factions of these groups battled one another when they were not fighting the Romans. Estimates of the number of Christians, Jews, and Muslims killed by one another reach into the millions, and the slaughter continues to this day.[13]

The most notable example of the internecine warfare among the descendants of Abraham was the carnage wrought by the Crusades. Spanning two hundred years in the Middle Ages from 1095 to 1291, a series of attempts were made to wrest control of the Holy Land from the Selcurk Turks, who threatened the Eastern Roman (Byzantine) Empire.

Muslims gained control of the Holy Land in 638 C.E. Pleas for help came from Byzantine Emperor Alexius I as the Turks gained control of all of the Middle East and most of Anatolia as well as Spain and Sicily. Pope Urban II called for the liberation of the Holy Land from the Muslims because "God will[ed] it." To further entice volunteers for the Crusades, it was generally believed that anyone who died for the cause would immediately ascend into Heaven.

Of the seven major tries, the first four were the most organized and significant, with the first being the most successful. Estimates of the number of people killed in these events vary, but one expert places the toll of Christians, Jews, and Muslims at three million.[14]

Perhaps one of the saddest chapters in this sequence was the Children's Crusade of 1212 led by a twelve-year-old French boy, Stephen of Cloyes. He claimed to have a letter from Jesus ordering him to establish a crusade to liberate the Holy Land. Thirty thousand children from France and Germany followed him, and none returned. A second Children's Crusade that year was organized by a boy named Nicholas from Germany, with 20,000 participants (including some unmarried women and men). They, too, met a similar fate, most perishing along the way.[15]

Another morbid clash among these faiths occurred in the fateful year of 1492. Known in the West as the year Columbus discovered America, it was also a fateful year for Jews and Muslims who had been living peacefully in Spain for centuries. That year Ferdinand and Isabella married, uniting Spain and sealing a victory over the last remaining Muslim cities in Andalusia in the south. This ended centuries of Muslim control in the region that began after Muslims secured Jerusalem in the seventh century.

After the Muslim conquest of the Holy Land, Islam spread quickly engulfing Sicily, Portugal, and Spain. Jews and Christians were allowed to practice their religion in Muslim-controlled Spain, but they had to pay an additional tax (*jizya*) and wear clothing that denoted they were not

Muslim. In an effort to unite their country, Ferdinand and Isabella secured permission from Pope Sixtus IV to undertake an inquisition to purify the Catholic faith by eliminating heretics and nonbelievers. The Spanish Inquisition began in 1478 and lasted until 1834. Under the guidance of Inquisitor General Tomas de Torquemada in 1483, over 2,000 people were executed.

In 1492 the Alhambra Decree was issued, forcing Jews to convert, face execution, or go into exile. In 1502 Muslims were banished, and later in that century Protestants were targeted. In all, 40,000 "heretics" were tried: 200,000 Jews and three million Muslims were expelled, leaving an immense intellectual vacuum. The very structure of Spanish society was uprooted by the Inquisition, despite the benefits bestowed upon it through religious diversity. For example, as early as 1100 C.E. the city of Cordoba had 5.6 million Muslims with 200,000 houses, 600 mosques, 900 public baths, 10,000 lamps, and 50 hospitals with lighted and paved streets.

Muslims and Jews were a vibrant part of Spanish society, making enormous contributions to art, science, literature, and medicine. Scholars visited Spain from all over Europe to study astronomy, science, geography, and medicine. This knowledge, along with the splendid architectural works, was all but lost in the fanaticism of a movement that consumed itself in hatred for "the other."[16]

There was a long tradition of tolerance for Jews and Christians under the Ottoman Turks who gained control of Jerusalem in 1517. Non-Muslims were allowed to practice their religion in their own houses of worship and give religious instruction in their schools and seminaries. While the *jizya* tax on Christians and Jews was required and Muslims were given preferential status, there was more religious tolerance in the territory they occupied than in Christian Europe.[17]

The Turks controlled a large swath of the world for four hundred years and made major social, educational, and scientific contributions to humanity. When the Spanish king began forcing out Jews, Sultan Beyazid II is reported to have said that if the Spanish king was mad enough to exile the most industrious of his subjects, the Ottomans would be glad to take advantage of his incapacity.

In the nineteenth century, Istanbul had churches of Bulgarian Orthodox, Greek Orthodox, Greek Catholic, Armenian Apostolic, Armenian Catholic, Roman Catholic, Assyrian Chaldean, Anglican, Congregational, and others, as well as Sephardic and Ashkenazic Jewish synagogues.[18]

CONSENSUS AND CONFLICT

Despite periodic conflicts among these groups, the Abrahamic faiths shared the concept of covenant, except their interpretation of the contract between God and their group varied. Jews contended that Abraham was blessed by God with the promise of many descendants and land for his people:

> I will establish My covenant between Me and you, and I will make you exceedingly numerous. As for Me, this is My covenant with you: You shall be the father of a multitude of nations. I will make you exceedingly fertile, and make nations of you; kings shall come forth from you. I will maintain My covenant between Me and you, and your offspring to come, as an everlasting covenant throughout the ages, to be God to you and to your offspring to come. I give the land you sojourn in to you and your offspring to come, all the land of Canaan, as an everlasting possession. I will be their God. (Genesis 17)

There were a number of problems related to Abraham's revelation, not the least of which surrounded the property rights of people already inhabiting Canaan. More importantly for our discussion were modifications made to the covenant by Christians and Muslims in later generations. These groups disputed and resented the claim of Jewish primacy as God's selected group to inherit His blessing—a sentiment reinforced by the reluctance of Jews to proselytize and convert non-Jews.

Early Jewish writings in what is known as the Babylonian Talmud meticulously established relationships between Jews and gentiles. This was to prevent Jewish absorption into the larger non-Jewish population. These processes were necessary to ensure the integrity of Jewish spirituality and traditions, and, most importantly, the covenantal relationship between Jews and God. [19]

For their part, Jews were expected to follow the tradition of *berit milah*, ritual circumcision of all males at the age of eight days as a demonstration of their faith in and allegiance to God. The Bible notes that upon hearing God's direction for a flesh/blood offering, Abraham, who was ninety-nine, circumcised himself, Ishmael, and all males in his household that very day.

Some scholars trace the origin of the conflict among these faiths to disputes over the role of Ishmael, who God also blessed. Though He bestowed His fuller blessing upon the yet-to-be-born Isaac:

> As for Ishmael, I have heeded you. I hereby bless him. I will make him fertile and exceedingly numerous. He shall be the father of twelve chieftains, and I will make of him a great nation. But My covenant I will maintain with Isaac, whom Sarah shall bear to you at this season next year. (Genesis 17)

Each of these faith traditions drew on scriptural writing believed to be divinely inspired, if not literally the word of the Almighty. For the Jews it was the Torah (the five books of Moses that Jews believe contain God's commandments about living and dying), and the Talmud, which defines how the laws of the Torah should be applied.

For Christians, a New Testament was developed with Gospels about the life of Jesus and his philosophy (Mark, Matthew, Luke, and John). This was said to form the basis of a new covenant between God and the followers of His Son: "I am the way, the truth, and the life: no man cometh unto the Father but by me" (John 14:6).

Muslims venerate the Holy Qur'an, with its 114 *Surahs*, or chapters, and 6,200 verses. They also draw on the *hadith*, which is an account of what the Prophet Muhammad said and did during his lifetime. It must be understood that, despite differences in texts, stories, interpretations, and prophetic messengers, all Abrahamic faiths believe in the same Supreme Being: God, Yahweh, the Almighty, the Father, Allah.

Each set of writing embellished and altered the central Jewish text. Through time the nature of the relationship/covenant between Abraham and God and Abraham's sons and descendants was reinterpreted and altered. This was done to accommodate the growth and striving of Christianity and Islam for supremacy. As new monotheistic religions grew and became institutionalized and bureaucratized, they became expansionist, seeking new converts, frontiers, social and political power.

Modifications were added to accommodate the throng of Christians who craved access to the Gates of Heaven. Although Judaism had a messianic component, it was not embraced by all adherents. Jewish rejection of Jesus's claim of the promise of salvation through him fed into the Christian charge of deicide. This allegation has tainted the relationship between Jews and Christians for two millennia.

For their role, Muslims may have been tolerant of Jews and Christians, but they believed in the infallibility of Muhammad's transcription of God's words in the Qur'an. They accepted Jews and Christians along with their holy men (prophets) as "people of the Book." But they prophesized the coming of a messiah, and emphatically concluded that Muhammad was the "seal," or last, of God's prophets on Earth. This belief supersedes Jewish and Christian scriptural writing and covenants. It also casts subsequent religious movements and would-be prophets as heretics. Muslim persecution of Baha'is in Iran and elsewhere is a direct result of the belief that there can be no other prophets beyond Muhammad.

HOW RELIGION BECAME INSTITUTIONALIZED

We can trace the expansion of Christianity to the Roman Emperor Constantine's embracing of the religion in 312 C.E. Although Christianity was legalized, it took many years to develop an infrastructure that assured its eventual ascendance over traditional Roman and other forms of worship. The path that Christianity took is instructive. It illustrates an important complementary relationship between religion and politics that eventuated in the institutionalization of religion in society.

Monarchs recognized and embraced the power of religion and its surrogates. Whether or not they were devoted to specific theological principles, they perceived the primacy of the normative power that religion
exerts over people. By providing a moral code that pacified the populace
through the promise of rewards or punishment in an afterlife based on
how they lived in the present, religion became the quintessential method
for placating and controlling the masses.

As religions grew and became institutionalized, assuming formal bureaucratic structures, so, too, did the complexity of rules, regulations, and
rituals that accompanied their routinization and ascendancy. It became
necessary to have teachers and arbiters (priests, pastors, rabbis, imams)
who could interpret cannon/clerical law and perform sacred rituals. They
would lead and train citizens in the correct practice of the faith to ensure
purity of tradition in the face of change. Eventually, religious institutions
were afflicted with the same challenges that plagued lay leadership and
institutions: greed, avarice, and corruption.

When Martin Luther challenged papal authority and the tradition of
selling indulgences in his ninety-five theses in 1517 in Wittenberg, Germany, it was an important precedent. It led to the Protestant Reformation
and provided the impetus for the efflorescence of other religions and
challenges to religious orthodoxy. A large swath of the Occident was
under the control of the Holy Roman Empire. Monarchs collaborated
with various popes in a mutually beneficial arrangement of power and
wealth.

Ossified, elitist religious, and State systems were plagued by internal
strife with competing factions that rent both Church and State. Competition for a share of power and privilege proved a formidable tool for
motivating people to demand change.

Some monarchs were able to discern the importance of acceding to the
desires of their subjects to improve their lot in life. The decentralization of
religion allowed the common man to practice his faith and established a
bond between the individual and the religious institution. The request/
expectation of deferred gratification (rewards in the afterlife for sacrifices
in the present) was a tactic seized by rulers and clerics who recognized
the utility of fusing religion and politics. This complementarity of purpose, namely, to perpetuate power and control by clerics and rulers, continues today.

The partnership between religion and government has, however,
undergone a series of transformations. Secularization has eroded the traditional roles of the parties. Religion still retains its normative control
over peoples' lives. But, the individualization of religion has gained
prominence. The focus now is often on how individuals can derive a
personal sense of fulfillment through acts of faith, sacrifice, and engaging
in mutually beneficial service for the commonweal. This trend, coupled
with the growth of evangelical and spiritual trends, (what sociologist

David Martin refers to as the secularization movement)[20] coincides with a reorientation of organized religion.

Individual freedom and a focus on improving the quality of life of the impoverished are emphasized (e.g., Catholic liberation theology popularized in the latter half of the twentieth century in Central and South America and in the perspective of Pope Francis I).

In a sense, the style of religion was transformed by the forces of change, but for many true believers, its theological soul remained. While established, organized religion became more secular, it morphed into New Age varieties of spirituality (e.g., in northern Europe and North America).

People in less democratic and technologically unsophisticated cultures reacted as if their society was under assault by forces that threatened to destroy the traditions and principles they espoused. This phenomenon, what some term provincialism, conservatism, or reactionary, finds expression in fundamentalism. It is an attempt to maintain the status quo in the face of perceived threats to spiritual orthodoxy and cultural traditions.[21]

We now discuss the characteristics of fundamentalism so we may understand the motives and similarities among such religious movements around the world.

THE CORE CHARACTERISTICS OF FUNDAMENTALISM

It has been said that fundamentalists define themselves by what they are against.[22] Their worldview is consumed with maintaining or reclaiming a social order that emphasizes stability and simplicity. They strongly believe in the literal interpretation of holy texts (the Bible, Torah, Qur'an) and view them as divinely inspired, as well as the prophets and messengers who brought God's word to the masses. In the tradition of reverence for holy men, most fundamental movements have charismatic leaders who interpret the divine message to the believers.

An important element of fundamentalism, and one relevant to our understanding of the challenges we face in reaching an accommodation with different cultures, is the emphasis among fundamentalists on the primacy of their views *often to the exclusion of all others*. Fundamentalism is an incubator for ethnocentrism. The only boundaries it respects are those that bind its followers together into a one-dimensional mindset that demands obedience to the *Word* as revealed by revered prophets through holy texts.

True believers are often fanatical in their commitment to theological principles that are held to be infallible because of their purported divine origin. They have a negative perception of modern society and science, which are perceived as corrupting, secular changes that threaten traditional inerrant theological precepts about good and evil, men and women, and the conduct of human interaction in society.

This fear of change and the agents of change—secularism, modernity, science, and human rights—is often manifested in a struggle between the in-group of true believers and the out-group of nonbelievers, heretics, and infidels. It has led to paranoia and acts of violence to protect the faith and faithful from the intrusions of outsiders who threaten core beliefs.

The thought process that leads fundamentalists to adopt an ethnocentric perspective of their group, namely their belief in the purity, sanctity, and infallibility of their spiritual/theological belief system, is inextricably intertwined with their interpretation of peoples' fates—their behavior in this life as it affects life after death. Fundamentalist movements are therefore able to exert a great deal of power over adherents. They reaffirm the bond between individual responsibility/behavior now and rewards or punishments in the afterlife, maximizing the normative compulsion of religion through the "Great Mystery."

Fundamentalists not only claim moral superiority on the basis of the jaundiced view of their theology, they are often explicitly chauvinistic, misogynist, and homophobic. Invariably, God is viewed as a male, and women are depicted as inferior and submissive. Strict codes governing morality, especially sexual behavior of women are enforced, limiting the full participation of women and the LGBT population.

Such views recall the work of Adorno in his conceptualization of the authoritarian personality,[23] and Merton's trained incapacity, which helps explain their inability and unwillingness to accept change.[24] More importantly, for our discussion, are the implications of such behavior for their perceptions of the efficacy of social change. There is a reluctance to accept "others" and "nonbelievers" as they are brought into close proximity through mass transportation and telecommunications.

As science and technology have transcended spatial and temporal boundaries, fundamentalist movements have, understandably, reacted negatively. They are threatened by ideas, beliefs, and behaviors that challenge their stable worldview and theology. Faced with an onslaught of unwanted images and immigrants, feeling beleaguered and victimized, their reaction is often hostile. This is to protect the faithful from what may be perceived as attacks on sacrosanct values which have, until the present, served to maintain the integrity and viability of the group.

In its attempt to restore what Tamas Pataki refers to as "the golden past,"[25] fundamentalism and its corresponding ethnocentrism may morph into an ideology of nationalism, creating social and political movements. These can have enormous consequences for stability in the modern world (e.g., the imposition of Shariah Law in some Muslim countries and purported attempts to implement it in the United States and Western Europe).[26]

We should remember that the defining characteristics of fundamentalism, notably its ethnocentrism, fear of change, and aversion to science are not restricted to Islam. They have been responsible for producing cataclysmic upheavals in societies characterized by diverse religious traditions. We now turn to a few illustrations of some of the most contentious contemporary situations associated with religious intolerance and the implications they have for perpetuating conflict around the world.

SUMMING UP

- Religion is a powerful force in societies around the world.
- Religion provides answers to questions that science cannot (e.g., life after death).
- Religious conflict continues to cause strife and suffering around the world.
- Abraham is a pivotal figure in Judaism, Christianity, and Islam.
- Religious fundamentalists share characteristics, regardless of their faith, and a reluctance to engage nonbelievers.

NOTES

1. Viktor Frankl, *Man's Search for Meaning*, revised ed. (New York: Pocket Books, 1997).
2. Sigmund Freud, *The Future of an Illusion*, ed. James Strachey (New York: W.W. Norton, 1989).
3. Johannes Climacus (Soren Kierkegaard), *Philosophical Fragments, Kierkegaard's Writing*, vol. 7 (Princeton, NJ: Princeton University Press, 1985).
4. Martin E. Marty, *When Faiths Collide* (Malden, MA: Blackwell, 2005), 28.
5. "Declaration on the Relation of the Church to Non-Christian Religions: Nostra Aetate," Proclaimed by His Holiness Pope Paul VI, October 28, 1965, http://www.vatican.va/archive/hist_councils/ii_vatican_council/document/vat-ii_decl_19651028_nostra-aetate_en.html.
6. Samuel P. Huntington, *The Clash of Civilizations and the Remaking of World Order* (New York: Simon & Schuster, 2011).
7. Amazingly, this sentiment was recently expressed by forty-year-old Marco Rubio, U.S. Senator from Florida. In a speech he made at the Ronald Reagan Presidential Library on August 23, 2011, Rubio, the son of Cuban immigrants, criticized the reliance of the poor on the federal government and noted, "We must begin by embracing principles that are absolutely true. No. 1—the free enterprise system does not create poverty. . . . The free enterprise system creates prosperity, not denies it. The second truism that we must understand is that poverty does not create our social problems, our social problems create our poverty." *St. Petersburg Times*, September 7, 2011, 9A.
8. Emile Durkheim, *The Elementary Forms of Religious Life* (Glencoe, IL: The Free Press, 1965).
9. Ferdinand Töinnes, *Community and Civil Society*, ed. Jose Harris (New York: Cambridge University Press, 2001).
10. Martin E. Marty, *When Faiths Collide* (Malden, MA: Blackwell, 2005).
11. Bruce Feiler, *Abraham: A Journey to the Heart of Three Faiths* (New York: William Morrow, 2002), 19.

12. "The Great Revolt," Jewish Virtual Library, http://www.jewishvirtuallibrary. org/jsource/Judaism/revolt.html.

13. Addressing participants at the Vatican's annual World Peace Day in December, 2010, Pope Benedict XVI proclaimed that Christians are the most persecuted religious group in the world today. Associated Press, "Pope Calls Christians the Most Persecuted," December 16, 2010, http://www.syracuse.com/news/index.ssf/2010/12/pope_calls_christians_the_most.html.

14. Matthew White, "Selected Death Tolls for Wars, Massacres and Atrocities Before the 20th century," http://necrometrics.com/pre1700a.htm.

15. "Children's Crusade," http://www.historylearningsite.co.uk/childrens_crusade. htm.

16. Webchron, The Web Chronology Project, "The Spanish Inquisition 1478–1834," Western and Europe Chronology, http://www.thenagain.info/webchron/westeurope/ spainqui.html; American-Israeli Cooperative Enterprise, "The Spanish Expulsion, 1492," Jewish Virtual Library, 2011, http://www.jewishvirtuallibrary.org/jsource/ Judaism/expulsion.html; Maryam Noor Beig, "Andalusia When It Was," http://www. hispanicmuslims.com/andalusia/adalusia.html.

17. "Turkish Toleration," The American Forum for Global Education, 2000, http:// www.globaled.org/nyworld/materials/ottoman/turkish.html.

18. Ibid.

19. See Tractate 8 of the Babylonian Talmud, *Abodah* Zareh, edited by Rabbi Dr. Isdore Epstein, for examples of this policy at http://www.come-and-hear.com/talmud/ index.html.

20. David Martin, *On Secularization: Towards a Revised General Theory* (Burlington, VT: Ashgate, 2005).

21. A contemporary example of this phenomenon is the conflict between conservative African Episcopalians and their more liberal counterparts in the West. See Miranda K. Hassett, *Anglican Communion in Crisis: How Episcopal Dissidents and Their African Allies Are Reshaping Anglicanism* (Princeton: Princeton University Press, 2007).

22. Jakobus M. Vorster, "Perspectives on the Core Characteristics of Religious Fundamentalism Today," *Journal for the Study of Religions and Ideologies* 7, no. 21 (2008): 44–65.

23. Theodore Adorno et. al., *The Authoritarian Personality* (New York: Harper and Row, 1950).

24. Robert K. Merton, *Bureaucratic Structure and Personality* (Glencoe, IL: The Free Press, 1957).

25. Tamas Pataki, *Against Religion* (Victoria, Australia: Scribe, 2007).

26. For a discussion of the attempt to Islamize the West through the imposition of Shariah Law and the malevolent intentions of some of the opponents, see: Andrea Elliott, "Behind an Anti-Shariah Push," *New York Times*, July 31, 2011, A1, A16, and the Summer 2011 issue of the *Intelligence Report*, no. 142, published by the Southern Poverty Law Center.

SEVEN

"Am I My Brother's Keeper?"

Inequality, Intolerance, and the Roots of Terrorism

There will always be desperate people as long as we have conditions that make people desperate.

— Archbishop Desmond Tutu

The legacy of conflict and hate reaches into our classrooms and affects the way teachers and students view themselves and one another. Knowing the origins of these conflicts will help us understand and relate to our students as they struggle to overcome burdens placed on them by previous generations.

THE SOURCE OF CONTEMPORARY RELIGIOUS FRICTION

The late Harvard political scientist Samuel Huntington predicted that the world of the twenty-first century would be rent by wars that originate over religious and cultural differences. He foresaw an unremitting cascade of conflict between the competing civilizations of East and West and North and South as the combatants struggle for political, economic, and theological hegemony.[1] Is this the world our children are destined to inherit?

Our preceding discussion helps to lay the foundation for understanding why the world seems to be seething with religious conflict. How could a set of principles designed to create moral relationships among people become inverted by some of the faithful? Under what guise can religion be used as a weapon to abet the destruction of the very things and beings it was invented to protect?

Our search for answers to these questions rests on contemporary social and psychological phenomena. We no longer have to dredge up his-

133

torical depredations. There are innumerable contemporary cases of man's inhumanity to his fellow men, women, and children, as well as the despoliation of nature that we were entrusted to preserve. Nor do we have to search for the usual suspects (Christians, Jews, and Muslims—people of the Book) to find offenders.

Supposedly peaceful, contemplative Eastern religions such as Hinduism have also become embroiled in internecine warfare with other faiths such as Islam. The seemingly never-ending conflict over Kashmir and Jammu between Hindu-dominated India and Muslim Pakistan has enveloped these countries since Pakistan separated from India in 1947. Estimates of the number of people killed range from 47,000 to 100,000. Fighting between Indians and Pakistanis periodically erupts over control of these Northern provinces.

THREE CONTEMPORARY CASES OF THE PERVERSION OF RELIGION AND POLITICS

Conflict between dominant, majority faiths and minority traditions has occurred throughout history. Even now, humanitarian organizations such as Amnesty International and Human Rights Watch receive numerous complaints about the persecution of the faithful of diverse religions. A recent PEW Center Report found that between 2006 and 2009 restrictions on religious beliefs and practices *increased* in twenty-three countries (12 percent) around the world, affecting nearly a third of the world's population.[2] Below, three cases of contemporary conflict are presented to illustrate how religion, government, and power can become intertwined to produce mayhem and carnage. In each case, the antagonists cannot be distinguished from one another from purely physical appearances. They differ in religious and political dogma. Their "true believers" have created a fanaticism that has led to the rationalization of horrendous violations of human freedom and dignity.

Yugoslavia, Ethnic Cleansing, and the Struggle for Identity

One of the most egregious examples of the negative consequences of the fusion of religion and politics to gain power and privilege were the conflicts among Serbs, Croats, and Muslims from 1991 to 2000 in the former Yugoslavia. To understand the intricacies and dynamics that led to them we must go back over 700 years to 1300 C.E. (common era). Then, the Ottoman Turks expanded their empire across the Middle East, into North Africa and Europe. They were stopped at Vienna where the Grand Vizier, Kara Moustafa's army, was defeated by Austrians and a coalition of German princes and Poles led by the Polish king, John Sobieski.[3]

Prior to the Turkish incursion, a multitude of different ethnic groups inhabited the territory that became known as Yugoslavia at the end of World War I. The first identifiable peoples known as Illyrians became residents around 700 B.C.E. (before the common era) in what is now Macedonia. Around that time, Tracians moved into present-day Serbia, and the Venti occupied what is now Croatia. A hundred years later, the Greeks founded colonies along the Adriatic. In the fourth century B.C.E. Celts forced the Illyrians southward and created a combined Celtic-Illyrian culture in present-day Slovenia, Croatia, and Serbia.

South Slavs entered the region around 500 C.E., but it was the Romans, who conquered and divided the region in the third century C.E., who made a lasting contribution to the cultural, and later religious, separation of the region. After vanquishing the Celts who had lived in modern Serbia and defeating the Macedonians under Philip II and Alexander the Great, Rome separated the Byzantine and Roman spheres of the region into Eastern (what became Orthodox Serbia) and Western empires (later Roman Catholic Croatia and Slovenia) respectively. This created a division that survived their empire and plagues the peoples of the region to this day.

Following the disintegration of the Roman Empire, the region was successively attacked and occupied by the Goths (fourth century C.E.), Huns (448 C.E.), Ostrogoths (493 C.E.), Slavs (fifth and sixth centuries C.E.), and Avars (sixth century C.E.).[4] The region became the battleground of numerous armies and at various times and places dwelled within the Holy Roman, Habsburg, and Austro-Hungarian Empires. Between 1359 and 1481 Mehmed II, the ruler of the Turkish Empire, acquired the territory formerly known as Yugoslavia. In 1453 he conquered Constantinople (now Istanbul) ending the Eastern Roman Empire.

In 1521 Sultan Suleiman the Magnificent conquered modern Yugoslavia, but the Turkish wave was halted at Vienna. The dissolution of the Ottoman Empire was hastened by their alignment with the Germans and the Central Powers in World War I. The breakup of the empire resulted in the creation of forty new countries, including twenty-two Arab states.[5]

A lot has been written and said about the state of religious freedom under the Ottoman Turks who controlled the region for five hundred years. Historians contend that non-Muslims were allowed to practice their faith. According to author Fred Singleton, religious leaders under the Turks had a great deal of influence in civic life and the affairs of their communities. This often led to a conflation of religion with nationalism. "Orthodoxy and national identity were inextricably intertwined, and religious leaders became the spokesmen of national revolt" against the Turks late in their occupation.[6]

During their long occupation of the region, the Turks employed the *millet system*, which allowed religious communities autonomy in regard to the practice of their faith. Leaders of the various faiths supervised the faithful, collected taxes for the Ottoman government, and maintained order. Singleton contends that it was not until the empire started to decline that restrictive pressure was exerted on non-Muslims. Christian subjects in the Balkans were, according to him, probably treated no worse than the peasants of central Europe by their feudal overlords.

Another practice of the Turks created a great deal of dissension among their Christian subjects and helps explain the large number of converts to Islam during their reign. This was the system of *Devsirme*, which encouraged the conscription of Christian boys ages 8–20 for compulsory military service. Known as *janissaries*, they became trusted fierce defenders of the empire.

Torn from their homes and parents, they were forcibly converted to Islam and often became fanatical Muslims. But exceptions to the practice were made through bribes to Muslim officials, and child orphans, married men, and some skilled tradesmen were excluded, as well as Muslims and Jews.

Most of the conscripts came from Orthodox Christian Slav, Greek, and Albanian families, sowing the seeds of future ethnic conflict that would torment the region. Yet, some families benefited from the practice. It improved their social and economic position in the realm as the youths progressed up the military leadership hierarchy. Several conscripted youths became prominent leaders of the Ottoman Empire, Grand Viziers such as Ibrahim, the Greek who served Suleiman the Magnificent in the 1500s; Macedonian Kocu Bey, who advised Murad IV in the seventeenth century; and Mehmed Sokollu, a Bosnian who advised several Turkish leaders in the middle of the sixteenth century.[7]

Following the fall of the Ottoman and the Austro-Hungarian Empires at the end of World War I, the victors created a new country—Yugoslavia (land of the South Slavs). It was composed of more than twenty ethnic groups. Joseph Broz Tito, a shrewd autocrat, emerged from the partisan opposition to the Nazis during World War II and became the country's leader from 1945 until his death in 1980. Simultaneously, he served as the head of the Communist Party, Marshall of Yugoslavia, head of the government, commander-in-chief, and president.

Political scientist, Aleksa Djilas, contends that Tito's policy of suppressing ethnic identities and cultural exchanges among the country's six republics (Slovenia, Croatia, Serbia, Montenegro, Macedonia, Bosnia-Herzegovina) created a "cultural and intellectual autarky," reinforcing nationalism among the disparate ethnic groups. Despite the population of twenty-four million in 1989, there was no university that represented the diverse nationalities, nor a policy that encouraged students to study outside of their republic.[8]

Once Tito's iron hand was removed from the throat of the nationalistic republics, age-old religious and political animosities surfaced pitting one ethnic group against the other. The country was torn apart in a civil war that raged from 1991 to 1995, when the Dayton Peace Accords were signed by some of the warring parties. Violent disputes were still occurring as late as 2001.[9]

Much of the contemporary antagonism among the Serbs, Croats, and Muslims can be traced to atrocities committed during World War II. The Croats and some Muslims aligned with the Nazis, and the Serbs with the Russians. During the war, atrocities were committed by all parties to the dispute as they vied for ethnic, ideological, theological, and regional supremacy.

Psychiatrist, Dusan Kecmanovic, a Yugoslav expatriate, fled the country in August 1992 after living a wretched existence in Sarajevo, which was under siege by the Serbs. In his book, *Ethnic Times*, he tried to understand and explain the process that led to the destruction of his homeland and the barbaric treatment of one ethnic group by another.

The brutality exhibited in the Yugoslav civil war was incomprehensible to him. As a therapist he struggled to heal the broken souls of his compatriots:

> Longstanding friendships and marriages disintegrated simply because the friends and spouses were not of the same ethnic origin. Violence became the order of the day. National myths were resurrected on all sides. Great effort was put into concocting differences between the cultures of the ethnonational groups, and differences that actually did exist were enormously inflated. Brotherhood by faith became the strongest tie. The inhabitants of far-off countries and continents were recognized as brothers. In some environments, religious circles began to play an important role in governing state affairs.[10]

Political scientist Huntington placed the responsibility for the protracted conflict on the historically adversarial alignment of religious kin groups that supported the various factions with arms, money, and soldiers. The world powers were drawn into an extension of the "Cold War" as resources from ethnic and religious kin around the world poured into the region.

Allied with Croatia (Roman Catholic) were Germany, Austria, the Vatican, European Catholic countries, and the United States. Allies of Serbia (Orthodox) were Russia, Greece, and other Orthodox countries (e.g., Bulgaria. Allied with the Bosnian Muslims were Iran, Saudi Arabia, Turkey, Libya, and other Islamic nations). "Reportedly a thousand or more Russians, along with volunteers from Romania and Greece, enlisted in the Serbian forces to fight what they described as the 'Catholic facists' and 'Islamic militants.'"[11] Huntington facetiously noted, "The combination of the lure of the dollar and the sympathy for cultural kin made a mockery of UN economic sanctions against Serbia as they also did to the UN arms embargo against all the former Yugoslav republics."[12]

The war, which rent the country into pieces, claimed some 150,000 lives. It was part of an age-old process of ethnocentrism, based on myths and stereotypes about the diverse people of other cultures and religions who inhabited the region. As Singleton noted:

> A potent influence in shaping national consciousness arises from the perception of their history which the subject peoples nurture, and which is led by folk traditions, by the preservation of the vernacular language and by the influence of traditional religious beliefs. Each national group had its own glorious epoch which it did not share with its neighbors; in fact, the glories of one medieval kingdom were often achieved at the expense of its neighbors. [13]

The human landscape of the region, with its cultural diversity and historical demonizing of "the other," fed into virulent ethnocentrism. It was exploited by rulers who practiced the adage "divide and conqueror." Life under the Turks, who dominated the region for half a millennium was not, as we have seen, as harsh as depicted in the descriptive phrase of their reign as "the long, black winter."

Regional and local animosities were exacerbated by the various groups who subjugated the indigenous people of the region. Throughout the centuries, age-old grievances were left to fester, forming putrid sores that spewed violence and mayhem as one group sought revenge for real or perceived injustices.

Left to simmer in their ethnocentric animosity for one another, the emotional contagion burst forth in a bloody scourge during World War II. Serbs, Croats, and Muslims engaged in a concatenation of atrocities that led to the death of an estimated one million people. The fractious parties still, to this day, cannot agree on the numbers of people who were slain. [14]

Still, we do know that many Croats and Muslims who sided with the Germans and Axis powers in the war slaughtered Serbs, Jews, and Gypsies living in their territory. The pro-Nazi *Ustashi* security force settled on a solution for the elimination of Serbs in Croatia: one-third would be deported, one-third converted to Roman Catholicism, and one-third liquidated. In fact, 125,000 Serbs were murdered there and in Bosnia-Herzegovina. Many perished at the notorious Croatian concentration camp in Jasenovac, where 77,000–99,000 people died between 1941 and 1945. [15]

The memories of such transgressions left an indelible mark on the consciousness of the offended groups. The passage of time did not remove it. In 1971 the Yugoslav Communist Party created semiautonomous regions to provide independence for each nationality. After Tito's demise Yugoslavia splintered into separate republics. In March 1989 Slobodan Milosevic, the strident Serb nationalist leader, revoked the constitutional autonomy of Slovenia, Croatia, and Bosnia-Herzegovina. This led them to declare their intention to secede. When he refused their request for independence a civil war erupted.

The carnage that ensued enveloped the region in another round of conflict that rivaled the atrocities of World War II. Wanton destruction of property, mass executions of ethnic minorities, and widespread sexual assaults against women from minority groups ensued. Concentration camps were created, and the removal of ethnic minorities from disputed territory that became known as "ethnic cleansing," was practiced.

University of California religion professor Michael Sells chillingly describes the details of the Serb assault on civilians in Bosnia. All vestiges of ethnic minorities in Serb-dominated regions were obliterated by targeting museums and libraries to eradicate the very history of other cultures.[16] One of the most heinous incidents involved the mass execution of Muslims by the Serbian majority in Bosnia-Herzegovina. The Red Cross estimates 7,079 Muslim men and boys were slain in Srebrenica in July 1995. The fighting among Serbs, Muslims, and Croats rekindled old animosities from World War II. It is difficult to pinpoint the number of people who were killed in this series of wars that lasted for a decade. Estimates range from 100,000 to one million.

The irony (or hypocrisy) of the Yugoslav situation was that the Yugoslav federal and republican constitutions guaranteed equal rights for all ethnic groups. This included the right to participate in public life, government, and the armed forces. Minority nationalities had the right to organize groups to exercise their cultural rights and promote their national interests. Article 119 of the federal criminal code prohibited propaganda and other activities that incited or fomented national, racial, or religious intolerance, hatred, or dissension between nations and nationalities. The federal and republican constitutions provided for proportional representation of the nations and nationalities in assemblies, commissions, the highest levels of the army's officer corps, and other government institutions.[17]

Under the leadership of Slobodan Milosevic, the Serbs continued a campaign of ethnic cleansing in regions around the former Federal Republic of Yugoslavia. Reports of atrocities against civilians in the autonomous province of Kosovo, with a population of 90 percent Albanians, led to Operation Allied Force, a North Atlantic Treaty Organization (NATO) offensive against the Serbs. It ran from March 24 to June 9, 1999.

The offensive was intended to stop the Serbs from spreading the conflict in the Balkans and halt their attack on civilians in Kosovo. Serb military activity was curbed by destroying their economic assets and infrastructure. NATO planes flew 38,004 sorties during this period and dropped 6,303 tons of munitions. Thirty-five percent of the bombs and missiles were precision guided. The strategy was effective, degrading Serb military command and control capabilities, munitions, and infrastructure, although approximately five hundred civilians were killed during the raids.[18]

The initial conflict ended after three bloody years of war when Bosnia, Serbia, and Croatia signed Peace Accords that had been worked out in Dayton, Ohio, on December 14, 1995, in Paris. They called for monitoring the agreement, security, and confidence-building measures in Bosnia and Herzegovina and arms control. A total of 54,000 troops from the United States, NATO, and eighteen non-NATO nations were stationed as a buffer between the warring factions. This number was reduced to 18,000 in 2003.

Each year a continuing resolution has been passed in the United Nations to maintain the presence of peacekeepers in that region. Speaking before the United Nations Security Council on November 18, 2010, Valentin Inzko, the high representative for Bosnia and Herzegovina told the group that there was still "insufficient" dialogue and compromise, fifteen years after the Accords were signed.[19]

The search for some of the most heinous villains in the series of conflicts in the former Yugoslavia has continued. After NATO degraded the Serbian military, and economic sanctions by the United States and the European Community threw the region into an economic tailspin, pressure was exerted on Serb leader, Milosevic, to resign. He refused until massive rallies occurred in Belgrade demanding his ouster. Vojislav Kostunica was elected to succeed him in October 2000. The economic sanctions were lifted, and Milosevic was arrested in April 2001. He was turned over to the United Nations International Criminal Tribunal for the former Yugoslavia in the Hague.

Milosevic refused to cooperate with the authorities in his trial and was found dead in his cell on March 11, 2006. But other renegades remained at large. It was not until July 21, 2008, that authorities arrested the ultranationalist leader of the Bosnian Serbs, Radovan Karadzic, and charged him with genocide in the ethnic cleansing of Bosnian Muslims. On May 26, 2011, Ratko Mladic, the reputed enforcer of ethnic cleansing operations in the region, was arrested. His trial for war crimes in the Hague is still in progress. All remain defiant and unapologetic for their actions.

The nature of this ethno-violence stands as a stark reminder of how terribly wrong human relationships can go when religion and ethnicity are subjugated to political ends. Too bad they did not heed Kant's dictum that the means are never justified by the ends. In this conflict, it was not only ethics that were abused; human beings were treated like excrement. Each side struggled to dehumanize the other in a futile attempt to gain what was left of the moral high ground.

Friends, even family members, participated in the depravity. "The others" were reduced to objects of ridicule and derision. Perpetrators were drawn into the maelstrom that devoured every semblance of their humanity. "My seven-and-a-half-year-old daughter was raped several times and my son, who was thirteen at the time, was raped for months, and that hurts the most," said a witness at Karadzic's trial in the Hague. He noted that he is still haunted by the thought that the men he knew, former friends and neighbors, committed the crimes. [20]

As expatriate Kechmanovic recalled, "Members of another religion who lived in the same neighborhood, worked at the same job, lived on the same street or in the same village became sworn enemies or simply unwelcome as people who could not and must not be trusted." [21] This sentiment even carried over into schools in the United States where the children of war refugees verbally and physically assaulted one another.

In 1996, I was called into a high school in St. Petersburg, Florida, to assist in defusing violence among Muslim, Serb, and Croat students. Over a hundred of them were fighting on campus in an extension of the conflict they had fled in their homeland. Fifty of the antagonists gathered in the library.

Tensions were high. The night before, at a PTA meeting, one of the parents threatened to "go home and get my gun" to resolve the conflict. Many of the teenagers had witnessed horrible atrocities. Their journey was a circuitous route from Yugoslavia to refugee camps in Germany, where they were located until admitted into the United States.

Derisive comments about one another could be heard by the ten teachers and administrators who lined the room as fifty students filed in. They were asked to sit in a large circle as they jockeyed to be with members of their own ethnic group. Bewildered American students were clueless about the circumstances that had created the animosity among them.

Their lack of awareness was compounded by their inability to perceive the markers the Yugoslav students used to differentiate one from another. There were no obvious signs of distinction among them. They were all white and spoke broken English; many were blonde, wore typical teen clothes, and looked like other kids from the States. But these kids possessed a kind of knowledge that transcended surface stereotypes used by American whites and blacks—a knowledge borne from centuries of myths and prejudices about "the other." These ideas nurtured over the ages created the violence they had endured:

"I don't know why you all are fighting so much," said Kenny, a blonde American kid sitting between three Serbs and four "Bosnians" (Muslims). "You all look alike to me."

"That's not so!" shouted Kiran, a tall dark-haired boy. "We're Muslims, and they hate our guts."

"Why shouldn't we?" shouted back Irina. "Look what your people did to us."

I could see where this was going, so I interjected: "Why don't we introduce ourselves as we go around the circle. Each person can tell how he or she got to the United States."

For the next hour we heard the sorrowful tales of violence—rape, murder, and mayhem—committed against them and relatives in their homeland.

"They took my father and brother from our home, and we never saw them again."

"They came to our village, the neighbors, and shot my uncle right in his house."

"They beat my father and left him there for dead."

The teachers and administrators who had been eavesdropping were crying, and the American students were also moved. When they finished, I observed, "I'm sorry that you had to endure these things. But you're here now. One thing you may have noticed is that you all, Serb, Muslim, Croat, had similar experiences. You all lost people you loved, and you all suffered because people mistreated you. Think about that before you say or do something to hurt someone. You don't have to relive that all over again."

"I can't forgive them for what they did," said Samir.

"I'm not asking you to right now, but I want all of you to try to get along with one another, to begin to understand that you're in a new country."

"We'd rather be at home, but there's a war going on there. They sent us to Germany, and they wouldn't even let us go to school in the camps," said Koschina.

"You've got a chance to learn now," I said. "Why bring all these old hatreds over here?"

"I can't ever forget what happened," she continued.

"I don't think anyone could, but I'm asking you to give one another a chance. Try to start something new. You don't have to love one another, but you've all experienced these things. Don't you see, you've all been victims of hatred. All I'm asking is that you try to get along so you can continue your schoolwork and move on."

That day was the beginning of a two-year project that brought seventy-five of the students together each week to dialogue and engage in teambuilding activities. At first many of them didn't like being in the same room, let alone talking civilly to one another. After a few meetings they were able to see common challenges they had living in America.

One day I showed them a video, *Land of the Demons*, about the war in their homeland, narrated by Peter Jennings. As he spoke, scenes of a concentration camp appeared on the screen, and one of the students gasped, "That's the place they took my father. We never heard from him again."

While the kids didn't become good friends, the derisive comments and blatant stereotypes gradually diminished. When the project wrapped up in May 1998, most were graduating and four had been admitted to college.

One fascinating footnote to this discussion is the finding that the warring ethnic groups in that region *are actually related to one another.* DNA research of modern-day inhabitants of the region point to a wide-scale migration/invasion by Indo-Europeans between 2,500 and 2,100 B.C.E. An analysis of the genetic markers (mtDNA and Y chromosomes) indicates strong genetic commonalities and linkages among the residents of the Balkans, in effect demonstrating their kinship dating back over 2,000 years.[22]

Figure 7.1.   Map of Yugoslavia[23]

NORTHERN IRELAND: THE GREEN LAND THAT KEEPS BLEEDING RED

The struggle for land, political rights, and religious freedom is not unique to the Balkans. The conflict in Northern Ireland between Catholics and Protestants has also raged for hundreds of years. The Emerald Isle was first populated by humans who migrated from Scotland and landed in Antrim on the coast around 8,000 B.C.E. Since it was an island, it was one of the last parts of Western Europe to be settled. Over the centuries, it has endured a succession of invasions from Scandinavia and the continent.

One of the most significant invasions of Ireland was the arrival of the Celts. They appeared around 300 B.C.E. Known by a variety of names attributed to their many tribes (e.g., Galatians or Gauls, the root origin of their name in Greek (Keltoi) and Roman (Celtae) means barbarian). Tall of stature and fair skinned, they had light-colored hair that was often bleached. They were fierce warriors who, it is said, often fought naked in battle and hung the heads of vanquished opponents above entrances to their homes.

They were also skilled artisans and metallurgists. Although they did not leave a written record, artifacts indicate they had a complex language and sophisticated culture that valued the arts and science. Their empire spanned a dozen countries in the contemporary world. They even defeated the mighty Roman Army and occupied Rome for three months in 390 B.C.E. They were ultimately defeated by Julius Cesar in 58 B.C.E. and merged with other groups in Europe.

As with other desirable locations, the ensuing struggles that plagued Ireland were over natural resources. In the ninth and tenth centuries C.E. the Vikings, known as Norsemen (later abridged to Normans) invaded, and a Danish invasion occurred in 853 C.E. The English invaded the island in 1168 C.E. and from the twelfth century to 1400 they maintained control of the country, with the center of power in Dublin. Although there were many English colonists on the island, and much intermingling, they were unable to wrest control from the indigenous Irish.

Under Norman rule the country was predominantly Catholic. When King Henry VIII of England separated from the Catholic Church and became the supreme head of the Church in England in 1534, it was a foreboding sign of strained relations between Protestant England and Catholic Ireland. An abortive revolt by Thomas, Lord Offaly, that year infused religion into Irish politics. He attempted to rally the Irish in a Catholic crusade against Protestant England. Henry imposed his reformation and created a further religious divide when he was declared king of Ireland by the Protestant-dominated Irish Parliament in 1541.

As Protestantism swept across the English landscape, Catholic Ireland held fast to its ties with Rome. Attempts by English monarchs to break the Papacy's hold on the island only strengthened resistance. Then Edward VI began confiscating Irish lands taken from rebellious families and redistributing them to English settlers.

In the 1560s, England suppressed a revolt in Ulster. Queen Elizabeth retaliated by expropriating the province and accelerated the practice of populating Irish lands with Englishmen. Over time, some of the best land was taken by the English, who also rose to prominence in the government and judicial system at the expense of the indigenous Irish.

Hugh O'Neill, earl of Tyrone, was an Irish chieftain who vainly fought for independence from England and Elizabeth in a war that lasted for nine years. When he and other Irish nobles fled to Rome in 1607, the country was bereft of indigenous Irish Catholic leaders. The "plantation" policy of settling Englishmen escalated, especially in Ulster, a verdant region of Northern Ireland. When dispossessed Catholics revolted in 1641 they were defeated by Oliver Cromwell's forces. He repaid supporters by offering them confiscated Irish lands.

In England, James II gained the throne in 1685. His ascendancy created consternation among Protestants in England and Ireland because his wife was Catholic. The prospect of a Catholic becoming the head of state was anathema. Anti-Catholic sentiment had already eventuated in the Test Acts passed by Parliament in 1673. These prevented Catholics from becoming members of Parliament or holding other high offices. Nevertheless, James attempted to place Catholics in important positions, only to be stymied by the laws.

When no clear successor to the throne emerged, James imprisoned the Archbishop of Canterbury and six other prominent Protestant bishops in the Tower of London for opposing his plan that would enable Catholics to gain power. Members of Parliament then implored Mary, James's daughter and her husband, Prince William of Orange, who were living in Holland, to come to England and take the throne. They arrived in 1688 with a Dutch army.

James ultimately fled to France, avoiding a civil war, but engaged William at the much storied Battle of the River Boyne in Ireland in 1690, where he was defeated. This battle has been immortalized to this day in the annual "Marching" (parades) of Protestants through Northern Ireland every July, perpetuating a centuries-old triumph of one denomination of the same faith over another.

Following William's victory, a rising Protestant "Ascendancy Class" implemented harsh laws in Ireland to prevent future uprisings. Catholic property ownership was restricted, as was their educational opportunities and right to bear arms. Catholic clergy were also driven out. These policies stoked the development of Irish nationalism in the seventeenth and eighteenth centuries. Although some of the most offensive laws were relaxed following the American and French revolutions, Irish Catholics still chaffed under the foreign rule of the English and Protestants.

In 1798 a failed rebellion by United Irishmen led to the creation of an "Act of Union" between Ireland and Britain in 1801. Protestant Irish members of Parliament took seats in Westminster and the Irish Parliament dissolved itself. It was not until 1829 that Catholic-dominated Ireland was emancipated from Britain with northern Ulster being declared a "special case," separated from the rest of the country.

When the Great Famine scourged Ireland from 1845 to 1850, further reforms were put on hold. Over a million people died of starvation and disease when the Irish potato crop failed. What is less spoken about was the reluctance of the British to intervene to prevent the loss of life.

Prior to the outbreak of the blight (*phytophthora infestans*) that decimated the Irish potato crop, 60 percent of the country's food was derived from that staple. When the crop failed, Britain's response was weak, restrained, and insufficient. British colonial policies prevented Irish Catholics from fully participating in Irish society (e.g., entering the professions, holding government offices, and purchasing land). Catholic farmers often leased small plots of farms from absentee British Protestant landlords and subdivided them further for their children. It is estimated that three million Irish farmers and their families survived through potato farming. When the crops failed they could not make payments to the owners, and over 500,000 people were evicted.

As the famine wore on, the suffering of the Irish people increased. Between 1845 and 1855, the population of Ireland was reduced by one-fourth, including one million deaths and two million emigrants. Some critics contend that Britain's slow and ineffectual reaction to the Irish crisis was equivalent to genocide. British policies favored free trade and encouraged the exportation of grain and other foodstuff during the famine. Some historians contend that sufficient food existed in Ireland but was not being adequately distributed.

Some of the same social and cultural dynamics that exacerbated this catastrophe have played a role in the similar mistreatment of minorities around the world. While formal structural policies prevented the Irish from gaining access to full participation in society, social and cultural ideologies held by the British about them were even more devastating. Recall our earlier discussion of the meaning and function of work. Popular Protestant theology of the time extolled the dignity of hard work and individual initiative. Success was equated with divine inspiration and reward for living a God-fearing, virtuous life.[24]

Restrictive anti-Catholic colonial British policies created a self-fulfilling prophesy. Protestant assumptions about the natural inferiority of the Irish depicted them as lazy, slovenly, filthy, lacking self-reliance, and dependent. This perspective led to "famine fatigue" among the British public, who did not support extensive relief aid to Ireland. Irish farmers, who were made destitute by British exclusionary trade and landholding policies, were blamed for their own immiseration and negatively stereotyped as inferior human beings.

With millions of Irish starving, the British responded by expanding a system of workhouses that had been established in 1838. Over 2.6 million Irish entered them and lived and worked under harsh, crowded conditions, and 200,000 people died during their stay. British Prime Minister Lord John Russell believed that the free marketplace would ultimately restore the imbalance in Irish society. But the misery of the Irish intensified as farmers owning more than a quarter of an acre were denied relief.

Though popular British sentiment held that the Irish were to blame for their own predicament, hard work was not enough to reverse the tragedy. One expert contends that even if all the exported grain had been retained it would have been insufficient.[25] At the time of the famine, Britain was the wealthiest nation in the world. Prevalent ideological and theological beliefs prevented the British from implementing the kind of comprehensive relief program that would have averted the disaster.

A soup kitchen program that fed three million people daily was discontinued after six months, reflecting ineptitude or callousness. Meanwhile, Sir Charles Trevelyan, the British civil servant responsible for the relief effort, wrote in his 1848 book *The Irish Crisis*, that the famine was "a direct stroke of an all-wise and all-merciful Providence."[26] Trevelyan's opposition to halting the evictions coincidentally led to restructuring Irish society in favor of British capitalists, demonstrating once again the subjugation of religious and theological beliefs to political ends.

The population of Ireland prior to the famine was eight million. During the decade 1845–1855 an estimated two million people immigrated to other countries, most to the United States, Canada, and Great Britain. Their journey was not without hardship. Perhaps as many as 100,000 people died in the "coffin ships" that ferried them to other lands. Today, more than seventy million people around the world are descendants of Ireland and the famine that affected the world.[27]

The Irish dream of freedom from Britain persisted throughout their tribulations. In 1870 the Home Rule League failed to gain support in Parliament for Irish self-government thanks largely to Protestant Ulster resistance. Some of the opposition was related to Protestant antipathy toward presumed backwardness of the Irish Catholics. The Industrial Revolution flourished more so in Ulster and England. Protestants also feared the resurgence of Irish nationalism and with it Irish culture and the Gaelic language.

In 1905 Irish Republicans founded Sinn Fein ("ourselves alone"), a political pro-independence organization, and revived the Republican Brotherhood. Irish Protestants responded stridently. Hundreds of thousands of pro-British unionists signed the Solemn League and Covenant that threatened their armed rebellion if Home Rule was implemented. Private armies were created—the Ulster Volunteer Force (Protestants) and the Irish Volunteers (Catholics) both claimed over 100,000 soldiers.

The country was tottering on civil war when World War I broke out and temporarily sidelined the issue. Then in 1916, the military council of the Irish Republican Brotherhood led an uprising that tore Dublin apart. It was crushed by the British, and the leaders were executed, further inflaming Irish Catholics.

Sinn Fein's popularity among Irish Catholics soared under the leadership of Eamon de Valera, unifying Republican groups. In the first postwar election, 73 Sinn Fein candidates were elected to Parliament but refused to attend Westminster. The British were antagonistic to Sinn Fein because of its separatist bent, and for backing Germany in World War I. When Republican Irishmen formed their own legislative assembly, the Dail Eireann, the Irish Republican Army (IRA) began a war against the British.

The British imposed curfews and deployed troops (the "Black and Tans" and the Auxiliaries). Atrocities were committed by both sides during the long struggle. In 1921 Britain partitioned Ireland with twenty-six predominantly Catholic counties in the south and six predominantly Protestant counties in Ulster to the north. An Irish Free State was created that had dominion status in the British Commonwealth but lacked full independence.

A civil war ensued between pro- and anti-nationalists. De Valera ultimately joined the political process and successfully steered Southern Ireland to full independence in 1949. Still, problems remained in Northern Ireland. The IRA continued the campaign of violence it had begun before the 1921 partition. The Ulster Volunteer Force, a Protestant organization, was a combatant in the sectarian violence.

One of the saddest days in the conflict occurred on January 30, 1972, Bloody Sunday, when British soldiers killed fourteen civilians in Derry. This event precipitated a truce between the British and the IRA, but it did not last. Public opinion was, perhaps, permanently turned against the British during the infamous Hunger Strike of 1981. Ten youthful IRA members starved themselves at the H Blocks of Long Kesh prison. The first "martyr" was Bobby Sands, a twenty-seven-year-old. He had been elected to the British Parliament six weeks into his hunger strike and died on the sixty-sixth day of his protest.

The thrust of the prison demonstrations centered on the British criminalization of IRA inmates who thought they should be treated as prisoners of war. After a series of protests occurred that included noncompliance to wearing prison clothes, rejection of prison work, and refusal to leave their cells, which led to the contamination of their quarters with human excrement, the hunger strikes began. They lasted from March 1 until October 3, 1981.

All of the young men who died were immortalized in song and verse. Their cause captured the attention of the world's media. Sinn Fein gained credibility and helped launch a peace process. After many fretful contretemps, a settlement was reached on April 10, 1998, known as the Good Friday Peace Agreement covering Northern Ireland. After two years of talks and thirty years of conflict, British Prime Minister Tony Blair and Republic of Ireland Prime Minister Bertie Ahern agreed to terms. Gerry Adams, leader of Sinn Fein, signed on a month later.

The agreement created a Northern Ireland Assembly, a cross-party cabinet, and cross border institutions to handle issues common to both the North and South. Some power was given to Catholics in the North. The Republic of Ireland in the South also received some input in the North. Direct British Rule of Northern Ireland ended in May 2007 when Rev. Ian Paisley, former outspoken Protestant union activist, was elected the first prime minister of Northern Ireland.[28] In a gesture toward reconciliation, Queen Elizabeth journeyed to Northern Ireland and shook hands with former IRA chief Martin McGuiness on June 27, 2012.

The wounds from hundreds of years of war heal slowly. Despite the valiant efforts of diplomats from Britain, north and south Ireland, and other countries, violence still erupts in Northern Ireland. In late 2012 and early 2013 some of the worst violence in fifteen years occurred in Belfast, ostensibly over the flying of the English Union Jack flag. As with the former Yugoslavia, stereotypes of religious and ethnic groups demonized for their differences still cloud the thinking of otherwise rational men and women. This self-inflicted fog continues to prevent the development of a safe and secure homeland for all Irish people. The persistent characterization of Irish Catholics as inferior human beings is paradoxical. The peoples who populate the Emerald Isle possess a strong genetic link to one another forged over 8,000 years of living together.[29]

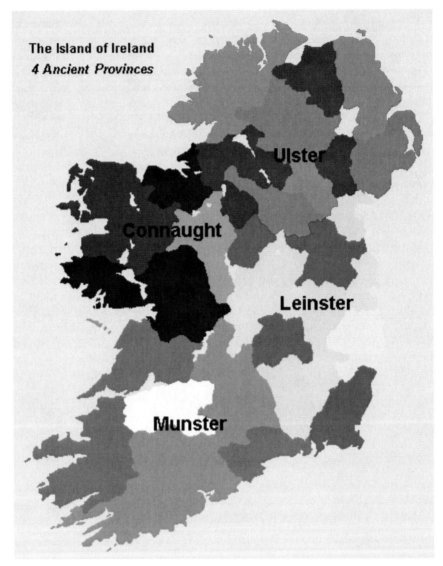

Figure 7.2.   Map of Ireland [30]

THE MIDDLE EAST: WHERE RELIGION, POLITICS, AND RATIONALITY COLLIDE

The Middle East is the acknowledged birthplace of monotheism. There Abraham entered into a covenant with God, which birthed Judaism, Christianity, Islam, and the Baha'i faiths. It was also the home of the first large cities—Mesopotamia, in the region now known as Iraq and Iran. The Fertile Crescent was an accommodating place. It contained many animals and plants that could be husbanded, leading to a surplus that enabled the rise of social classes and the division and specialization of work.

Prehistoric man first ventured into the region around 40,000 years ago. This early migration from Africa was followed by a second wave that ultimately led to the population of Europe and the rest of the world. Throughout human history, the Middle East has been home to countless groups of humans who fought or coexisted in the region that became the cradle of civilization. They were known by many names that appear throughout our holy books: Cannanites, Sumerians, Akkadians, Hittites, Hebrews, Israelites, Assyrians, Chaldeans, Babylonians, Persians, Phoenicians, Amorites.

The first written language, known as cuneiform, is attributed to the Sumerians, who lived in the region beginning around 4000 B.C.E. The great Sumerian King Sargon united Mesopotamia (Greek for "land between the two rivers," the Tigris and Euphrates) around 2300 B.C.E. From that time onward a succession of groups including the Babylonians, Persians, Greeks, and Romans, populated the region. They attempted to gain hegemony over the human and ecological resources that made it so desirable.

Inhabitants of the region in the early millennia of recorded history practiced a variety of religions characterized by polytheism. Then an itinerant shepherd by the name of Abraham founded monotheism some 4000 years ago. Judaism and its descendants, Christianity and Islam, all trace their origin to Abraham and monotheism, believing in the same universal deity. They have, however, from their inception, waged an unceasing struggle with one another (and even within their own ranks). The battle has been over the interpretation of purportedly divine scriptures, purity of message, and methods for obtaining salvation in the Great Mystery that awaits us all. Numerous wars and atrocities were committed by these groups against one another in the name of religious purity and piety, but more often for theological supremacy and territorial hegemony.

Nowhere has the theological cauldron of hate and prejudice been stirred more than in the very area that birthed these faith traditions. And there is more misinformation and misunderstanding surrounding the origin and belief system of the youngest of these faiths—Islam.

The acknowledged and revered founder of Islam (literally "I surrender to God's will") was a boy born into the Quraysh tribe in Makkah (Mecca) in 570 C.E. by the name of Muhammad. His father died before his birth, and his mother succumbed when he was only six years old. For the next two years his grandfather cared for him. When his grandfather passed, his uncle assumed the responsibility.

Muhammad became a successful merchant and caravan manager who was given the title of al-Amin, "the trustworthy one," because of his honesty and piety. Early on he eschewed polytheism and embraced the monotheistic tradition of Abraham. When he was forty he received a revelation while meditating in a cave in Hira in the mountains above Makkah.

He devoted the next twenty-three years of his life explaining his revelations from God (Allah) as he travelled throughout the region, advocating for Islam. In essence, it was a refined, purified version of Jewish and Christian theology. He believed they had strayed from the form initially presented to humanity by God. His followers transcribed his revelations, said to have come through the angel Gabriel, into the holy book of Islam, the Qur'an.

Persecuted by neighboring polytheists in Makkah (Mecca), he moved 210 miles north to the city of Yathrib, where he established Islamic rule and renamed the city Madinah (Medina, City of the Prophet). When he died in 632 C.E. the youngest branch of monotheism had spread throughout the region, uniting diverse Arabic tribes. Within one hundred years of his death, Islam had spread to Europe, North Africa, and central Asia.

Today, Islam has approximately 1.6 billion adherents (nearly a quarter of the world's population) found in virtually every nation. Contrary to popular belief, only 15 percent of the world's Muslims are Arabs. There are fifty-seven predominantly Muslim countries in the world, the largest being Indonesia (203 million), followed by Pakistan (174 million), India (161 million), Bangladesh (145 million), Egypt (78 million), and Iran and Turkey each with approximately 74 million.[31]

Second only to Christianity, with approximately 2.1 billion followers, Islam, like Christianity and Judaism, is composed of diverse denominations and cultures. But it is not nearly as diverse as Christianity, which has 38,000 denominations. Still, there is a significant division among Muslims dating back to the death of the Prophet Muhammad.

After his passing there was disagreement among his followers over succession. The Sunnis ("one who follows the traditions of the Prophet") believed that the first four caliphs (leaders of the faith) were Muhammad's rightful successors. They ruled continuously in the Arab world until the breakup of the Ottoman Empire at the end of World War I.

The Shiites ("the party of Ali") believe that only the heirs of the fourth caliph, Ali, Muhammad's cousin and son-in-law, are legitimate successors to Muhammad. Tensions between the two groups escalated when, in 656 C.E., Ali's supporters killed the third caliph and Sunnis killed Ali's son, Husain. In 931 C.E., the twelfth Imam (religious leader) disappeared. Shiites believe this was a loss of divinely inspired leadership in Islam. Contrary to their wishes, the Sunnis (who account for 90 percent of the world's Muslims) selected Abu Bakr, a close adviser of the Prophet, to succeed him and lead the Islamic State (caliphate).

In effect, the schism between the two groups is based on hereditary (Ali) versus elected (Abu Bakr) leadership succession. Shiites also believe that the Mahdi ("the rightly guided one") who will bring about a just and global caliphate has already arrived and is in hiding, awaiting the appropriate time to emerge. Sunnis believe he hasn't arrived yet. While there are other areas of differences between the two groups (e.g., veneration of Imams, fast days, significance of shrines), they concur on the essential elements and practices of the faith. Shiites are concentrated in Iran, Iraq, and Lebanon, while Sunnis predominate in the rest of the Muslim world.

The end of World War I saw the dismantling of the Ottoman Empire and the decline in the international influence of Islam. Western powers scrambled to control the Middle East region and its rich oil resources. Upon seeing a series of secret agreements among the Allies, Colonel Edward House, an advisor to President Woodrow Wilson, prophetically commented this would be "a breeding place for future wars."

As the Western powers struggled to gain control over the region, little attention was given to the religious, cultural, and political differences within areas demarcated for division. Mandates were established that rewarded factions, clans, and tribes for their loyalty to the victors. Kuwait, Qatar, Bahrain, Oman, Egypt, Yemen, Iraq, and Palestine came under British domination. Most of the Arabian Peninsula went to the British ally Ibn Saud, who created the nation of Saudi Arabia in 1932. Libya fell to Italy, while France gained control over Syria, Morocco, Algeria, and Greater Lebanon, which was later partitioned to protect the Maronite Christians.

The British divided Transjordan in half, installing the Hashimite family as rulers. The other half of the region was, under the British Balfour Declaration of 1917, considered Palestine. Jews from around the world were, under the Zionist movement, encouraged to immigrate and make it a Jewish homeland. Even after the Diaspora following the second destruction of the sacred temple in Jerusalem by the Romans in 70 C.E., a small number of Jews remained in the area.

In 1915 there were approximately 83,000 Jews living in what was then known as Palestine, prior to its division, compared to 590,000 Muslim and Christian Arabs. By 1922 their number grew by only 1,000. Jewish immigration began to increase dramatically in the mid-1920s because of anti-Jewish economic legislation in Poland, restrictive immigration policies of the United States, and the rise of Nazism in Germany. Prior to the entry of the United States in World War II, the peak of Jewish immigration occurred in 1935 (66,472), as can be seen in table 7.1.

The desire for Jewish immigration to Palestine surged after the war as survivors of the Holocaust sought refuge in "the promised land." The British steadfastly refused to resettle Jewish refugees in the region. President Truman urged them to reconsider their restrictive policy. British Foreign Minister Ernest Bevin exclaimed that the United States wanted displaced Jews to settle in Palestine "because they did not want too many of them in New York."[32] Nevertheless, an estimated 70,000 Jewish immigrants filtered into the region, many illegally on ships, between 1945 and 1948. The Jewish State of Israel was inaugurated on May 14, 1948.

A cultural and moral morass was created among Muslims in the region because of these several developments, as well as the dissolution of the Ottoman Empire. In addition, the division of the region into arbitrarily contrived fiefdoms, self-serving secret agreements among the Allied victors of World War I, and fratricidal struggles among competing Muslim tribes, Sunnis and Shiites, increased tension and conflict in the region.

Table 7.1. Jewish Immigration to Palestine, 1919–1941

Year	Jewish Immigrants to Palestine
1919	1,806
1920	8,223
1921	8,294
1922	8,685
1923	8,175
1924	13,892
1925	34,386
1926	13,855
1927	3,034
1928	2,178
1929	5,249
1930	4,944
1931	4,075
1932	12,533
1933	37,337
1934	45,267
1935	66,472
1936	29,595
1937	10,629
1938	14,675
1939	31,195
1940	10,643
1941	4,592

Source: Mitchell Bard, "British Restrictions on Jewish Immigration," Jewish Virtual Library, http://jewishvirtuallibrary.org/jsource/History/mandate.html.

Partitioning Palestine through the Balfour Declaration and increasing immigration of Jews into Palestine also contributed to the distress among Muslims.

To counter this blow to Muslim self-esteem, an Egyptian school teacher, Hasan al-Banna, founded the Muslim Brotherhood (Jamaat al-Ikhwan al-Muslimun) in 1928. His reaction testifies to the validity of the nature of the clash of civilizations thesis described by Harvard political scientist Samuel Huntington.[33] Banna espoused some of the concepts promoted by Muhammad ibn Abdul Wahhab, who was born in what is now known as Saudi Arabia in 1703.

In what is commonly termed the *Salafist* movement, both men sought to take Islam back to its roots and pure form. Salafis contend that Islam has not been properly understood and practiced since the Prophet Muhammad and his early disciples. Wahhab was obsessed with what he considered heretical influences that had crept into Islam. He viewed most Muslims as apostate. Along with Westerners and other nonbelievers, they were considered infidels and could be objects of scorn and abuse.

The Wahhabis' search for Muslims' return to the original faith and practices was based on their belief in the uniqueness of Allah (God). The conditions for obtaining the pure form of Islam could only be obtained through establishment of a Muslim caliphate run on Shariah law. Other cultures, even variations of Islam (Shiites), were rejected as polytheist for their veneration of saints, shrines, and tombs. The Wahhabis gained control over Mecca and Medina and destroyed sacred Shiite sites before being driven off by the Egyptians in 1818. In 1744, Wahhab formed an alliance with the Saud family. With the help of the British, they established the Kingdom of Saudi Arabia.

One of the most important postulates of Wahhabism is the linking or juxtaposition of religion and politics, a concept that Banna incorporated in the Muslim Brotherhood. In what has become a recurrent phenomenon, both groups used religion as a means for accomplishing political ends. Wahhabis pledge (Bayah) to follow the dictates of a pure leader as long as he observes the laws of Islam. Fanatical suicide bombers who obliterate themselves and other humans to prevent secularism from polluting Islam are tolerated, even at times encouraged, in the cause of creating a Muslim caliphate around the world.

To that end, nonbelievers (infidels) are viewed as interlopers and colonial imperialist powers targeted as defilers of the faith. But Banna lived in a different era from Wahhab and was a pragmatic strategist. He sought to unite Muslims in a common jihad against intruders. Banna toned down the more puritanical and extremist elements of Wahhabism. This allowed Muslims of different sects to unite in a common goal of ridding infidels from their midst. The Brotherhood's motto says it all:

God is our purpose,

The Prophet our leader,
Jihad our way of dying for God's cause our supreme objective.[34]

One of the disturbing byproducts of the Muslim Brotherhood's indigenous drive for nationalism, self-rule, and self-esteem was an infusion of anti-Semitism. It was directed against Jewish immigrants who flooded the region during the Holocaust, bringing different cultures and, significantly, secularism. It was this last sin that was the most unforgiveable for, as Banna observed, the Europeans "imported their half-naked women into these regions, together with their liquors, their theatres, their dance halls, their amusements, their stories, their newspapers, their novels, their whims, their silly games, and their vices."[35]

Banna contended that the fight against secularism and colonialism would go on:

> We will not stop at this point [freeing Egypt from secularism and modernity], but will pursue this evil force to its own lands, invade its Western heartland, and struggle to overcome it until all the world shouts by the name of the Prophet and the teachings of Islam spread throughout the world. Only then will Muslims achieve their fundamental goal . . . and all religion will be exclusively for Allah.[36]

In a paradoxical way, Banna acknowledged the achievements of Western civilization but believed it was morally and spiritually bankrupt:

"The civilization of the West, which was brilliant by virtue of its scientific perfection for a long time, and which subjugated the whole world with the products of this science to its states and nations, is now bankrupt and in decline."[37]

What better target to select for derision than the age-old scapegoat, the Jews. Banna's anti-Semitism was no doubt fueled by the increasing number of Jewish immigrants into the region. Many Arabs believed the Balfour Declaration amounted to a political double-cross after Britain had promised the territory to them.[38]

Banna's Muslim Brotherhood aligned with fascism and the Nazis against the Jews and the Allies, even using anti-Semitic cartoons and Nazi propaganda. Historian Matthias Kuentzel traced the infiltration of Nazis and their propaganda in the Middle East prior to and during World War II. He blamed the Mufti (Muslim legal advisor) of Jerusalem, Haj Amin el-Husseini, for the infusion of anti-Semitism in the region during and after World War II.

According to Kuentzel, from 1939 to 1945 the Nazis conducted an unremitting stream of anti-Semitic shortwave radio broadcasts from Zeesen, Germany (not far from Berlin), aimed at the Arabs, Turks, and Persians. Under the guidance of the Mufti, the Allies were presented as lackeys of the Jews, and the Jews were depicted as enemies of Islam. The Nazis contributed funds to the Palestinian revolt in 1936–1939 against the British and Jews. They gave money to the Muslim Brotherhood to disseminate anti-Semitic propaganda and develop its military. In turn, the Brotherhood assisted General Rommel in his campaign in North Africa.[39]

A common thread running through the beliefs of Wahabb, Banna, the Mufti, and Sheik Izz al-Din al-Qassam, a close ally of the Mufti who in 1931 began a movement in the Haifa region to return to original Islamic teaching, was their disdain for Western secularism and antimodernity. They embraced fundamentalism and anti-Semitism, believing that Jewish values and behavior represented a threat to their way of life.

"The cinema, the theatre and some shameless magazines enter our houses and courtyards like adders, where they kill morality and demolish the foundation of society," said the Mufti. And the Jews were, once again, blamed for this immorality: "They [the Jews] have also spread here the customs and usages which are opposed to our religion and to our whole way of life. The Jewish girls who run around in shorts demoralize our youth by their very presence."[40]

In a speech given by the Mufti in November, 1943 he tried to rally Muslims against the Jews by invoking centuries-old verses from the Qur'an:

> This people has been the enemy of the Arabs and Islam since it came into being. The Holy Koran expressed this old enmity in the following words: "you will find that the most hostiley-disposed toward the believers are the Jews." They tried to poison the praiseworthy Prophet, put up resistance to him, were filled with hostility to him and plotted against him. This was the case over 1300 years ago. Since then they have never ceased to hatch plots against the Arabs and Mohammedans.[41]

Western and Jewish penetration into the Middle East, with its challenge to control the land and its natural resources was an important ingredient in the Middle East cauldron. It continues to produce a toxic pall over the region. As Kuntzel incisively points out, elements of contemporary Islamism are tainted with anti-Semitism reflected in the widely watched Al-Manar Arabic satellite channel (second-largest behind al-Jazeera), which broadcasts blatantly anti-Semitic material designed to inflame Arab emotions against Israel and the Jews.

The Jews aren't the only religious/ethnic group besieged in the region. Tension between Christians and Muslims existed almost from the beginning of the introduction of Islam there 1,400 years ago. Many of the inhabitants of Egypt at the time of Muhammad were Coptic Christians who now number more than eight million (10 percent of the Egyptian population). Later, Catholic Maronites inhabited the region, growing to more than 1.5 million (35 percent) of the population of modern Lebanon. While Christians enjoy many of the rights and privileges afforded Muslims in contemporary Middle Eastern countries, this was not always the case in previous Muslim caliphates.

The Qur'an affectionately refers to Christians and Jews as "people of the book." But relations between Muslim overlords and Christians inhabiting the region have been tumultuous at times, especially during the Crusades (1095–1291 C.E.) when Christians invaded the region to wrest the Holy Land (Jerusalem) from Muslim domination.

The political, economic and social status of Christians living in the Middle East fluctuated with changes in the Muslim ruling establishment. Some rulers were more liberal than others. The Ummayad caliphs (661–750 C.E.) afforded Christians (and Jews) many of the same rights and privileges as Muslims, but Christians couldn't hold office, pray aloud, or be witnesses against Muslims in court. Financial arrangements were also abolished for Christian churches, threatening their viability.

The Abbasid Era (750–1258 C.E.) was comparatively harsher. Christians and Jews were restricted from participating in civic affairs and forced to wear yellow on their clothes. Churches constructed since the Muslim conquest of the area were destroyed.

Under the Ottomans, relations improved, but Christian boys were, as noted, subject to conscription in the military (*janissaries*). In 1860 there was a civil war in Lebanon between Muslim Druze and Christian Maronites over land ownership. Over 15,000 Christians died and 10,000 were left homeless. Intent on maintaining stability in their empire, the Ottomans imprisoned Druze leaders and punished Ottoman officers and officials for not preventing the conflict. The French also intervened to protect the Maronites in Beirut, establishing a modern precedent repeated to this day.

Although there are still large numbers of Christians living in the Middle East, many have fled the region since the Gulf Wars of 1991 and 2003, the Arab Spring, and the recent civil war in Syria. Christians complain of being treated as second-class citizens. Religious freedom is often guaranteed (except in Saudi Arabia, which even bans the construction of churches). Religious expression is limited by laws and practice. For example, Christians are not allowed to visit the cities of Mecca or Medina.

In recent years there has been an increase in violence directed against Christians in Egypt, Iraq, and Lebanon. In March 2008 the Catholic Archbishop of Mosul, Iraq, Faraj Rahho, was kidnapped and murdered by al Qaeda. On October 9, 2011, following the Arab Spring in Egypt, twenty-seven Coptic Christians were killed as they demonstrated peacefully in Cairo. A march commemorating the tragedy led to more injuries forty days later. The Egyptian military accused the Copts of inciting violence and arrested Coptic Christians following the incidents.[42]

Years of conflict among the various ethnic and religious groups are taking their toll. The high Muslim birthrate and Christian emigration have dramatically reduced the percentage of the region's Christian population. Barring political and demographic changes, they, like the Jews seem destined to be swamped by the Muslim population explosion.[43]

The ongoing Syrian civil war not only threatens Christians, but also Shiites, as the predominantly Sunni rebels threaten to wreak vengeance as they conquer territory.[44]

RELIGIOUS STRIFE AND SOCIAL CHANGE

These three snapshots of interreligious strife have been provided to give readers a glimpse of the interrelated historical, theological, and political turmoil that embroils large numbers of people around the world. There are several commonalities among them. First, the groups in conflict are all Abrahamic and monotheistic—descended from the biblical tradition of the patriarch Abraham.

Despite their common origin, Judaism, Christianity, and Islam have, for nearly 2,000 years, been competing with one another for theological supremacy. This war for believers originated in the realm of ideas. Now the struggle for dominance involves fratricidal conflict among competing denominations within a faith tradition as in Ireland (Catholics and Protestants), the former Yugoslavia (Orthodox Serbs and Roman Catholic Croats), and Middle Eastern Muslims (Sunnis versus Shiites).

The engine that drives much of this madness emanates from the belief that one's theological framework is the only true path to salvation. It must be shared with or impressed upon nonbelievers. Associated with this is a corresponding impulse among some in positions of power (monarchs and prelates) to proselytize because they benefit from the expansion of natural and human resources that come with religious hegemony. The common thread that continues to stoke the fires of religious conflict around the world is the juxtaposition of religion, theology, ideology, and politics. Each element reinforces the others in an acquisitive campaign to engulf and dominate competing perspectives.

Religious diversity is a challenge to the theological purity of some faith traditions. It is a threat to the base from which religions and elites derive their power—land and capital. The prospect of gaining or losing adherents becomes more than an ethereal search to save souls. It is played out in the age-old struggle for power and privilege *under the guise of salvation.*

Linking struggles in this life with the promise of a better existence in the hereafter continues to be a powerful method of social control. It is invoked as needed by spokesmen of diverse creeds around the world. This strategy is being challenged in the modern world by technological innovations that usher in social change on a scope unparalleled in human history. How our secular and spiritual leaders address this issue will, ultimately, have a profound effect on the outcome of mankind's journey.

Figure 7.3.　Map of Middle East[45]

SUMMING UP

- Religious conflict has been responsible for contemporary strife in the former Yugoslavia, Northern Ireland, and the Middle East.
- Religion and politics frequently form alliances that can promote hatred and conflict.
- Religious conflict today is the result of political and economic policies of yesterday.
- Contemporary anti-Semitism and Islamophobia as well as anti-Christian violence are frequently linked to irrational fear and hatred of strangers and secularism.
- Understanding the cause of religious conflict can help teachers relate to diverse students and improve their classroom environment.

NOTES

1. Samuel P. Huntington, *The Clash of Civilizations and the Remaking of World Order* (New York: Simon & Schuster, 1996).

2. "Rising Restrictions on Religion," The PEW Forum on Religion and Public Life, PEW Research Center, August 9, 2011.

3. For a fascinating account of King Sobieski's triumph over the Grand Vizier, see the letter to his wife at http://personal.ashland.edu~jmoserl/siegeofvienna.htm.

4. "Yugoslavia—Pre-Slav History," Yugoslavia Index, http://www.mongabay.com/history/yugoslavia-pre-slav_history.html; Fred Singleton, *A Short History of the Yugoslav Peoples* (London: Cambridge University Press, 1985).

5. "Ottoman Empire," Encyclopedia of the Middle East, http://www.mideastweb.org/middle-east-encyclopedia/ottoman.htm.

6. Singleton, *Short History of the Yugoslav Peoples*, 21.

7. Ibid., 38.

8. Aleksa Djilas, "Tito's Last Secret: How Did He Keep the Yugoslavs Together?" *Foreign Affairs* 74, no. 4 (1995), http://www.foreignaffairs.com/articles/51216/aleksa-djilas/tito-s-last-secret-how-did-he-keep-the-yugoslavs-together.

9. For a summary of these accords, go to "Summary of the Dayton Agreement on Bosnia-Herzegovina," Online Backgrounds, PBS, http://www.pbs.org/newshour/bb/bosnia/dayton_peace.html.

10. Dusan Kecmanovic, *Ethnic Times: Exploring Ethnonationalism in the Former Yugoslavia* (Westport, CN: Praeger, 2002), 2.

11. Huntington, *Clash of* Civilizations, 284.

12. Ibid.

13. Singleton, *Short History of the Yugoslav Peoples*, 23.

14. For an analysis of the disputed numbers, see C. Michael McAdams, "Croatia: Myth and Reality," http://mirror.veus.hr/myth/victims.html.

15. "Jasenovac," *Holocaust Encyclopedia*, U.S. Holocaust Museum, http://www.ushmm.org/wlc/en/article.php?moduleId=10005449.

16. Michael A. Sells, *The Bridge Betrayed: Religion and Genocide in Bosnia* (Berkeley, CA: University of California Press, 1996). For a sociological explanation of ethnic cleansing, see Michael Mann, *The Dark Side of Democracy: Explaining Ethnic Cleansing* (London: Cambridge University Press, 2004).

17. "Yugoslavia—Ethnic Composition," Yugoslavia Index, http://www.mongabay.com/history/yugoslavia/yugoslavia-ethnic_composition.html.

18. W. J. Fenrick, "Targeting Proportionality During the NATO Bombing Campaign against Yugoslavia," *European Journal of International Law* 12, no. 3 (2001): 489–502, http://www.ejil.org/pdfs/12/3/1529.pdf.

19. "Security Council Extends Mandate of European Force in Bosnia and Herzegovina," UN News Centre, November 18, 2010, http://www.un.org/apps/news/story.asp?NewsID=36798&Cr=bosnia&CR1.

20. "Trial of Radovan Karadzic—Bosniak Children Ruthlessly Raped by Serbs," Institute for the Research of Genocide in Canada, September 26, 2011, http://www.instituteforgenocide.ca/trial-of-radovan-karadzic-bosniak-children-ruthlessly-raped-by-serbs/.

21. Kechmanovic, 2.

22. "Origins, Age, Spread and Ethnic Subclades," *Eupedia*, http://www.eupedia.com/europe/origins_haplogroups_europe.shtml.

23. See www.srska-mreza.com/MAPS/Ethic-groups/map-NatGeogr-1990.html.

24. Max Weber, *The Protestant Ethic and the Spirit of Capitalism* (New York: Routledge, 2001).

25. Jim Donnelly, "The Irish Famine," BBC History, http://www.bbc.co.uk/history/british/victorians/famine_01.shtml.

26. Cited in ibid.

27. The following sources were also used for this summary: "The Irish Potato Famine," *Digital History*, http:www.digitalhistory.uh.edu/historyonline/irish_potato_famine.cfm; "British Policies During the Great Famine, http://www.mtholyoke.edu/~ebstork/famine.html#anchor24222."

28. I have drawn heavily on the concise chronology about Ireland provided by the BBC History website's "The Road to Northern Ireland, 1167–1921," at http://www.bbc.co.uk/history/recent/troubles/overview_ni_article_01.shtml (accessed October 29, 2011). Other research materials used in this summary were "Travel through Ireland . . . The Mesolithic Stone Age," accessed October 28, 2011, http://www.Wesleyjohnston.com/users/ireland/past/pre_norman_history/mesolithic_age.html; John Holwell, "A Brief History of Ireland," accessed October 28, 2011, http://genealogypro.com/articles/irish-history.html; "King James Biography," Spartacus Educational, accessed October 28, 2011, http://www.spartacus.schoolnet.co.uk/STUjames2.htm; Martin Wallace, "The Battle of the Boyne," *A Little History of Ireland* (Belfast: Appletree, 1994); "The Irish Potato Famine," Digital History, accessed October 30, 2011, http://www.digitalhistory.uh.edu/historyonline/irish_potato_famine.cfm; "British Policies During the Great Famine," accessed October 31, 2011, http://www.mtholyoke.edu/~ebstork/famine.html#anchor24222; James Donnelly, "The Irish Famine," BBC History, accessed October 31, 2011, http://www.bbc.co.uk/history/british/victorians/famine_01.shtml. Also see Donelly's book on this topic, *The Great Irish Potato Famine* (Gloucestershire, UK: 2002).

29. For genetic evidence of these links, see Stephen Oppenheimer, "Myths of British Ancestry," *Prospect* 127, October 21, 2006, http://www.prospectmagazine.co.uk/2006/10/mythsofbritishancestry/; Stephen Oppenheimer, *The Origins of the British* (New York: Carroll & Graf, 2007); Bryan Sykes, *Saxons, Vikings, and Celts* (New York: W.W. Norton, 2007); "Origins, Age, Spread and Ethnic Subclades," *Eupedia*.

30. See www.wesleyjohnston.com/users/ireland/geography/counties.html.

31. "Mapping the Global Muslim Population: A Report on the Size and Distribution of the World's Muslim Population," PEW Research Center, October 7, 2009; Robin Wright, *Rock the Casbah* (New York: Simon & Schuster, 2011). These figures have been rounded to the nearest million.

32. Cited in Mitchell Bard, "British Restrictions on Jewish Immigration," *Jewish Virtual Library*, at http://www.jewishvirtuallibrary.org/jsource/History/mandate.html (accessed November 17, 2011).

33. Huntington, *Clash of Civilizations*.

34. "Hassan al-Banna," *Encyclopedia of the Middle East*, accessed November 8, 2011, http://www.mideastweb.org/middle-east_encyclopedia/hassan_al_banna.htm.

35. Quoted in R. Scott Appleby, "History in the Fundamentalist Imagination," *Journal of American History* 89, no. 2 (2002).

36. Cited in Mary Habeck, *Knowing the Enemy: Jihadist Ideology and the War on Terror* (New Haven, CT: Yale University Press, 2006), 120.

37. "Hassan al-Banna," *Encyclopedia of the Middle East*.

38. For a summary of the political machinations prior to and after the Balfour Declaration from an anti-Zionist anti-British perspective, see Avi Shlaim, "The Balfour Declaration and Its Consequences," in *Yet More Adventures with Britannia: Personalities, Politics and Culture in Britain*, ed. William Roger Louis, (London: I. B. Tauris, 2005), 251–270, accessed November 11, 2011, http://users.ox.ac.uk/~ssfc0005/The percent20Balfour percent20Declaration percent20and percent20its percent20consequences.html. For a similar view, see Christopher Hitchens and Edward Said, eds., *Blaming the Victims: Spurious Scholarship and the Question of Palestine* (London: Verso, 2001). For a different perspective of this history and the role of Zionism in the formation of Israel, see Ami Isseroff, "The History of Zionism and the Creation of Israel," *MidEastWeb* for Coexistence, Middle East Resources, http://www.mideastweb.org/zionism.htm.

39. Matthias Kuentzel, "National Socialism and Anti-Semitism in the Arab World," *Jewish Political Studies Review* 17 (Spring 2005), http://www.matthiaskuentzel.de/contents/national-socialism-and-anti-semitism-in-the-arab-world.

40. Cited in ibid.

41. Cited in ibid.

42. For a review of the event and critique of the Egyptian military's role, see Mary Abdelmassih, "Egypt Randomly Arresting Copts for Maspero Massacre," *Assyrian International News Agency*, November 5, 2011, accessed November 18, 2011, http://www.aina.org/news/20111105173122.htm.

43. For more information on the demographic status of Christians in the Middle East, see Robert Fisk, "Exodus: The Changing Map of the Middle East," *Independent*, October 26, 2010, http://www.independent.co.uk/opinion/the-changing-map-of-the-middle-east-2116463.html. See the following for information on the treatment of Christians in the Middle East: "Lebanon: Treatment of Christians, Particularly Maronites; the Availability of State Protection," *Refworld*, UNHCR, February 19, 2007, http://www.unhcr.org/refworld/country,,IRBC,,LBN,4562d8cf2,469cd6ba15,o.html, and for the historical treatment of Christians, see "Shattered Christian Minorities in the Middle East," http://phoenici a.org/christiansmea.html.

44. For an eyewitness account of the internecine civil war among the various ethnic and religious groups in Syria, see James Harkin, "The Battle for Aleppo," *Nation*, June 24/July 1, 2013, 11–17.

45. See www.worldatlas.com/webimage/countrys/asia/printpage/measiamain.html.

Act 3

Reunification

EIGHT

Technology, Freedom, and Religious Fundamentalism

Millennia of human history have shown that religion is not a "small difference" but possibly the most profound difference that can exist between people. The frequency, intensity, and violence of fault line wars are greatly enhanced by beliefs in different gods.
—Samuel P. Huntington, *The Clash of Civilizations and the Remaking of World Order*

Technology in the classroom poses the same challenges and risks as it does in larger society. It can inform and instruct, but it can be misused and abused. Educators must seek a balance that inspires creativity and camaraderie.

FEAR OF SOCIAL CHANGE

The specter of social change through immigration, mass transportation, and telecommunications has elicited fear, fight, and flight among religious and ethnic groups bent on preventing the infusion of new ideas, cultures, and "strangers" into homogeneous societies. Technology threatens to disrupt the compact among monarchs, prelates, and the masses. Sociologist William F. Ogburn posited the concept of *cultural lag*, the notion that technology changes faster than human values and beliefs, almost a century ago. He could not foresee how prescient it would be in our evolving society.

Technological innovation is a double-edged sword. It promises to improve the lot of humanity while simultaneously challenging established moral, social, and cultural standards. The journey toward the reunification of mankind has been impeded by conflict among competing ethnic and religious groups. The future of mankind is inextricably linked to the evolution and diffusion of technological innovation.

Past conflicts pale in comparison to the scope of the contemporary intrusion of diverse cultures with their technological and social challenges to societies around the globe. Our discussion now focuses on how these engines of change affect the viability of religious and ethnic groups as they try to maintain the purity of their message and gene pool in an age of instantaneous transparency and interaction.[1]

THE REJECTION OF TECHNOLOGICAL INNOVATION

The problems that threaten the stability of our world today cannot be solved by the introduction of technology alone. They are human problems and must be addressed on interpersonal levels. Technology may increase our longevity and improve the quality of our lives. It may also precipitate other, sometimes more serious, problems or be spurned because of social and cultural taboos.

The lead researcher on the team that created the first birth control pill, Dr. John Rock, was a devout Catholic. He hoped his discovery, which regulates hormones in women, would be an acceptable method of fertility control to the Roman Catholic Church. The Church rejected the pill because of its concept of natural law. Man's attempt to interfere with nature's processes was unacceptable. God's divine plan, as interpreted by the Holy See, takes precedence over worldly scientific endeavors. No matter that poverty, suffering, and human misery might be attenuated through Rock's scientific discovery. Ecclesiastical matters pertaining to Natural Law are, in the Church's perspective, immutable and inviolable.[2]

The Catholic Church's opposition to the use of artificial methods of contraception like the birth control pill continues. It is apparent in the contentious debate over President Barack Obama's Affordable Health Care Act, which mandates that employers, e.g., hospitals, clinics, and universities, provide contraceptive services without copayments to their employees. The Catholic Church is opposed to this facet of the new legislation. A recent report by the Guttmacher Institute, however, found that over half (58 percent) of the women in the United States who take oral contraceptives do so *exclusively* for noncontraceptive purposes (e.g., regulating their menstrual cycle and reducing pelvic pain, migraines, acne, and endometriosis).[3]

The pill also helps women regulate and control their fertility. This enables them to make more effective reproductive choices about if and when they will conceive. Such decisions have had a liberating effect on women. On the other hand, the introduction of the pill may have led to an increase in sexually transmitted diseases (STDs) that accompanied the sexual revolution of the 1960s. It was not hedonistic impulsive behavior that spread STDs. Sexual partners who had been using other methods of contraception prior to the pill such as condoms were exposed to STDs when they abandoned traditional barrier forms that had provided some measure of protection against infections.

For some women the pill is medically contraindicated because they smoke. This can lead to cardiovascular disease and stroke. The pill has also been linked to increases in liver and cervical cancer in women. But it has also been found to reduce the incidence of ovarian and endometrial cancer.[4]

Arguably, the introduction of oral contraception precipitated one of the most important changes in social relationships in the history of mankind. This example illustrates the unanticipated consequences associated with technological innovation. It reflects the tension between religion and science and the struggle to prevent the erosion of traditional sacrosanct values in the face of social change—cultural lag.

THE FLOW OF PEOPLE AND IDEAS

The modern-day equivalent of the Four Horsemen of the Apocalypse for racists, religious fundamentalists, and antimulticulturalists are variations in skin color, ethnicity, religious diversity/secularism, and social change. These phenomena are anathema to groups and individuals who are intent on preserving the status quo. But their struggle against the winds of change is like the Dutch boy trying to stop a leak in the dike with his finger. The magnitude of technological innovations being introduced into the world is so immense, their parameters so large, and their pace of intrusion into daily life so rapid that they cannot be stopped. Rearguard retrogressive actions can only slow the introduction and utilization of science and technology. The genie is out of the bottle and can't be forced back in.

Today, people are more mobile than ever. Interaction among diverse cultures is occurring on an unprecedented scale. The World Tourism Organization of the United Nations estimated that 940 million people (approximately 7.5 percent of the planet's population) traveled internationally in 2010, a 6.6 percent increase over the previous year. The World Health Organization estimates that half a million people are in the air at any given time.[5]

Tourism and immigration account for a large amount of human interaction. Even more astounding are the figures for telecommunication, which projects ideas and cultural images electronically and *instantaneously*. According to the International Telecommunications Union, in 2011 there were an estimated 5.981 billion mobile cellular subscriptions in the world. Nearly four times as many cell-phone users are in the *developing* world as in the developed countries, signifying a forthcoming sea change in human relations.

The use of the Internet provides another index of the globalization of ideas. Worldwide, 2.4 billion people were plugged in during 2011, bringing a cascade of diverse cultures into the lives of strangers around the planet.[6] The nightly news has demonstrated how handheld electronic devices have been used for a variety of purposes, documenting civil unrest during the Arab Spring of 2011 and the ongoing agony of Syria.

They have been the catalyst for social change despite efforts of ruling elites to stifle them. Journalist Robin Wright noted that in Tunisia, "to quell dissent, the government deployed police who used tear gas and then live ammunition. But as protestors started to die, the opposition only got angrier. Many cell phone videos of the shootings and their bloodied victims ended up on Facebook, the only video-sharing platform beyond the government's control. The images shocked Tunisians." In Egypt over 50,000 people signed up on a Facebook page to support the "Day of Rage" protest on January 28, 2011.[7]

The Soviet Union was among the first modern governments to grapple with the problem of information control. Its attempt to withhold news about the Chernobyl nuclear disaster in April 1986 was, perhaps, a critical juncture in the struggle of governments to impede the flow of information.

The totalitarian Soviet regime had been waging a fight to limit information about Soviet society before Chernobyl. A form of underground press known as *Samisdat* (literally self-publishing) arose there in the 1980s. Dissidents used this to spread information about the regime, current events, and other prohibited or censored material. Through handwritten manuscripts, carbon copies, typewriters, and nighttime printing on mainframe computers, information was surreptitiously passed throughout Soviet society.

In 1985, then General Secretary of the Communist Party Mikhail Gorbachev initiated a policy of *glasnost* that encouraged openness in Soviet society and reduced censorship, but the entrenched regime was still resistant. The old adage "where there's a will there's a way" helps to describe the dissidents' pursuit of freedom of expression. The sheer magnitude of the disaster, combined with changes in information technology, in particular the electric typewriter, computer, and photocopying machines, overcame censorship, and the world learned more about the horrendous accident.

The facts about Chernobyl and subsequent revelations about Soviet society might not have been known without the courageous dissidents whose love for freedom led them to rebel against despotism. Their cause was in no small part facilitated through technology. The centralized government sought to maintain control over the use of photocopying machines and computers. But the drive for freedom of speech overwhelmed the system's attempt to control information. *Glasnost* prevailed, and the structure of Soviet society was transformed.

A contemporary counterpart of this situation has been unfolding in the Peoples' Republic of China. The government has sought to censor Internet communications and the widely used search engine Google. The Internet threatens the ability of totalitarian governments to control the content and flow of information and allows for the introduction of ideas.

Google, the world's largest search engine, began service in China on January 27, 2006. China (and other nations) censors Internet content and political speech; and Google initially agreed to self-censor its search engine results. "Our decision was based on a judgment that Google c.n. will make a meaningful—though imperfect—contribution to the overall expansion of access to information in China," said Elliot Schrage, then vice president of Google Communications, as he attempted to rationalize the corporation's position.

China is the largest Internet user in the world with over 420 million people online and growing. Google made over $300 million there in 2009 and did not want to lose that market. In March 2010, Google promised never to censor its searches in China again. It initially redirected queries from the mainland to its uncensored service in Hong Kong. Then it developed a new site—www.google.cn, which allows users to perform uncensored searches by linking them to Hong Kong. It also threatened to abandon China rather than engage in censorship. Google is the second-largest Internet search engine in China behind Baidu. The Chinese government recognized the importance of the service and renewed Google's ICP license in July 2010.[8]

The government shut down the Google search engine again for twelve hours in November 2012 during the Communist Party's week-long National Congress. Some observers speculated that it was a test to ascertain the public's reaction to the move that might presage similar actions in the future. Then, in late December 2012, the Standing Committee of the National People's Congress issued new rules that required Internet users to give their real names to service providers. Internet companies were required to delete forbidden postings and to report them to the authorities.

Shortly before the implementation of these new rules the websites of the *New York Times* and Bloomberg were blocked to prevent the public from learning about corruption in the government. The *New York Times* reported that the Chinese government was especially focused on limiting information on Virtual Private Networks (VPNs), which are used by individuals to protect against government and state-owned business attempts to pry into their communications.[9]

Conservative Islamic countries like Saudi Arabia also censor material. They block access to websites deemed offensive to what they interpret as Islamic cultural and political and moral values. The United Arab Emirates announced in August 2010 that the government intended to block features on the popular BlackBerry smartphone because it could not adequately monitor transmissions. This prevents users from accessing their email and the Web. The stated purpose of the government's action, which took effect on October 11, 2010, was for security reasons. The government of Saudi Arabia announced it would follow suit. [10]

Today, over a third of the world's population is using the Internet, creating an enormous potential to spread ideas and change culture. Technology poses challenges to the political and cultural stability of closed societies. It threatens to disrupt them by infusing information on an unparalleled scale. From radios to cell phones and other handheld electronic devices, from televisions to computers, symbols of secularism bombard the consciousness of young and old in a nonstop barrage of words and images. [11] This stream of information has drawbacks. On the one hand, it is capable of informing and liberating; on the other hand, it panders materialism that may be perceived as a perverse, even sacrilegious, attack on traditional values.

THE LONG ARM OF TECHNOLOGY

Despite Gil Scott-Heron's warning in his 1974 song "The Revolution Will Not Be Televised," and the documentary of the same name about the brief ouster of the late Venezuelan President Hugo Chavez in 2002 by Irish filmmakers Kim Bartley and Donnacha O'Briain, revolutions, as well as every other facet of human interaction, are being recorded and televised today. In fact, WikiLeaks and similar Internet sites are demonstrating that very little information—government, corporate, and personal—is private or secret.

"We were just two guys with an out-of-date, tiny server. For the first time, I realized that we could stand up to anyone in the world," wrote Daniel Domscheit-Berg, former associate of Julian Assange, the founder of WikiLeaks. [12] Revelations about illicit corporate and government activities posted on the WikiLeaks site, most notably information pertaining to United States foreign policy decisions in Iraq, rocked the world. They revealed the machinations conducted in the inner sanctums of corporate boardrooms and government offices. [13]

The implication of technological outing of corporate and diplomatic secrets goes beyond specific revelations, for as Domscheit-Berg noted, "When I finally did realize how few people really were involved, my sense of being invaluable grew. And it motivated me to think that so few people could set such great things in motion." [14] Whether for personal gain, revenge, notoriety, patriotism, or treason, the Information Age is becoming the Dissemination Age. Through technology the people of the world are gaining access to knowledge, current events, culture, and one another. Domscheit-Berg contended that he and Assange leaked privileged information for altruistic reasons:

> What connected Julian and me was the belief in a better world. In the world we dreamed of, there would be no more bosses or hierarchies, and no one could achieve power by withholding from the others the knowledge needed to act as an equal player. That was the idea for which we fought. It was the project that we started together and watched grow with enormous pride. [15]

In the Age of Dissemination human interaction is becoming unnecessary as a method of gathering information. A variety of technological gadgets are used to gather and diffuse information of the most sensitive type, often without knowledge of those affected. Facebook, with over one billion participants, and other social media services, as well as commercial sites such as eBay and Craigslist, have the capacity to track the addresses of users as well as their preferences, browsing behavior, past purchases, contact information, and identity.

Handheld electronic devices such as phones were used to televise social unrest in the Middle East during 2011–2012, natural disasters in Chile and Japan, as well as police brutality in the United States and other nations. They also have the ability to provide information on the user's identity and location.

Even though industry and government have assured users their privacy will be protected, there are no iron-clad guarantees of that. As long as fear, greed, and the pursuit of power motivate some people, the Dissemination Age will facilitate the intrusion of third parties into private lives. This will create a challenge to freedom using the free flow of information against the very people it was meant to liberate.

A recent report in the *New York Times* revealed that cell phone carriers responded to 1.3 million demands for subscriber information in 2011 from law enforcement agencies seeking a variety of information ranging from text messages, caller locations, and other personal user information. Edward Markey, U.S. Congressman from Massachusetts, who requested the information from nine carriers was shocked. "I never expected it to be so massive." He feared that "we've already crossed the line" in compromising the privacy of many customers. AT&T reported an average of seven hundred requests a day, triple the number it received in 2007. Sprint reported averaging 1,500 requests a day. Law enforcement requests have been rising at the rate of 12 to 16 percent annually in the last five years. [16]

Even without such devices our privacy is at risk. Sophisticated tracking and listening machines can photograph and record our every move from satellites in space or drones circling above. Already closed-circuit cameras are becoming as ubiquitous as pigeons in some cities. The United Kingdom is thought to be the leader in their use. Estimates put their number at about 1.85 million private devices, with an additional 33,433 cameras used by local authorities and 115,000 used by the transit police.[17]

One report noted that public authorities in London had, by 2007, spent over 200 million pounds ($300 million) on 12,000 cameras in high-crime traffic areas. But 80 percent of the crimes were still unsolved—the same proportion as neighborhoods without them.[18] A study of the use of surveillance cameras in San Francisco reported that they did not reduce violent crime. This questions the rationale for using them for that purpose. They did reduce property crimes, burglary and larceny, over two years by 24 percent in areas within one hundred feet of the cameras.[19]

Technological innovations hold the promise of increasing the flow of information in societies around the world, potentially leading to democratization. They can also restrict freedom and foment conflict through clashes among cultures. The negative impact that technology has on society is amplified under real or perceived internal and external pressures for social change. For example, terrorist threats or actions can have a chilling effect on freedom of movement and privacy.

This scenario materialized in the United States as a reaction to the September 11, 2001, attacks. The passage and reauthorization of the Foreign Intelligence Surveillance Act (FISA) of 1978, the Patriot Act of 2001, and the National Defense Authorization Act allow monitoring of correspondence and phone calls, detention of suspected terrorists and accomplices, and trials without full disclosure of evidence and knowledge of one's accusers. These actions conflict with Constitutional safeguards. Defenders of such practices note the necessity for preempting future attacks on the United States by clandestine terrorist groups such as al-Qaeda.

The American Civil Liberties Union (ACLU) has been an outspoken critic of attempts to diminish individual rights bestowed by the Constitution of the United States. A recent ACLU analysis of government surveillance in that country revealed that the Federal Bureau of Investigation (FBI) has increased its use of National Security Letters. These allow the government to obtain a wealth of information on people without a warrant. It was also found that the FBI is using census data to map minority communities for surveillance, e.g., Muslims in Detroit, Chinese and Russian Americans in San Francisco, African-Americans in rural Georgia, based on race, ethnicity, national origin, and religion.

> Since 9/11, protections against domestic spying developed post-Watergate have been blasted full of loopholes. FBI guidelines now allow preliminary investigations called "assessment"—which can include physical surveillance, informants, high-pressure interviews, commercial database searches, and subpoenas for phone and e-mail information—on the basis of nothing more than an agent's unsubstantiated hunch. The FBI conducted over 80,000 assessments in a two-year period, with fewer than 5 percent yielding any basis to justify further inves-

tigation. The FBI also issued 143,074 NSLs [National Security Letters] over a two-year period—potentially obtaining the private data of millions of Americans that is accessible to librarians, telecommunications providers, and Internet service providers—without a single terrorism prosecution to show for its efforts. And the FBI can retain all the personal information it collects indefinitely.[20]

The conundrum the government and population face in the United States and elsewhere is linked to the prospect of terrorist success. The vast majority of inquiries and investigations appear to be unnecessary. But the public does not know the exact number of investigations and terrorist plots that were preempted because such information is too sensitive to release. Nevertheless, testimony on June 18, 2013, by Gen. Kenneth Alexander, director of the National Security Agency, revealed that fifty attacks were aborted with the help of intrusive investigative techniques.[21] It only takes one successful attack to wreak havoc on society, undermining government authority, credibility, the economy, and public confidence.

This position was recently made by President Obama following revelations about the widespread mining of Internet and phone communications by the National Security Agency's PRISM program: "You can't have 100 percent security and also have 100 percent privacy and zero inconvenience. We're going to have to make some choices as a society" (June 7, 2013). Since 2007, PRISM has collected information on millions of people in the United States and other countries through surveillance of Apple, Google, and Facebook servers. Another program, MAINWAY, has been used by the U.S. government to collect telephone information on millions of Americans. Both programs were revealed by former National Security Agency contractor Edward Snowden in 2013.

The U.S. public has consistently chosen increased government surveillance over confidentiality. A 2007 public opinion poll found 71 percent acquiescent. A national poll was conducted after the PRISM revelation by the PEW Research Center for the People and the Press. Released on June 10, 2013, 62 percent of respondents said it was important for the federal government to investigate possible terrorist threats, even if it intrudes on personal privacy. Only 32 percent disagreed.

Even more distressing was the column by Charles Blow[22] that reported four out of ten Americans favor expanded camera surveillance in public places and the use of facial-recognition technology to scan for suspected terrorists at public events.

After reviewing the literature on this issue, various distinguished study groups concluded that public opinion in the United States was becoming less accepting of government surveillance as time passed from the 9/11 attacks, but "most people are more tolerant of surveillance *when it is aimed at specific racial or ethnic groups,* when it concerns activities they do not engage in, or when they are not focusing on its potential personal impact. We note that people are not concerned about privacy in general, but rather with protecting the privacy of information about themselves."[23]

That Americans are more favorably disposed to accept surveillance of minority groups is cause for consternation. Stereotypical conceptions of "the other" as deviants harkens back to the mid-1800s when the pseudoscience of phrenology was used to identify potential criminals.[24]

The London riots in the summer of 2011 generated thirty-six million minutes of video, captured by 8,000 closed circuit television cameras.[25] Without the aid of computerized scanning programs searching for preselected characteristics the authorities might still be reviewing them. Even more pause for concern may be the number of youths who perpetrated crimes and were overlooked because they did not fit the preselected stereotypes.

The public should be alarmed, for, as security expert Bruce Schneier noted, "We are entering the era of wholesale surveillance."[26] Ominously, Jay Stanley of the ACLU believes "We are heading toward a total-surveillance society in which your every move, your every interaction, is duly registered and recorded by some computer."[27]

WHY TECHNOLOGY THREATENS THE STATUS QUO

The infusion of technology into homogeneous cultures is like the flow of water over Niagara Falls—a rush of images and ideas that cannot be suppressed. They wend their way into every nook and cranny of our lives, leaving memories with the potential to tear the fabric of society. In their attempt to maintain control over their followers and subjects, political and religious leaders may feel compelled to close ranks and embrace antimodernist values. They shun or misuse the very technology that could improve the quality of their lives.

No doubt the thousands of school/seminaries known as Madrassas in Pakistan, India, Afghanistan, and the Middle East have contributed to anti-Western, antimodernity sentiment among segments of the Muslim population. Funded by oil-rich Saudi Arabia, at times linked to al-Qaeda, many of these schools embrace a Salafist, Wahhabist fundamentalism that appeals to disenfranchised illiterate youth. Critics contend they preach a distorted form of Islam that leads to militancy and violence. Such institutions have influenced the Taliban and pose a threat to the world.[28]

On the other hand, Westerners should consider the impact their culture may be having on people in developing nations. What they assume to be enriching and liberating may be interpreted as an assault on the beliefs and culture of others. Rejection of Western values and technology should not be interpreted as a rejection of Westerners. It may be a rational attempt to preserve one's culture and traditions in the face of a perceived threat to change it.

Journalist Robin Wright contends that the burgeoning youth population of these countries is attempting to bridge traditional Islamic religious values and Western secularism. The large number of youth and their high under- and unemployment, combined with despotic rulers and rampant poverty, provided the impetus for the Arab Spring of 2011. Labeling them Generation U, she observed, "The Muslim young under age thirty who were unfilled, unincluded, underemployed or underutilized, and underestimated . . . have been thoroughly unhappy with the status quo. And they are totally into YouTube."[29]

The reference to the popularity of YouTube and the use of other forms of social media among youth in Islamic countries testifies to the ubiquity of telecommunications. But this phenomenon is not restricted to the Middle East. It is stretching across the face of the planet. It envelops the youth of all nations in a spider-like web of information and promises. It draws them into an electronic universe with impermeable boundaries that transcend chauvinism and nationalism, threatening theological fundamentalism.

The revolution of the streets was preceded by the revolution of technology. It is being followed by the revolution of rising expectations—the clamor for materialism and democracy. The right to use, consume, and dispose of things, people and ideas as they will, regardless of efforts to preserve traditional cultures and political systems.

We would be remiss if we ignored the prevalent condescending smugness that characterizes the West's view of developing nations, especially the presumed backwardness of Middle Eastern Islamic societies. The possessor of superior technology is not necessarily the repository of moral superiority. As the United States pressures Iran to forego the development of nuclear weapons, we should not forget that it is, to this date, the only nation that ever used them on another.

FUNDAMENTALISM: A TALE OF TWO CULTURES

Picture, if you will, a large-scale society with millions of people representing many different cultures. This society has a long history of democratic institutions steeped in the rule of law that protects the rights of minorities from political and social abuse. People move about freely, interact in public and private without restrictions. They are free to practice their religious beliefs as they wish. But the people of this society are under pressure from fundamentalist religious groups who spend large sums of money to influence public opinion and gain political power—and not without success.

Public opinion polls reveal the people in this country are socially conservative and scientifically naïve. Only slightly more than a third subscribe to Darwin's theory of evolution, with little more than half even knowing about his contribution to science. In fact, only 15 percent believe humans evolved without God's intervention. Nearly half believe that humans were created by God in their present form. Perhaps this is related to the fact that the people there are very religious, more so than any other industrialized nation. Eight out of every ten of them are absolutely certain there is a God. Six out of ten are sure there is a heaven. About half the population is certain there is life after death, and a similar number believe there is a hell.

Among the most religious residents of this society, less than 2 percent believe that human beings developed over millions of years from less advanced forms of life. Indeed, over three-fourths of these people reject the very concept of evolution. They believe that God created human beings less than 10,000 years ago. This belief is even shared by 16 percent of the least religious there. Nearly nine in ten of the residents believe in miracles and 31 percent think witches exist.

Western media portray Islamic societies as backward havens of remorseless fundamental heathens. But abundant evidence casts doubt on the intellectual level of discourse in so-called technologically advanced societies. The above figures are actual numbers derived from surveys of people in the United States.[30]

THE POLITICIZATION OF RELIGION

It is no secret that people in the United States have been engaged for many years in a cultural war between religious conservative fundamentalists and secular humanists, mainline believers, agnostics, and atheists.[31] On issues of premarital sex; abortion; contraception; sex education; LGBT rights; educational curricula; prayer in public places; the government's role in taxation; the delivery of health care; assistance for the poor, disabled, elderly, and children; and a host of other social issues, there is profound disagreement as to approaches and solutions.

A report by the PEW Foundation on religious lobbies in the United States revealed that 212 religiously oriented groups spent $390 billion lobbying Congress in 2008–2009. The largest amount by far was spent by the pro-Israeli American Israel Public Affairs Committee, AIPAC ($88 million), followed by the U.S. Conference of Catholic Bishops ($26.6 million), the conservative Family Research Council ($14.2 million), the American Jewish Committee ($13.3 million), Concerned Women of America ($12.5 million), Bread for the World ($11.3 million), National Right to Life Committee ($11.3 million), the Home School Legal Defense Fund ($11.3 million), Citizen Link (associated with the conservative group Focus on the Family) ($10.8 million), the Traditional Values Coalition ($9.5 million), and the National Organization for Marriage ($8.6 million).

The top spenders were primarily conservative groups and collectively spent $64 million in an effort to influence legislation and public opinion.[32] While Jewish groups outspent such organizations, their focus was primarily on influencing foreign, as opposed to domestic, policy.

In 2009, evangelicals and Roman Catholics joined forces to issue the Manhattan Declaration. It asked the U.S. government to adopt conservative theological views on social issues. The initiative was led by recently deceased convicted felon of Watergate fame Charles Colson. He once warned participants at an Atlanta conference for the Association of Classical and Christian Schools that today's evangelicals were becoming moderate and guilty of "worshipping at the alter of the bitch goddess of tolerance." The document has been described as "an effort to draw a line in the sand against the surging tides of secularism and the growing hostility in many quarters toward Christianity, and to defend religious freedom for all persons of faith."[33]

Journalist Rachel Tabachnik has been chronicling the war for the souls of Americans being waged by fundamentalist Christian "Dominion" groups. They believe that evangelical Christians must gain control over these critical sectors of society: government, education, the media, arts and entertainment, the family, business, and religion in order to establish a "proper" Christian reign in the United States and prepare for the coming of the Messiah. Also known as the New Apostolic Reformation, with affiliates in all fifty states, followers of this movement believe that the Earth is controlled by Satan and demons and it is necessary to conduct spiritual warfare to remove them.[34]

These groups advocate anti-intellectual theories about science such as creationism and intelligent design that reject Darwin's theory of evolution and fly in the face of modern DNA research. They actively promote school vouchers and homeschooling for their own children to avoid secular influences on the one-dimensional perspective they use to indoctrinate them. The National center for Education Statistics estimates there were 1.5 million homeschooled children in the United States in 2007, and their number has been increasing steadily to over two million in 2010.[35]

Not all of these children are being schooled in religious fundamentalism. But it is safe to assume that a significant number of them are, since many of their parents are reluctant to have their children in the more secular public school environment. A survey of homeschooling parents conducted by the National Homeschooling Education Research Institute revealed that 83 percent homeschooled their children so they could provide religious and moral instruction to them. Nearly nine out of ten parents said they were concerned about the public school environment, and approximately three-quarters said they were dissatisfied with other schools.[36]

Considering children who are educated in private religious schools gives us another indication of the influence that conservative Christian religious organizations have in our society. There are 33,366 private schools in the United States, one-fourth of all schools. Ten percent of all children in the United States attend them. Eighty percent of these private schools are religiously affiliated, and 82 percent are Christian. In the 2009–2010 academic year, Catholic schools enrolled 43 percent of private school students, followed by 15 percent in conservative Christian schools, 5 percent in Baptist schools, 4 percent in Lutheran, 2 percent in Episcopalian, 1 percent in Seventh Day Adventist, and about half a percent each in Calvinist and Friends schools. Jewish student enrollment accounted for 5 percent, and nonsectarian enrollment was 14 percent.[37]

For the record, it is worth noting that, overall, private school students outperform public school students at all levels of the National Assessment of Educational Performance standardized tests (the Nation's Report Card) including math, science, reading, writing, civics, and history. It should also be noted that private school students' demographics do not reflect those of the public school population. There is an underrepresentation of children of color and a lower percentage of students enrolled in private schools who live in poverty. Black and Latino enrollment in private schools in 2009 accounted for 18 percent, compared to 38 percent in public schools, and their rate of poverty is considerably higher than white students.[38]

The thin veil of presumed Western intellectual and technological superiority fades in light of such findings. Yet, fundamentalist movements continue to create problems around the world. When author Salman Rushdie published his *Satanic Verses* novel in 1988 with unflattering characterizations of Islam and Muhammad, it caused a furor in the Muslim world. The late Ayatollah Ruhollah Khomeini of Iran called for his execution.[39]

The publication of twelve cartoons depicting the Prophet Muhammad in various disparaging poses by the Danish newspaper *Jyllands-Posten* ignited a firestorm of protest among Muslims. Churches and embassies were burned, and two hundred people died. Rioting in February 2012 in Afghanistan over the burning of Qur'ans led to the deaths of six NATO servicemen and thirty Afghans.

Such demonstrations confirm the link between religious and political objectives as they morph into anti-American sentiment.[40] They reveal the emerging impact that telecommunications are having around the world as disparate cultures and peoples collide. Even more disturbing were the demonstrations in more than thirty countries in September 2012 as Muslims protested an amateurishly produced portrayal of the Prophet Muhammad as a womanizer and pedophile.

The complexity of this case was rarely explained to the American public, which was misled into believing that the principal source of the conflict was the film "The Innocence of Muslims." In fact, the film was a vehicle for the expression of decades of discontent among unemployed and underemployed individuals. Many of them had been struggling to create new democratic institutions and wrestling with the concepts of free speech and freedom of expression.

True enough, many Muslims were insulted by the film. Their outrage was fueled by Western support for dictatorial, repressive regimes in return for rights to exploit oil and other natural resources in their homelands. Misunderstandings over legal and cultural standards governing speech between predominantly Muslim and Western nations also existed. We may never know the extent to which terrorist groups manipulated these demonstrations to fuel anti-American dissent.

While these incidents cause Westerners to recoil, it should not be forgotten that similar expressions of outrage have occurred in the West. Literary productions, such as Rolf Hochhuth's 1963 play "The Deputy," which alleged Pope Pius XII's anti-Semitism and sympathy with the Nazis, precipitated protests and generated discussion about the legitimacy of the allegations.[41]

When Martin Scorsese adapted Nikos Kazantzakis's 1955 book, *The Last Temptation of Christ*, into a movie of the same name in 1988, Universal Studios was deluged with petitions and phone calls threatening reprisals and pleading for the movie's removal. Kazantakis was excommunicated by the Greek Orthodox Church, and the Roman Catholic Church banned the book.

Conservative Christian groups in the United States also railed against the production. Bill Bright, then head of the Campus Crusade for Christ, offered to reimburse Universal Studios for its investment in exchange for all existing prints, which he promised to destroy. Twenty-five thousand people from religious groups in Orange County, California, protested against the movie at Universal's headquarters in Los Angeles. Edwards Theaters refused to show the movie at its 150 locations, and United Artists' and General Cinemas' combined 3,500 theaters declined to air it.

The film was actually banned in a number of cities, including Savannah, New Orleans, Oklahoma City, and Santa Ana. Demonstrations occurred around the world, and protestors in Paris hurled Molotov cocktails inside the Saint Michel Theater, injuring thirteen people. The leader of a Roman Catholic group who opposed the film commented, "We will not hesitate to go to prison if it is necessary."[42]

Although critically acclaimed, the movie was not financially successful, grossing only $8.3 million. Even Blockbuster Video declined to carry it in its stores, bowing to public pressure. Protests against the film were reignited in the mid-1990s when it was aired nationally on Canadian and Russian television.[43]

More recently, controversy over Dan Brown's 2003 book, *The Da Vinci Code*, and Ron Howard's film adaptation of it in 2006 sparked worldwide criticism. Its plot centered on a conspiracy theory that Jesus was married to Mary Magdalene and fathered a daughter. Cited as blasphemous, the movie was criticized by the Roman Catholic Church, which depicted it as a sinister force suppressing supposed authentic facts about Jesus's life. It was banned in Manila and Chennai, India, and castigated by fundamentalists in the United States. It received mixed reviews but became a box-office winner, garnering over $200 million.

On the other hand, Mel Gibson's 2004 movie, *The Passion of the Christ*, which appealed to Christians, grossed $370.2 million in the United States and $611.8 million worldwide—the highest earnings of any independent film in history.

The preceding discussion reveals how sensitive the issue of religious freedom is and how the power of technology transmits and foments images of cultural conflict. Once again we see the influence that religion has on people around the world and the similarities of attitudes and behavior among the faithful. The expressed outrage over perceived offenses to one's religion is instructive. Threats and censorship have led to the curtailment of freedom of expression. The potential for renewed attacks on unpopular perspectives persists.

The world of the twenty-first century is destined to witness an increase in the spread of ideas that threaten the establishment. The flow of information is inexorable. With it come conflict, accommodation, and change. We must try to understand why people feel so strongly about such things. It is important to know how their sensibilities can be addressed in a world where information flows freely and cultures regularly interact and collide. We must create an environment that at once values "the other," is nonthreatening, nonjudgmental, and inclusive. That is the subject of the final chapter in mankind's journey.

SUMMING UP

- The "clash of civilizations" or conflict among nations is the result of cultural differences and competition for resources.
- Immigration and technological innovations are bringing people from diverse cultures into greater contact with one another.
- It is impossible to reverse the increase in migration and technology.
- The nature of societies around the world are being transformed by immigration, travel, and technology.
- Technology can help educate and break down myths and stereotypes about strangers.

1. For a discussion of technology, social change, and cultural lag, see William F. Ogburn, *Social Change*, revised ed. (New York: Viking, 1950.)

2. For a further discussion of Rock's dilemma, see Malcolm Gladwell, "John Rock's Error," *New Yorker*, March 13, 2000, 52–63, and Loretta McLaughlin, *The Pill, John Rock, and the Church: The Biography of a Revolution* (Boston: Little, Brown, 1983). See also Rock's case for using the pill in his book *The Time Has Come: A Catholic Doctor's Proposal to End the Battle over Birth Control* (New York: Alfred A. Knopf, 1963).

3. Rachel K. Jones, *Beyond Birth Control: The Overlooked Benefits of Oral Contraception Pills* (New York: Guttmacher Institute, 2011).

4. "Birth Control," Mayo Clinic.com, July 21, 2010, http://www.mayoclinic.com/health/birth-control-pill/wo00098/nsectiongroup=2.

5. "Facts and Figures," United Nations World Tourism Organization, 2011 edition, www.unwto.org/facts.

6. "Key Global Telecom Indicators for the World Telecommunications Service Sector," International Telecommunications Union, accessed November 29, 2011, http://www.itu.int/ITU-D/ict/statistics/at_glance/KeyTelecom.html.

7. Robin Wright, *Rock the Casbah* (New York: Simon & Schuster, 2011), 18, 21.

8. "Google vs. China, Sequel," *New York Times*, editorial, July 1, 2010, http://www.nytimes.com/2010/07/02/opinion/02fri3.html; John D. Sutter, "Tech 101:What You Need to Know About Google vs. China," CNN SciTechBlog, March 24, 2010, http://scitech.blogs.cnn.com/category/china/.

9. Keith Bradshaw, "China Toughens Its Restrictions and Use of Internet," *New York Times*, December 28, 2012, http://www.nytimes.com/2012/12/29/world/asia/china-tough.

10. Adam Schreck, "United Arab Emirates to Block Key Features on BlackBerrys,"*Washington Post*, August 2, 2010, http://www.washingtonpost.com/wp-dyn/content/article/2010/08/01/AR2010080103087.html/?hpid=to. On April 23, 2012, President Barack Obama announced sanctions to be imposed on foreign nationals who use new technologies (e.g., cell phone tracking and Internet monitoring) to abuse human rights, noting, "These technologies should be in place to empower citizens, not to repress them" (Scott Wilson, "In Holocaust Memorial Visit, Obama Outlines Policies Aimed at Preventing Genocide," *Washington Post*, April 23, 2012, http://www.washingtonpost.com/politics/obama-announces).

11. See Benjamin Barber, *Jihad vs. McWorld* (New York: Ballantine Books, 1996).

12. Daniel Domscheit-Berg, *Inside WikiLeaks*, trans. Jefferson Chase (London: Jonathan Cape, 2011), 32.

13. For a fascinating glimpse at the consequences of these leaks on Latin America, see the collection of articles on this topic in the *Nation*, vol. 295, nos. 7 and 8, August 13/20, 2012.

14. Domscheit-Berg, *Inside WikiLeaks*, 24.

15. Ibid., 4. Private Bradley Manning, the source of the massive leak of sensitive U.S. diplomatic information, was held for nine months in solitary confinement in the Marine Corps brig in Quantico, Virginia. On February 28, 2013, he pled guilty to ten of the charges against him that carry a possible twenty-year sentence. The military intended to continue with its prosecution of him under the Espionage Act, calling 141 witnesses. Manning's trial began on June 3, 2013, in Ft. Meade, Maryland. On August 21, 2013, he was sentenced to thirty-five years in prison.

16. Eric Lichtblau, "More Demands on Cell Carriers in Surveillance," *New York Times*, July 8, 2012, http://www.nytimes.com/2012/07/09/us/cell-carriers-see-uptick-in-requests-to-aid-surveillance. For a discussion of the issues concerning the use and abuse of the Internet and telecommunications, see Rebecca MacKinnon, *Consent of the Networked: The Worldwide Struggle for Internet Freedom* (New York: Basic Books, 2012).

17. Tom Reeve, "How Many Cameras in the UK? Only 1.85 million Claims ACPO Lead on CCTV," *Security News Desk*, March 2011, http://www.securitynewsdesk.com/2011/03/01/how-many-cctv-cameras-in-the-uk/.

18. Justin Davenport, "Tens of Thousands of CCTV Cameras, Yet 80 percent of Crime Unsolved," *London Evening Standard*, September 9, 2007, http://www.

thisislondon.co.uk/news/article-23412867–tens-of-thousands-of-cctv-cameras-yet-80–of-crime-unsolved.do.

19. David Kravets, "Report: U.S. Surveillance Society Running Rampant," *Wired*, January 12, 2009, http://www.wired.com/threatlevel/2009/01/us-surveillance/.

20. Susan N. Herman, "Who's Watching the Watcher?" *Civil Liberties*, American Civil Liberties National Newsletter, Winter 2012, 6–7. Also see E. D. Kain's critique of the National Defense Authorization Act legislation, "President Obama Signed the National Defense Authorization Act—Now What?" *Forbes*, January 2, 2012, http://www.forbes.com/sites/erikkain/2012/01/02/president-o.

21. For a discussion of these issues, see Jonathan Schell, "The Surveillance Net," *Nation*, July 8/15, 2013, 3–4, 6, and Marcy Wheeler, "Trust Us," *Nation*, July 8/15, 2013, 6, 8.

22. Charles Blow, "Slippery Slope of Losing Liberty," *Tampa Bay Times*, June 11, 2013, 9A.

23. Committee on Technical and Privacy Dimensions of Information for Terrorism Prevention and Other National Goals and National Research Council, *Protecting Individual Privacy in the Struggle against Terrorists: A Framework for Program Assessment* (Washington, DC: National Academies Press, 2008), 284. Italics added.

24. See, for instance, Franz Joseph Gall and Johann Gaspar Spurzheim, *Phrenology and the Moral Influence of Phrenology* (Philadelphia: Carey, Lea, and Blanchard, 1835), and George Combe, *A System of Phrenology* (Boston: B.B. Mussey, 1851).

25. Rebecca Rosen, "London Riots, Big Brother Watches: CCTV Cameras Blanket the UK," *Atlantic*, August 9, 2011, http://www.theatlantic.com/technology/archive/2011/08/london-riots-big-brother-watches-cctv-cameras-blanket-the-uk/243356/.

26. Quoted in James Vlahos, "Surveillance Society: New High-Tech Cameras Are Watching You," *Popular Mechanics*, October 1, 2009, http://www.popularmechanics.com/technology/military/4236.

27. Ibid.

28. See the interview with the late Ambassador Richard Holbrooke and Vali Nasr, an authority on Islamic fundamentalism, "Analysis Madrasses," *Frontline*, PBS, accessed Feruary 17, 2012, http://www.pbs.org/wgbh/pages/frontline/shows/saudi/analyses/madrassas.html.

29. Wright, *Rock the Casbah*, 91. See pp. 124–126 for data on unemployment in Middle Eastern nations.

30. For information on the numbers of people in the United States who embrace Darwin's ideas about evolution, see "Poll Finds More Americans Believe in Devil than Darwin," *Reuters*, November 29, 2007, http://www.reuters.com/article/2007/11/29/us-usa-religion-beliefs-idusn2922875820071129, and the recent Gallup public opinion poll, along with comparative longitudinal analyses, conducted during May 3–6, 2012, http://www.gallup.com/poll/21814/evolution-creationism-int. Information on religious beliefs and practices of people in the United States can be obtained in the Faith Matters survey reported in Robert D. Putnam and David E. Campbell, *American Grace: How Religion Divides and Unites Us* (New York: Simon & Schuster, 2010).

31. The Faith Matters representative survey of 3,108 people in the United States found 17 percent of the population claimed no religion. See Putnam and Campbell, *American Grace*, 16.

32. "Lobbying for the Faithful: Religious Advocacy Groups in Washington, D.C.," PEW Forum on Religion and Public Life, PEW Research Center, November 21, 2011, http://www.PEWforum.org/lobbying-religious-advocacy-groups-in-washington-dc.aspx?src=prc-headline.

33. *Church and State* 64 no. 6, (2011), 19–20.

34. "The Evangelicals Engaged in Spiritual Warfare," National Public Radio, August 24, 2011, http://www.npr.org/2011/08/24/139781021/the-evangelicals-engaged-in-spiritual-warfare.

35. National Center for Education Statistics, Institute of Education Sciences, accessed February 16, 2012, http://nces.ed.gov/fastfacts/display.asp?id=91. Brian D. Ray,

"Research Facts on Homeschooling," National Home Education Research Institute, January 11, 2011, http://www.nheri/content/view/199/.

36. Janice Lloyd, "Homeschooling Grows," *USA Today*, January 5, 2009, http://www.usatoday.com/news/education/2009–01–04–homeschooling_N.htm.

37. "Private School Statistics at a Glance," Council for American Private Education, accessed February 16, 2012, http://www.capenet.org/facts.html.

38. "Private School Enrollment," National Center for Education Statistics, Institute of Education Sciences, accessed February 16, 2012, http://nces.ed.gov/programs/coe/indicator_pri.asp; "Children Under 18 Years Living in Poverty, 1959–2010," Institute for Research on Poverty, http://www.irp.wsc.edu/faqs/faq6.htm; Sophia Addy and Vanessa R. Wright, "Basic Facts about Low-income Children, 2010," National Center for Children in Poverty, accessed February 16, 2012, http://nccp.org/publication/pub_/049.htm.

39. Salman Rushdie, *The Satanic Verses* (New York: Picador, 2000).

40. For a review of the Rushdie saga, see Andrew Anthony, "How One Book Ignited a Culture War," *Observer*, January 10, 2009, http://www.guardian.co.uk/books/2009/jan/11/sa/man-rushdie-satanic-verses. See also Patricia Cohen's piece and the sampling of articles about the Danish controversy in "Danish Cartoon Controversy," *New York Times*, August 12, 2009, http://topics.nytimes.com/topics/reference/timestopics/subjects/d/danish_cartoon_controversy/index.html.

41. See, for example, Eric Bentley's collection of essays, *The Storm over the Deputy* (New York: Grove Press, 1964).

42. Steven Greenhouse, "Police Suspect Arson in Fire at Paris Theater," *New York Times*, October 25, 1988, http://www.nytimes.com/1988/10/25/movies/police-suspect-arson-in-fire-at-paris-theater.html.

43. "Martin Scorsese's *The Last Temptation of Christ*," Theater, Film, Video on PBS, http://www.pbs.org/wgbh/cultureshock/flashpoints/theater/lasttemptation.html.

NINE
How You Can Make Reunification a Reality

The great faiths provide meaning and purpose for their adherents. The question is: can they make space for those who are not its adherents, who sing a different song, hear a different music, tell a different story? On that question, the fate of the twenty-first century may turn.
—Jonathan Sacks, *The Dignity of Difference*

Teachers have an obligation to kindle the spirit of inquiry in every student, to inform, enrich, and nourish their academic and intellectual growth by making them aware of social inequality at home and abroad and helping them commit to justice and equality.

VIEWING THE BIG PICTURE

An appropriate final chapter to this book might be couched in terms of what we have learned on our journey, or more importantly, what we have accomplished. Mankind's rendezvous with destiny has not yet happened. We do not know what that destiny will be. All of the preceding discussion has been an attempt to identify historical and contemporary trends that brought us this far on our way.

We have seen how some of our ancestors left the motherland in search of food and adventure. Branching out into uncharted territories, they huddled together and developed cultures that gave them distinct ethnic identities. Differences in pigmentation, facial, and other physiological characteristics occurred over thousands of years as the groups adapted to their new environments.

Adaptations were evolutionary changes that aided the survival of the group. These changes were minor in relation to the complex organism we

187

know as *Homo sapiens*. There is only one race of humans on this planet. They are social animals preferring to live in groups for protection and collaboration. But mankind's history has been marked by interminable conflict over social, psychological, and physiological differences that are, in the big picture, insignificant. Yet, these differences precipitated conflict that has enveloped the world. With modern technology, the very existence of the species and all others on this planet are endangered.

The modern age has brought a healthier, more comfortable life to some, but at what price? The growing disparity of wealth is creating a vast underclass of people unable to participate in the abundance that technology has brought. Even more ominous is the prospect of increased conflict between the haves and have-nots. As aspirations and expectations grow, people from different cultural backgrounds are exposed to new ideas through telecommunications and transportation.

Humanity cannot afford to ignore the plight of the poor and dispossessed. Disparities in wealth, education, health, and housing within and among nations are increasing. Three billion people live on less than $2.50 a day. Over 80 percent of the people on this planet live on less than $10 a day. The wealthiest 20 percent of the world's population accounts for three-fourths of the world's consumption. The poorest 20 percent accounts for just 1.5 percent. According to UNICEF, 24,000 children die each day because of poverty-related issues.

Just 12 percent of the world's population uses 85 percent of its water, and they don't live in developing countries. Over 1.5 billion people live without electricity. The gross domestic product of the forty-one heavily indebted poor countries, with a combined population of 567 million people, is less than the wealth of the world's *seven richest people combined*. Less than 1 percent of what the world spends every year on weapons could educate every child on the planet.[1]

Realizing the plight of mankind and the gap between the rich and poor, the United Nations convened the Millennium Summit in New York City on September 9, 2000. Attended by heads of state and government from 189 countries, they signed a document called the Millennium Declaration. It established eight goals and eighteen targets containing forty-eight technical indicators of progress toward the goals set for 2015. The event was the largest gathering of world leaders in history.

The document was adopted by the World Bank, the International Monetary Fund, and the Organization for Economic Cooperation and Development. The major focus of the goals is the alleviation of poverty, including hunger and disease, and the provision of adequate shelter, gender equality, education, and environmental sustainability.[2]

The declaration also called for extending basic human rights to all people:

1. Eradicate extreme hunger and poverty

2. Achieve universal primary education
3. Promote gender equality and empower women
4. Reduce child mortality
5. Improve maternal health
6. Combat HIV/AIDS, malaria and other diseases
7. Ensure environmental sustainability
8. Develop global partnerships for development

A second summit to assess progress was attended by 170 heads of state and government. It was held under the auspices of the United Nations in New York City from September 14–16, 2005. In 2010, a report card on the millennium development goals was issued by the Overseas Development Institute, a UK organization subsidized by the Bill and Melinda Gates Foundation. It noted that significant progress had been made in reducing extreme poverty and increasing basic health, education, water, and other essential services "unparalleled in many countries' histories." Some of the millennium development goals (MDGs) remained elusive, but the report noted that many developing countries were making progress, such as in reducing child mortality (the rate fell from 101 to 69 per 1,000 live births between 1990 and 2007) and in increasing access to maternal health services by 80 percent.[3]

The World Bank recently reported that significant progress had been made in reducing extreme poverty. Still, over 1.29 billion people lived that way in 2008, but this was a decrease from 1.94 billion in 1981. Preliminary data for 2010 revealed that the first MDG, reducing the number of people living in extreme poverty in 1990 by half, would be achieved prior to the 2015 deadline. Nevertheless, 43 percent of the people in developing countries still live on less than $2 a day.[4]

Clearly, if the people and nations of the world choose to collaborate they can accomplish amazing things. Yet, we have seen that ethnic and religious differences may impede progress toward noble objectives. If religion, as Rabbi Jonathan Sacks has noted, is not part of the solution, it will be part of the problem.

Even as this is being written, people are dying around the world as they struggle for freedom of religious expression. They are our genetic brothers and sisters, bound to us through the very DNA that brings us all life. Their desires are no different from ours—to live in peace and with dignity.

It is no longer possible to live in isolation from our kin, no matter how far away they may be. The challenges we face—population growth and immigration, technological innovation and cultural lag, racial and ethnic prejudice, ethnocentrism, and religious fundamentalism—are all human problems that must be addressed on a personal level. Men and women are social animals. No amount of technological innovation can change that fact of life. In the final analysis, we crave acceptance, recognition, and respect. We now turn to a discussion of how this can be accomplished.

UNDERSTANDING OUR MULTICULTURAL FUTURE

After the collapse of apartheid in South Africa, Bishop Desmond Tutu worked with Nelson Mandela to create truth and reconciliation hearings around the country, listening to the heart-rending testimony of victims of the previous white, racist regime. Accusers and accused poured out their stories of torture, abuse, and mayhem. All that was expected was honesty about their experiences. Forgiveness for even heinous crimes was granted if admissions were truthful. The most disarming gesture of the new black South African leadership was its magnanimity. Mandela himself, after being held in solitary confinement for twenty-seven years on Robben Island, forgave his captors, demonstrating the unique human ability to empathize and commiserate with his former enemies.

Selfless men like Mandela, Mahatma Gandhi, and Martin Luther King Jr. are rare. The pressure to gain hegemony over land, resources, and human capital are great. To be able to triumph over human foibles and the pull of materialism, we must learn to appreciate the differences in values, behavior, appearances, and culture that have arisen over the 60,000 years since some of our ancestors left Africa. We must be willing to challenge the myths and stereotypes that separate and divide us. We have to acknowledge that our way may not be suitable for everyone. Even seemingly irrational, senseless behavior has an origin that must be studied and understood. As Bishop Tutu remarked, "There will always be desperate people as long as we have conditions that make people desperate."

To begin with, we must recognize and accept the demographic facts of life about our world. This means that we must face the reality that the number of light-skinned people will continue to decline as a percentage of the world's population. Dark-skinned nations have a larger population base and higher fertility rates.

United Nations projections indicate that the world's population, given current rates of growth, will increase to 9.3 billion by mid-century. The map in figure 9.1 reveals that the countries with the highest fertility, those places where the average woman is having more than 1.5 daughters, are predominantly located in Africa. Thirty-nine of the fifty-five countries fall into this category.

Taking a medium projection of population growth, the UN estimates that the population in countries with high fertility will triple between 2011 and 2100, from 1.2 billion to 4.2 billion. On the other hand, low fertility growth countries found predominantly in Europe, China, Russia, Canada, and Australia, where women are not having enough children to ensure they will be replaced by a daughter, comprise 42 percent of the current world's population. Their population will decline from 2.9 billion to 2.4 billion people during this century.

Intermediate-fertility countries, including the United States, India, Indonesia, Bangladesh, Mexico, and Egypt, where each woman is having 1–1.5 daughters, currently account for 40 percent of the world's population. Given medium levels of growth, they will experience a population increase of 26 percent from 2.8 billion to 3.5 billion people.[5]

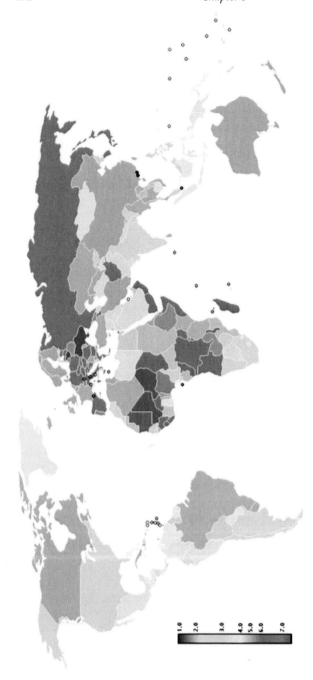

Figure 9.1.   Map of Fertility Rates of the World[6]

We have seen that immigration, tourism, and telecommunications are transmitting the culture and values of people throughout the world at an unprecedented level. We are experiencing an unremitting pushback against this unstoppable trend. Governments and religious and ethnic groups are scrambling to maintain their cultural identity, job opportunities, and share of the world's depleting resources.

European nations and the United States are struggling to fashion policies to deal with the influx of Muslim, African, Asian, and Latino immigrants. Their presence is perceived by some whites as anathema. This assault on social change is a rearguard attempt of historically white nations to turn back the demographic clock. But low-to-intermediate-growth countries will require immigrant labor in the coming decades to fill vacant jobs because of their low birth rates and aging population.

For most politicians and economists, stagnation is not an option. No growth or slow growth is a formula for political oblivion. The nature of contemporary societies with their production and consumption orientation emphasizes growth. If politicians do not level with their constituents about the necessity for conserving natural resources and controlled slow growth, the world will continue on a collision course with a sobering reality.

Four decades ago, the late economist E. F. Schumacher tried to establish a framework for a rational slow-growth society.[7] Then, as now, his views were regarded as heretical by some of his colleagues and politicians who remained ardent proponents of the consumption-production nexus with its materialistic ethos. Events have borne out the wisdom of his position, and movements espousing his ideas thrive around the world.

Even more sobering were his criticisms of the industrial age and the abuse of technology. He foresaw trends that perverted the activity of work by subordinating it to materialism. In his last book, *Good Work*, Schumacher proposed that people should reorder their priorities, eschew materialism, and redesign the nature and function of work so that it is more humanistic and fulfilling.[8] His message has resonated for decades. It reemerged in the Occupy Wall Street phenomenon that captured the imagination of idealists in the fall of 2011.

If the youthful exuberance waned from the early days of the Occupy Movement in Zucotti Park in New York City, the spirit of the movement has become a clarion call of the disenfranchised and alienated. They seek balance and rationality in their daily struggle to survive the rat race known as contemporary work.

Work as most people think of it today is a means to an end—a pejorative four-letter word. For many, it has lost its intrinsic capacity to offer satisfaction of higher level needs. It has become an instrument through which we obtain the means of escape and for which we willingly agree to relinquish our autonomy and creativity. Such an activity bullies people into compliance daily with organizational rules. It forces them into super-ficial relationships for the sake of obtaining rewards that are used to purchase satisfaction away from the job. It is inherently alienating and dehumanizing.

Contemporary work nurtures competition that fosters hedonism and materialism. It creates an environment where anti-immigration sentiment has found expression in the rise of political movements intent on preserv-ing the privilege of the few, mostly whites, over the needs of the many (mostly people of color). The call to nationalism is being sounded by demagogues around the world (e.g., the British National Party [BNP] led by Nick Griffin, Germany's National Democratic Party [NPD] led by Udo Voigt, France's National Front [FN] led by Jean Marie Le Pen, the Nether-lands' Freedom Party led by Geert Wilders, the Belgian National Front led by Patrick Cocraimont, Timo Soini of the Finnish True Finns Party, and Marton Gyongyosi of Hungary's Jobbik Party [Movement for a Bet-ter Hungary]).

Even Sweden experienced a rise in anti-immigrant sentiment follow-ing riots among immigrants in May, 2013. A majority of the residents of the country still support liberal immigration policies, but the rightist Sweden Democrats polled third in popularity following the riots. It is expected to fare well in the 2014 elections, increasing the stature of its leader, Jimmie Akesson.

Recent European parliamentary elections showed inroads into main-stream voters made by these and other anti-immigrant parties. As the world economic situation continues precariously, austerity measures im-posed by the World Bank, International Monetary Fund, and govern-ments are exacerbating tensions and inciting anti-immigrant hostility.[9] On March 31, 2012, a rally against Muslims was held in Aarhus, Den-mark, attended by representatives from Defense League white suprema-cist organizations from Norway, Switzerland, Sweden, Germany, Italy, Poland, France, Bulgaria, and the United States.

In some countries, such as France, Belgium, and Canada, laws have passed restricting clothes that some Muslims wear (e.g., the burqa, which covers a woman's face and body). Public opinion polls show widespread support for such restrictions in the United Kingdom, Spain, Italy, and Germany.[10]

The banning of such dress and religious icons is ostensibly intended to apply to all groups. The obvious target has been the growing Muslim community, whose population in the European Community doubled in the past thirty years. By 2050, 20 percent of Europeans will be Muslim.[11]

While some Muslims seek to assimilate into Western society, their religious practices (e.g., praying five times a day) and clothing signify to some people their rejection of Western secularism and culture. Hostility toward Muslims has been heightened by terrorist incidents in Western nations that involved Muslim perpetrators. The vast majority of Muslims are law-abiding and industrious. They chose to live in their host country and have provided important information on potential terrorists.

The United States has experienced a similar increase in anti-immigration sentiment, most notably directed toward Latinos. Muslims, too, have been the targets of hate crimes and discrimination, especially following the terrorist attack on the World Trade Center in New York City on September 11, 2001. Nearly 3,000 people were killed, including 327 foreign nationals.

Self-styled vigilante groups like the minutemen, have been "protecting" our borders against the wave of illegal immigrants from Mexico and Central and South America.[12] The Southern Poverty Law Center has documented a 755 percent increase (from 149 to 1,274) in the number of "patriot" groups, including armed militias, from 2008 to 2012.[13]

The epitome of anti-immigration sentiment in the United States is expressed in the racist symbols, signs, and comments of the Tea Party and draconian anti-immigration laws like those in Arizona and Alabama.[14] Hate websites like Stormfront.com, AryanNations.com, and Vdare.com post anti-immigrant information and host blogs containing overt racist rants. As in European nations, these are fringe elements. But they are becoming increasingly vocal and intrusive thanks to the ubiquity of the Internet, social media, and personal communication devices.

As in Norway, the constant anti-immigrant barrage can lead to violence, like the attack on a Wisconsin Sikh temple in August 2012 by forty-year-old Wade Michael Page. A neo-Nazi, he murdered six worshippers and wounded several others before being killed by police. His twisted worldview is, unfortunately, shared by others influenced by the torrent of hate on the Internet and TV and radio shows that depict immigrants and minorities as unwanted parasites.

FACE THE FEAR OF "THE OTHER"

Noted U.S. Supreme Court Justice Oliver Wendell Holmes observed, "A mind stretched by a new idea never returns to the same shape." It is true that immigrants and people of different ethnic groups, cultures, and religions leave an imprint on us. They present us with challenges to our usual way of behaving. Living in homogeneous societies creates a mindset that leads to ethnocentric beliefs about the superiority of one social system over others.

We fear "the other" because they represent the unknown. We resent "the other" because they threaten to push us out of our cultural comfort zone. It is a disruption in the normal/usual way we engage one another. Being unfamiliar with people from different cultures presents challenges to us on a number of intimate levels of understanding and interaction.

Encounters with "the other" force us to engage people who are different from us.

We may feel awkward or uncomfortable because we do not know or understand their cultures and how to interact with them. We may feel ill at ease and reluctant to encounter strangers because the outcome of such interaction is less predictable than with people we are accustomed to. We are reluctant to engage "the other" because we fear that our ignorance or naïveté about them will be revealed. Fear of "the other" also comes from the competition for our materialist lifestyle.

In the final analysis, it is the threat to our way of life posed by the introduction of "the other" that lies at the heart of the matter. It kindles within us the fear that our privileges are transitory—an awareness that change is the "new normal." The usual way of doing business is no longer usual.

We must learn to accept change if we are going to compete and participate in a multicultural world. Within the deepest recesses of our mind, we sense that what we believe and the way we have been behaving is questionable. These thoughts stoke the fear of "the other" and reinforce the white supremacists' sacred fourteen words: "We must secure the existence of our people and a future for white children."

Galileo and Darwin were targets of the establishment because they raised the possibility that the popular perception of reality was incorrect. The first was forced to recant his view of the solar system, and the latter endured derisive comments and scorn from colleagues and established religious bodies. But change is inevitable. No amount of physical bullying or intellectual gymnastics can prevent it from occurring. Eventually the truth will out in the Information Age.

The dilemma facing the world today is one of time and technology. They are inextricably linked. The people of the world are running out of time to create a collaborative global society. Rising levels of consumption and mobility facilitated through technology are reducing the window of opportunity to save the planet from resource depletion and interpersonal conflict. How ironic that the late political scientist Samuel Huntington concluded his magnum opus with, "On a worldwide basis Civilization seems in many respects to be yielding to barbarism, generating the image of an unprecedented phenomenon, a global Dark Ages, possibly descending on humanity."[15]

It was neither the fear of resource depletion nor geopolitical rivalries that prompted his dire assessment, but multiculturalism. The inclusion of different ethnicities into previously homogeneous societies, or "rejection of the Creed of Western civilization," in his words, to Westerners "means the end of the United States of America as we have known it. It also means effectively the end of Western civilization."[16]

For this planet to survive, we must practice the mantra of unlearning ethnocentrism and the stereotypical images we have of one another, or

Huntington's warning may become the swan song of humanity. We must figure out a way of engaging one another in meaningful dialogue, not to proselytize but to understand, not to tolerate "the other" but to learn and collaborate with them.

As a precondition for engaging "the other," no matter the nature of the differences that divide us, participants must be willing to suspend preconceived ideas of one another. They must contemplate the possibility that their perception of social reality, including historical and contemporary views of self, society, and "others," is, to put it euphemistically, incomplete. This, most necessarily, includes preconceptions about students.

Participants engaged in dialogic activities must be willing to concede the possibility that their worldview may be inaccurate. It is amenable to change, even transform, provided one enters into discussions with an open mind and heart. This is the message eloquently delivered in the works of Gustave Niebuhr and Eboo Patel, who implore readers to engage "the other" in dialogue and community-service activities.[17]

Sincere interethnic and interreligious communication is predicated on the assumption that participants have no ulterior motive to engage in dialogue. They sincerely wish to learn about one another and improve communication toward promoting inclusivity. Participants must avoid the temptation to lecture, preach, and proselytize.

To engage in meaningful, productive dialogue, participants must also be willing to learn and assimilate ideas about other religions. They must weigh the possibility that there may be alternative views that exist outside of their normal frame of reference. Such views deserve a hearing out of respect but also because they offer a different perspective that may be liberating and transformative.

Much as quantum physics views the world and universe differently from Einstein's paradigm, participants in dialogue must consider the existence of valid alternative universes of discourse. Different beliefs and behaviors based on systems of faith and culture can, if we allow them a voice by lowering our defenses, help us create a more meaningful collaborative society.

The fear of accepting the possibility that alternative realities exist is anathema to some individuals and organizations steeped in the lore of bygone civilizations, much as Huntington lamented the intrusion of other cultures into Western society: "Western culture is challenged by groups within Western societies. One such challenge comes from immigrants from other civilizations who reject assimilation and continue to adhere to and to propagate the values, customs, and cultures of their home societies."[18] This xenophobic refrain displays a Eurocentric fear of the foundation of our society—pluralism. Without immigration Western society will surely decline as its population ages and birthrate falls below the replacement level.

RULES OF ENGAGEMENT

Below are some ground rules and considerations that might help teachers and community leaders create productive interfaith and intercultural dialogue. The location may be in the classroom or somewhere in the community, but the goals, rules, and techniques are essentially the same.

1. The first and most important rule is that there be no preconditions governing the exchange of ideas. The dialogic encounter can be a form of proselytizing. The fact that and individual or group wants to draw "the other" into a dialogue may be viewed as coercive with the intent to modify values and beliefs. The desire to engage "the other" may be viewed as hostile and offensive—a move by members of a majority group who represent the seat of power and privilege in society. There is no simple panacea for avoiding this sentiment. Sincerity, meeting at a neutral place, utilizing the good will of esteemed members of both majority and minority communities as go-betweens, and agreeing on ground rules governing the interaction may help to desensitize the situation. Couch the invitation in carefully chosen words that are culturally sensitive and respectful. Meet at times that are inoffensive. Use music, food, art, and dance representative of participating groups to attract participants and establish rapport.

2. White participants should recognize that dialogue in the context of engaging people from different religious and ethnic traditions is principally a white, middle-class activity. It may be perceived as an activity to enlighten and entertain them, even if the initiators do not conceive it in these terms. To engage people from diverse religious and ethnic groups in meaningful nonthreatening dialogue there must be a quid pro quo. A fair exchange should exist based on perceived tangible benefits for all participants, not just the enrichment of the host.

   Conducting the dialogue in the dominant language places "the other" in the subsidiary role of being a minority. They are less powerful and unequal. In this context, "others" invited to dialogue may take on the character of pawns. They may be used to reinforce dominant values by demonstrating their cultural differences and presumed inferiority. Even when pressure is not used to coerce them into changing or acknowledging the superiority of the dominant culture, they may be perceived as cultural curiosities, eccentricities, or backward.

3. Fear of change or the threat of change may dissuade some participants from joining dialogue. This challenge is particularly relevant to faith groups with a strong belief in the infallibility of their theology. Believing in the superiority or special quality of their spiritual

framework may lead to denigrating or disparaging other belief systems, casting them as naïve, heretical, and apostate.

Paradoxically, true believers who cling to such perspectives may feel threatened by the presence of people from other faith and ethnic communities. People who have been stigmatized and denigrated for their differences may present a challenge to their own intransigent views. Interacting with "the other" may cause them to question "infallible" assumptions, challenging long-held stereotypes that insulated their group from the intrusion of "the other." Avoidance helps perpetuate ethnocentrism and the group's belief system from contamination with outsiders whose presence might contradict or dilute the message of the in-group.

Rather than risk threatening encounters that challenge racial and religious stereotypes, people refrain from participating. They prefer the safety and security of their cultural, racial, or religious group. Respecting the message of participants from diverse perspectives is difficult when prospective participants have avoided people because of the characteristics they bring to the dialogue. Therefore, dialogue attracts like-minded individuals who already embrace the concept of diversity. The question remains: how do we get diverse groups to the table?

Although different ethnic groups share the quality of being human, with DNA common to us all, there are a wide variety of cultural differences among us. Religion professor Stephen Prothero makes the cogent point that there are significant theological differences among the world's religions. Even though most have moral codes extolling the virtues of charity, humility, piety, and fairness, underneath the similarities lie different theology and rituals that distinguish them from one another. While it may feel reassuring to believe that we all want similar things out of life, our methods for obtaining them vary greatly. It should not be assumed that Abrahamic religions are basically alike any more than it is accurate to imply that Eastern religions such as Buddhism, Confucianism, Hinduism, and Sikhism are innately similar or compatible.[19]

The answer to the question about how to get diverse people to the table depends on why you want them there. Even the most noble intentions (to improve understanding, reduce tension and conflict in the community, combat prejudice and discrimination, open lines of communication and opportunities to enable everyone to participate in the community) may be necessary factors in the dialogic equation for success. But they are not sufficient to entice some people.

They may perceive their role as that of an insect being lured into a web spun of dominant social norms and customs that threaten the integrity of their group. In the case of religious discourse, the stakes are even higher. Members of faith communities may perceive the dialogue as threatening their beliefs about the afterlife. The fear of the unknown, the "great mystery," transcends mortal concerns about custom and tradition.[20]

WORKING TOGETHER TO ACHIEVE COMMON GOALS

Dialogue is a useful activity because it may accomplish some of the desirable ends above. It need not be the end or even the beginning of encounters with "the other." An alternative approach to improving understanding about people from diverse backgrounds and creating a more inclusive community is through engaging in community-service activities. Talking with one another is fine for some people, but others want to promote social change.

Even when the outcome of communal projects seem mundane (such as making a playground safer by installing nonabrasive surfaces; painting houses for older or infirm members of the community; planting flowers and shrubs to beautify pedestrian areas, nursing homes, or hospitals; and serving meals to the sick, poor, and elderly), they are needed. They also provide opportunities for students and people from diverse backgrounds to pool their talents and time in a mutually agreed upon civic endeavor.

More than half a century ago, psychologist Gordon Allport demonstrated that people from different ethnic groups can create meaningful interaction when they collaborate in activities that promote mutual respect. What he termed the "Contact and Acquaintance" premise, lends itself to community service where people collaborate on mutually agreed upon projects designed to enhance their community.[21]

Cooperative social action is the proverbial twofer. It focuses the community on addressing needed projects and simultaneously breaks down barriers by creating friendships among participants as they collaborate. Participants derive a sense of accomplishment from their work. Communication and mutual respect are promoted as they collaborate. Research over half a century involving over 200,000 participants indicates that such interaction has a beneficial impact on the participants and society *and* the process reduces prejudice toward members of stereotyped groups.[22]

WHAT WE MUST DO

Mankind's journey toward reunification will continue to be characterized by the intermingling of cultures as people and ideas circulate around the planet. The future, our future, will be one of multicultural diversity facilitated by transportation and telecommunications. The demographic and technological processes contributing to this transformation are already in progress. They cannot be stopped or reversed.

It is normal to be apprehensive about change. Fear of the unknown is powerful. That is why religion is so pervasive. We have two choices— embrace the inevitable, welcome diversity, and reach an accommodation with "the other" or resist change in an attempt to recreate bygone civilizations that recapitulate the worst experiences mankind has endured. The cycle of fear and hate does not have a positive outcome. There is no scarcity of demagogues willing to capitalize on these emotions in their quest for power and privilege.

For guidance, we have only to look to the "Golden Rule" and its many variations among the world's religions—treat people the way you wish to be treated. The Biblical admonition to "welcome the stranger," is as relevant today as it was thousands of years ago.[23] We will be far better served if we accept the reality of pluralism and multiculturalism, stop pining for the past, and recognize the value of diversity. The train has already left the station. You can get on at the next stop, but you can't hold it back.

Once we realize that these trends are inevitable, that we can control our destiny by the rational use of technology and the inclusion of diverse groups and individuals in our society, we will be able to utilize the immense potential that resides in humanity—a potential that languishes in the morass of racism, poverty, and prejudice.

Mankind has survived for thousands of years because we are social animals. Although the history of our species has been marked by violence, conflict, and war, we could not have gotten this far without sharing our cultures and collaborating. We now have the means to improve the quality of life of everyone on the planet, but do we have the will? The diminution of scarce resources and increasing social inequality threaten to tear our world apart. It is our choice—do we use the accumulated knowledge of the ages for the betterment of mankind or wipe our species from the planet?

Although there have been many detours along the road to reunification, man's journey has, throughout history, reflected his attempt to obtain a better life for himself and his posterity—a life with dignity and respect. When we recognize that, despite cultural differences, our goals are similar and when we work in unison to remove obstacles preventing the development of our potentialities, we will overcome the final obstacle on our path to reunification.

SUMMING UP

- The Millennium Summit goals to reduce poverty and inequality can be attained if teachers educate students about social inequality.
- We must use education and work for positive change in our lives and the world.

- We can overcome fear of strangers through dialogues in class and the community.
- We live in a global multicultural community and should help our children respect themselves and one another.
- Community service activities that engage students and adults from diverse backgrounds can lead to positive outcomes for people and society.

NOTES

1. For a summary of poverty statistics and relevant sources, see Anup Shah, "Poverty Facts and Stats," Global Issues, http://www.globalissues.org/article/26/poverty-facts-and-stats.

2. For a summary of the document and related events, go to http://www.un.org/millenniumgoals/bkgd.shtml.

3. "Millennium Development Goals Report Card: Learning from Progress," Overseas Development Institute, http://www.odi.org.uk/resources/docs/6014.pdf.

4. "World Bank Sees Progress against Extreme Poverty, but Flags Vulnerabilities," The World Bank, Press Release #20, February 29, 2012, http://web.worldbank.org/WBSITE/EXTERNAL/NEWS/0,,contentMDK:23130032~pagePK:64257043~piPK:437376~theSitePK:4607,00.html.

5. United Nations Press Release, May 3, 2011, http://esa.un.org/unpd/wpp/Documentation/pdf/wpp2010_Pres.

6. Fertility rate world map, United Nations, public domain.

7. E. F. Schumacher, *Small Is Beautiful: Economics As If People Mattered* (New York: Harper & Row, 1973).

8. E. F. Schumacher, *Good Work* (New York: Harper & Row, 1979).

9. See "The Neo-Nazi Surge: Right Wing Parties Sweep to Power in the European Parliament as Voter Turnout Plummets to Record Low," *Daily Mail*, June 11, 2009, http://www.dailymail.co.uk/news/worldnews/article-1191533/Right-wing-parties-sweep-power-European-Parliament-voter-turnout-plummets-record-low.html.   In April 2012, right-wing parties made significant electoral gains in France and the Netherlands, and in May, the fascist Golden Dawn Party made inroads in Greece.

10. See James Joyner, "French Burqa Ban Widely Supported in Europe," *New Atlanticist*, March 1, 2010, http://www.acus.org/new_atlanticist/french-burqa-ban-widely-supported-europe.

11. Adrian Michaels, "Muslim Europe: The Demographic Time Bomb Transforming Our Continent," *Telegraph*, August 8, 2009, http://www.telegraph.co.uk/news/worldnews/europe/5994047/Muslim-Europe-the-demographic-time-bomb-transforming-our-continent.html. See also the PEW Research Center, "Mapping the Global Muslim Population: A Report on the Size and Distribution of the World's Muslim Population," The PEW Forum on Religion and Public Life, October 2009, Washington, DC, that provides one of the most comprehensive estimates of the Muslim population around the world.

12. The Southern Poverty Law Center has represented a number of immigrants who were victims of hate crimes and published a scathing report of the treatment of migrant workers: Mary Bower, "Under Siege: Life for Low-Income Latinos in the South," Southern Poverty Law Center, April 2009, Montgomery, Alabama.

13. Richard Cohen, "Harsh Anti-Obama Rhetoric Fuels Extremism," *SPLC Report*, Winter 2012, 2.

14. For a collage of racist Tea Party signs, go to http://www.youtube.com/watch?v=s38vioxnBaI.

15. Samuel P. Huntington, *The Clash of Civilizations and the Remaking of World Order* (New York: Simon and Schuster, 2011), 321.

16. Ibid., 306–307.

17. Gustav Niebuhr, *Beyond Tolerance* (New York: Viking Press, 2008); Eboo Patel, *Acts of Faith* (Boston: Beacon Press, 2007).

18. Huntington, *Clash of Civilizations*, 304–305.

19. For a discussion of this logic, see Stephen Prothero, *God Is Not One* (New York: HarperOne, 2010).

20. Everyday Democracy, formally known as the Study Circles Resource Center, is a wealth of useful information for conducting dialogues as well as sponsoring important seminars on critical social issues. Go to http://www.everyday-democracy.org/en/index.aspx.

21. Gordon W. Allport, *The Nature of Prejudice* (Reading, MA: Addison-Wesley, 1979, first published 1954).

22. Thomas F. Pettigrew and Linda R. Tropp, "A Meta-Analytic Test of Intergroup Contact Theory," *Journal of Personality and Social Psychology* 90, no. 5 (2006): 751–783.

23. Leviticus 19:34.

Postscript

How to Create Inclusive Classrooms

I don't have a single American friend. I don't understand them.
— Tamerlan Tsarnaev (Boston Marathon bomber)

Every classroom must be a place where teachers and students create a collaborative community forged out of respect for self and others — a safe haven where intellectual activities are valued and community members feel wanted and important.

CREATING BETTER PEOPLE

If this book was simply an academic exercise it would have little practical relevance other than providing interesting bits of information about how humans evolved and society developed. But these words are more than historical snippets for cocktail chatter. The implication of our preceding discussion is magnified by current events that daily confirm the importance of the necessity for becoming a more tolerant and inclusive society. The process begins in our homes and schools.

The pressures of a burgeoning population, immigration, mass transportation, and telecommunications are, as we have seen, heightening tensions among diverse ethnic and cultural groups in society *and our schools*. The choice facing us is clear: improve our understanding and communication with people from diverse backgrounds or risk increasing conflict and social trauma. The magnitude of this dilemma is similar to the proverbial puzzle about eating an elephant: one accomplishes it a bite at a time.

This metaphor can help teachers overcome the pressures they experience (large classes, diverse students, emphasis on standardized tests, diminished resources, bureaucratic rules and regulations) if they focus on making their classrooms safe and respectful learning environments. Teachers cannot hope to solve intransigent problems like hunger and poverty. They can create classrooms where children and adolescents develop self-esteem, self-respect, and respect for one another. Creating a community of sharing and caring students in each class builds a bridge for them to cross over into the larger society. There they can utilize these skills in other areas of their lives.

It is imperative that teachers realize the important role they play in creating better people. In this vital endeavor they should focus on their own sphere of influence—their classroom. Out there, on the school campus, in students' homes, and the larger society, there are grave inequities. These can be best addressed by teachers helping students learn to value themselves and one another and modeling behavior that exemplifies the values and character that will lead to a more equitable and inclusive society.

Creating inclusive societies begins in the classroom. Teachers do not have control over students' families or social lives. They can lay a foundation that forms the basis of a more tolerant and inclusive world—one classroom at a time. Helping students learn about different cultures does not detract from standard lesson plans. If students do not feel respected or safe they are not ready to assimilate the information teachers want to impart to them. Empowering students with knowledge about their own and others' cultures through multicultural activities is an essential step on the path toward academic and social success. As we see below, the process must begin early.

OVERCOMING RACISM AMONG CHILDREN: THE CASE OF THE BLACK BARBIE DOLL

Leslie, a thirty-eight-year-old social worker who counsels children with stressful life situations, found her four-year-old daughter, Sophia, engage in animated play with her dolls. She watched incredulously as Sophia invited the four white dolls with blonde hair to a tea party while the dark-skinned doll with black hair lay alone across the room.

"Why isn't that doll going to the party?" she inquired.

"She's dead," replied Sophia matter-of-factly.

"Dead? How can that be? She's just like the other dolls. Why can't she play with them?"

"They don't want to play with her."

"Why is that?"

"Because she has dark skin," replied Sophia.

Leslie's mouth dropped to the floor as she fought back tears. How could this be? Hadn't she and her husband worked diligently to teach her child to be inclusive? Sophia had a variety of multicultural toys and books. She was only allowed to watch progressive television shows like *Sesame Street, Dora the Explorer, Diego, The Backyardigans,* and *Yo Gabba Gabba.* An only child, she attended an expensive, supposedly inclusive prekindergarten school that had a few children of color, but no staff of color.

"Sweet Pea," said Leslie plaintively, "you're hurting that doll's feelings. You've got to let her play with the other dolls."

"She can't. She's in jail," Sophia replied as she rationalized her decision to exclude the dark-skinned doll.

This scenario could be repeated in countless homes and classrooms around the nation. It was a real situation that wrenched Leslie *and me*, as we tried to come to a resolution to the problem. You see, Sophia is my granddaughter. I happened to be visiting when this incident occurred. As an advocate for civil rights and a diversity trainer, the family looked to me for an answer.

Eurocentric Culture Dominates Our Society

I recalled the doll experiments in the 1940s of Drs. Kenneth and Mamie Clark that revealed a preference for white dolls by both black and white children. Their research influenced the landmark U.S. Supreme Court decision *Brown v. Board of Education* in 1954 that led to desegregation of schools in the United States.

Despite attempts to integrate schools and create equal educational opportunities for all children, replications of the Clarks' work in the 1980s by another team of psychologists, Darlene Powell-Hopson and Derek Hopson, revealed a continued preference for white dolls among African-American children. The affinity for whiteness among black children and adolescents was dramatically revealed once again in 2006. An African-American teenager in New York City, Kiri Davis, produced an award-winning video, "A Girl Like Me," that replicated the Clarks' experiment.

Although Barack Obama, the forty-fourth president of the United States, is a man of color, race relations in this country remain volatile, punctuated by periodic outrages (e.g., hate crimes like the murder of James Byrd in Texas) and racial profiling and unequal sentencing of African Americans (e.g., the "Jena Six" African-American teenagers in Louisiana; stop-and-frisk policies that target blacks and Latinos in New York City; the refusal to allow black children to swim in a Pennsylvania country club pool; reference to President Obama as a Negro by Senate Majority Leader Harry Reid; and public outrage over the remarks of U.S. Attorney General, Eric Holder, who claimed that Americans were "cowards" when it comes to discussing race relations).

Taking a cue from these incidents, the Cable News Network (CNN) aired a number of specials on race relations in the spring of 2010 in an attempt to reveal the depth of the problem. In a variation of the Clarks' doll experiment, 133 kindergarten and middle school black and white children from the northeast and southeast United States were asked a range of questions about paper dolls with various skin tones.

The research found strong preferences among white children for light-skinned dolls as well as some preference for light skin among black children. One touching segment showed a white teacher in tears as her young son exhibited racist sentiments about dark skin. She noted that she's been teaching inclusiveness for fifteen years only to find it absent in her own son's attitudes.

SURVIVING WHITE CULTURE

What is the origin of such attitudes? Why do they persist despite our efforts to alter them? And why is it important for parents and educators to change them? Social scientists attribute negative attitudes toward blackness to historical and cultural processes in our society that perpetuate perceptions of dark skin as inferior to white.

Prior to the Civil Rights Era (1950–1970) many Southern states had Jim Crow laws designed to perpetuate the superior status of whites and the inferior position of blacks. Life in Northern states also contributed to the second-class status of African-Americans and other ethnic minorities. Informal, de facto forms of discrimination, such as policies and traditions that stigmatized minorities as being lazy, shiftless, and uneducable, still exist according to public opinion polls. These affect the achievement gap in educational attainment between blacks and Latinos versus whites and Asians.

These attitudes have been referred to as symptoms of *systemic racism*. They are reflected in the behavior of the dominant white society toward people of color. What is even more distressing is the internalization of negative stereotypes by groups who have been victimized by them. This process is called *stereotype threat*, and it can impede the academic performance of groups assumed to be inferior.

It is difficult for white people to recognize the impact that the white Eurocentric culture has on people of color. They are accustomed to viewing the world through their own perspective, assuming everyone's experiences and perceptions are similar to theirs. This phenomenon, known as *white privilege*, may deceive white parents and teachers into assuming that their way of behaving and experiencing the world is the norm. This helps explain the disconnect experienced by some children of color when their Eurocentric educational experience excludes contributions made by their own ethnic group.

A distressing conclusion that emerges from doll-type studies and the attempts of teachers and parents who conscientiously try to make their classrooms and homes more inclusive, is the stubborn persistence of negative stereotypes despite their efforts to change them. On the surface it seems that multicultural education is ineffectual—the achievement gap persists, African-American and Latino male graduation rates have been improving but remain abysmally low, and racist attitudes and incidents continue in our schools and communities. But this great American experiment at pluralism, the inclusion of hundreds of cultures and ethnic groups in a unified society, is still a work in progress.

Demographic changes in our population—currently over 309 million people, with half of all public school children African-American, Latino, Asian, Native American, and biracial (in forty years one of every three people in this country will be Latino)—make it imperative to continue our efforts to teach and practice inclusive behavior in our schools. If our nation is to survive we must afford equal opportunities to all our residents.

WHAT ARE EFFECTIVE STRATEGIES FOR TEACHING INCLUSIVENESS?

As with Sophia's experience, research from the doll experiments indicates that prejudice and racism intrude into children's lives at an early age. Sometimes our efforts through games, multicultural materials, and the media do not seem to interrupt the cycle. It's analogous to people voting along party lines, disregarding the qualifications of candidates. Tradition often guides our decisions.

But logic can be used to promote change. A large and growing body of evidence indicates multicultural education has a positive impact on children by improving their interpersonal interaction in school *and their academic achievement.* Unfortunately, many educators don't know about the beneficial effects of multicultural education. Others feel constrained by the demands of teaching to standardized tests, and public policy emphasizes science, technology, engineering, and math (STEM) curricula.

Some teachers and administrators are obsessed with catering to the whims of the corporate world at the expense of humanism in the classroom. Making better people should transcend making better students. The ubiquity of bullying and violence in schools and society indicates that our educational energies and resources are being misplaced. Providing teachers with multicultural materials they can integrate into their courses should also be accompanied by the rationale and benefits for doing this.

But what should be done when children like Sophia resist our efforts to teach inclusiveness? We may never know the incident that triggered her exclusionary behavior, but she adamantly refused to include the dark-skinned doll despite our prodding. Then Leslie had an "aha" moment. She left the room and returned with a photograph of Sophia and her cousin. The picture showed Sophia sitting alongside eight-year-old Dabney, a Haitian child adopted by Sophia's aunt and uncle.

"Isn't that you with Dabney?" asked Leslie. "Doesn't she have dark skin?"

A broad smile creased Sophia's face as she acknowledged her older cousin. She reached for the dark-skinned doll and pushed her into the toy car with the others. "They're all going to the party now," she said cheerfully.

Threats, cajoling, logic, and the use of multicultural materials such as books and videos may seem inadequate in the face of prejudicial attitudes that have an origin in experiences. While a picture may say a thousand words, an unkind act may leave a lasting impression—a scar on someone's personality. Educator Jane Elliott recognized this more than forty years ago when she segregated her third grade class in Riceville, Iowa, based on eye color. The classic video of this experiment, *The Eye of the Storm*, revealed how quickly children learn to discriminate and mistreat one another, and the negative effects of prejudice on academic achievement.

More than half a century ago, psychologist Gordon Allport, contended that prejudicial feelings could be overcome by having people from diverse backgrounds engage in community service together. A review of 515 studies in 38 countries involving 200,000 people by psychologists Thomas Pettigrew and Linda Tropp led them to conclude that intergroup contact reduces prejudice and creates positive effects *beyond* the specific activity for the entire group. Husband and wife psychologists Art and Elaine Aron, at New York University at Stony Brook, demonstrated that, after only a few hours, beneficial effects from cross-racial encounters occurred and created lasting friendships.

Clearly, children as well as adults benefit from engaging in diverse interaction. But our schools are, according to the UCLA Civil Rights Project headed by Gary Orfield, more segregated today than before the Supreme Court's *Brown* decision. What can parents and teachers do?

Research suggests that parents and teachers should model the appropriate behavior they want their children and students to adopt. This includes using inclusive language when they refer to people from different ethnic and cultural backgrounds. They should combine didactic and experiential activities at home and in the classroom, promote an understanding and appreciation of diversity, give children an opportunity to learn about and value differences and begin to accept them as normative.

Integrate and infuse multicultural materials into the home and school. Use materials that reflect the history and contributions of people from diverse ethnic and cultural backgrounds. Teach children that our nation is the product of many people who arrived here in various ways and at different times. Children will begin to understand that the United States, like the world, is becoming a global society. One made possible through the contributions and collaboration of people who come from different places, with diverse languages, customs, and traditions.

Including diversity goes beyond the celebration of ethnic holidays. A conscientious attempt to make our homes and classrooms inclusive incorporates an understanding of the social and psychological traditions of other cultures. We must learn the origin of ethnic holidays and understand why they are celebrated. How they approximate our own celebrations, and how and why they differ. Children must be exposed to a variety of historical, cultural, and scientific personalities and achievements—contributions of people from around the world who may or may not look like them.

This strategy can be assisted by involving speakers from different cultures, taking class trips to museums, utilizing multicultural materials from online sources such as Tolerance.org and the PBS Kids website. Lesson plans should emphasize inclusivity and teach skills that engage children. Small group, participatory problem solving and experiential activities help them become interdependent, trusting, and empathetic, much as the children in Jane Elliott's class long ago.

Every child should be given the opportunity to demonstrate her/his uniqueness through self-esteem building activities. Each child should have the chance to talk about something they like or excel at such as their favorite place to have fun or favorite book or TV show. Such activities demonstrate that they have similar hopes, aspirations, and feelings—humanity.

These activities should become part of the culture of your home and classroom. They should be continually reinforced through praise and positive action that rewards children for doing the right thing. By creating a helpful, inclusive environment, your home and classroom will become a welcoming place where every child is valued and respected. And, like Sophia, they will realize that we're all better together.

The challenges teachers and students face in schools across this nation are a microcosm of the issues confronted by people around the world. As our population expands, the pressure to conform to majority norms in schools and society sacrifices individuality and creativity for the sake of servicing large numbers of students and people in social systems overburdened with debt and diminished resources. We must resist pressures that seek the homogenization of students and culture into an amorphous entity. That destroys the vitality and integrity of the very parts that contribute to its uniqueness and humanness.

As our world and society become increasingly diverse, administrators and teachers must learn and practice skills that promote inclusion in their schools, modeling behaviors that value all students *and their colleagues*. They should incorporate the axioms in chapter 9 and engage one another and students regularly in dialogues on a variety of topics to promote understanding and inclusion.

Living in a multicultural world requires us to engage in introspection about our self-perception and rethink our relationships with one another. This process can be illuminating and painful. Historical and contemporary myths about who we are, where we came from, and what our lifestyle has done and is doing to the environment and those around us may threaten traditional ways of thinking and teaching. But the truth will set us free and light the way to human equality and, hopefully, peace on the road to reunification.

FURTHER READING

- Gordon Allport, *The Nature of Prejudice* (Reading, MA: Addison-Wesley, 1954). A timeless classic, this book provides insight about how prejudice is created and what we can do to alleviate it.
- James A. Banks, *Cultural Diversity and Education: Foundations, Curriculum and Teaching*, 5th ed. (Boston: Pearson, 2006), and James A. Banks, *An Introduction to Multicultural Education*, 4th ed. (Boston: Pearson, 2008). Indispensable resources on using multicultural education in the classroom by a pioneer in the field.
- Marvin W. Berkowitz, *You Can't Teach through a Rat* (Boone, NC: Character Development Group, 2012). Teachers can learn the virtues of infusing core values in their classrooms.
- Steven Brill, *Class Warfare* (New York: Simon & Schuster, 2011). A caustic look at what is wrong with American education.
- Kenneth B. Clark and Maime P. Clark, "Emotional Factors in Racial Identification and Preferences in Negro Children," *Journal of Negro Education* 19, no. 3 (1950), 341–350. Landmark study of the dominant effects of white culture on black children.
- Joe R. Feagin, *Racist America*, 2nd ed. (New York: Routledge, 2010). An in-depth look at the nature and impact of systemic racism in the United States.
- Darlene Powell-Hopson and Derek Hopson, *Different and Wonderful: Raising Black Children in a Race-Conscious Society* (Upper Saddle River, NJ: Prentice-Hall, 1990). A replication and expansion of the Clarks' doll experiment and its implications for black families and children in our society.
- H. Roy Kaplan, *Failing Grades: The Quest for Equity in America's Schools*, 2nd ed. (Lanham, MD, 2007). A look into cultural clashes in the classroom and how to avoid them.
- Baruti K. Kafele, *Motivating Black Males to Achieve in School and Life* (Alexandria, VA: ASCD, 2009). A hands-on approach to helping teachers connect with and motivate black male students.
- Jonathan Kozol, *The Shame of the Nation* (New York: Broadway, 2006). A perceptive analysis of the glaring inequalities in educational opportunities for the poor and children of color in our society.
- James Loewen, *Lies My Teacher Told Me* (New York: Touchstone, 2007). An iconoclastic review of misinformation being taught in our nation's schools.

- Peggy McIntosh, "White Privilege: Unpacking the Invisible Knapsack," http://www.nymbp.org/reference/WhitePrivilege.pdf. The original statement outlining the nature of white privilege in our society.
- Sonia Nieto and Patty Bode, *Affirming Diversity: The Sociopolitical Context of Multicultural Education*, 6th ed. (New York: Pearson, 2011). A look at social equity issues that affect the utilization and effectiveness of multicultural education and techniques for implementing it in the classroom.
- Gary Orfield and Chungmei Lee, *Historical Reversals, Accelerating Resegregation, and the Need for New Integration Strategies* (Los Angeles: UCLA Civil Rights Project, 2007). An analysis of the causes of the resegregation of America's schools.
- Thomas F. Pettigrew and Linda R. Tropp, "A Meta-Analytic Test of Intergroup Contact Theory," *Journal of Personality and Social Psychology* 90, no. 5 (2006): 751–783. A review of social science studies that demonstrates the importance of interacting and working with culturally diverse people.
- Diane Ravitch, *Left Back: A Century of Failed School Reform* (New York: Simon & Schuster, 2000). A critical analysis of our short-cited educational policies.
- Claude Steele and Joshua Aronson, "Stereotype Threat and the Intellectual Test Performance of African-Americans," *Journal of Personality and Social Psychology* 69, no. 5 (1995): 797–811. How stereotypes are internalized by victims.
- Hal Urban, *Life's Greatest Lessons* (New York: Touchstone, 2002). An educator's humanistic approach to understanding and working with students.
- Todd Whitaker, *What Great Teachers Do Differently*, 2nd ed. (Larchmont, NY: Eye on Education, 2012). A look at how master teachers connect with students and transcend problems in the classroom.

VIDEO RESOURCES

- CNN Doll Study, http://ac360.blogs.cnn.com/2010/05/17/ac360-series-doll-study-research/.
- Kiri Davis, "A Girl Like Me," http://www.youtube.com/watch?v=zOBxFRu_SOw.
- Jane Elliott's videos, including *The Eye of the Storm*, can be found on her website: http://www.janeelliott.com/.
- Multicultural lesson plans and related materials can be found on the PBS website: http://pbskids.org/.

- For lesson plans, antiprejudice advice, and tolls for classroom inclusion, go to the Southern Poverty Law Center's website: www. tolerance.org.

SUMMING UP

- All children are susceptible to popular stereotypes about people of color.
- Parents and teachers need to recognize and correct antisocial attitudes in children.
- Creating inclusive classrooms and homes can reduce prejudice and discrimination among children.
- Experiential activities are effective tools for overcoming prejudiced attitudes among children.

Index